CREATIVE CURRICULUM

Y0-BGG-527

CREATIVE CURRICULUM
Kindergarten Through Grade Three
Ellen S. Marbach

Brigham Young University Press

Library of Congress Catalog Card Number: 77-295
International Standard Book Number: 0-8425-0049-9
© 1977 by Brigham Young University Press. All rights reserved
Brigham Young University Press, Provo, Utah 84602

77 15M 20120

To
Merritt G. Marbach

Contents

1
Individualizing and Expanding the Curriculum

Individualizing instruction has been under way for more than three-quarters of a century. This movement was based upon the assumptions that (1) each child is different from every other child, and (2) these differences imply that each child should be allowed to learn at his/her own pace. Although many teachers of young children agree with these assumptions, they are puzzled as to how to individualize the curriculum creatively and meaningfully.

Individualizing does not mean necessarily that the curriculum has to be redesigned for each individual. To prepare a separate science experience for each of twenty-five or thirty children daily would be a tremendous task for any teacher. This extreme interpretation of individualizing the curriculum is not necessary.

    Nor does individualizing have to be a switch from presenting to large groups to presenting to smaller groups of children. The problem with this approach to individualizing is that simply reorganizing children into smaller groups still leaves an enormous range of individual differences within each group. This method is too simplistic and usually means the teacher assigns some children to groups on an arbitrary rather than a scientific basis. A child might be put in one group and his/her best friend in another group simply to prevent disruptive behavior. This type of grouping negates the goal of individualized instruction in favor of teacher convenience. If total individualization of instruction is too time-consuming, and often arbitrary on a small group basis, how can a curriculum be individualized?

What Individualizing Does Not Mean

Begin with the curriculum, not the instruction. The problem with most curricula is that they do not have individualization built in. The teacher is expected to individualize the curriculum.

    This book contains a curriculum with built-in individualization for the teacher. The subject matter is similar to that of other kindergarten curricula except for three new areas: nutrition, career awareness, and economic awareness in family living. The teacher may choose to enter this curriculum at any point, depending on an assessment of the needs

How to Individualize a Curriculum

of a given group of children or a particular child.

Each module or unit of learning includes a preassessment that enables the teacher to establish quickly which children already know the learnings in the unit, which children know only parts of it, and which children know little or none of what is contained in the unit. The postassessment determines which children are ready to exit from the module and enter another one. The preassessment gauges the curricular entry point of each child, and the postassessment gauges each child's pace through the curriculum. Even the activities are designed with the differences in individual pace in mind.

To individualize instruction the teacher needs to start with a curriculum that has built-in techniques for assessing student knowledge and pace. The curriculum in this book is designed in a modular form that accomplishes that goal.

The Scope of Such an Individualized Curriculum

Although this book is primarily a curriculum for kindergarten and primary-grade teachers, the modularized format as a method of individualizing instruction is an appropriate curricular design for nursery school through college. The concept of individualizing curriculum through a modular structure is not limited to early learning, nor to any particular group of students. Nor is individualizing curriculum the only element needed in the consideration of a good design. Whether or not the curriculum can be expanded must also be considered.

Expanding the Curriculum

Expanding the curriculum means allowing it to grow when it should. A teacher using the curriculum in this book is challenged to design activities and even modules when the need arises. In an area such as number concepts, each teacher might have a mental list of what should be covered for five-year-olds or a particular group of children. This list might be similar to what is covered in this book, but each teacher would probably want to expand the curriculum in his/her own way. This is exactly what the teacher should do. Expanding a curriculum gives it a dynamic force rather than a static quality.

Deleting curriculum is as important as expanding curriculum. Deletions should be based on the teacher's knowledge that certain children have already had enough exposure in a certain area or have achieved mastery. Children who already know how to read do not need to go through modules concerning prereading skills. Deletion in this curricular sense means skipping unnecessary parts of a curriculum and rerouting individual children into units of learning more appropriate to their present achievement level. Deletion does not mean getting rid of parts of the curriculum. Instead it means being more selective in exposing an individual child to the curriculum.

There is another way to expand the curriculum to facilitate individual learning. Within each module in this book are many activities that should help most children meet a particular learning goal. However, these activities might not be sufficient for every child. Consequently, each module contains the message that the teacher must design an activity to fit the learning style of each child. The teacher must ask whether this is a child who needs to repeat activities over a period of time in order to learn or one who requires an activity unlike any in the module. The teacher expands the curriculum by designing activities.

2

Enjoying a puppet that is part of a preassessment

Most curricula are dead because they are "frozen" in printed form. An alive and dynamic curriculum must have the built-in flexibility of fitting individual learners and of being expanded by the teacher. The curriculum in this book has this dynamic force because of its modular and performance-based structure. The teacher begins with the parts of this curriculum that create a curricular setting suitable to the individual learners at hand.

The Dynamic Force of Individualizing and Expanding the Curriculum

A creative curriculum is a purposeful curriculum. The goals must be known before they can be evaluated, redefined, merged, etc. Educational goals are usually vaguely stated and often forgotten as the learning process proceeds. The curriculum in this book uses the power of the stated goal by restating it in every activity. The teacher is not taking children on a field trip simply to be doing something, but for a purpose. In the Career Awareness units, the goal of the field trip to the firehouse might be to interview the chief and a fireman about their jobs. In the Social Living unit, the purpose for going to the firehouse might be to find out how the personnel are community helpers. The power of the stated goal enables the teacher to evaluate the goal as well as to keep it in mind when planning and evaluating activities.

The power of the stated and restated goal enables the teacher to determine the nature of a particular goal in the curriculum. Is it an end goal or a "stair step" goal to an end goal? If it is a "stair step" goal, how valid is it, or how efficient, as a way of reaching an end goal? A curricular end goal for early learning is to facilitate growth in language development as a part of language mastery. In this book's language development component, the major subdivisions are "stair

The Power of the Stated Goal

Teacher working with one group while another group works independently

step" goals called *modules*, and within each module are smaller "stair step" goals.

In education there has almost always been better agreement about the end goals of a curriculum than about the "stair step" goals leading to those end goals. Few educators question the importance of learning to read or learning to get along with others, but there is considerable controversy as to how curriculum should be designed to meet these end goals. The fact that this controversy exists is itself a strong argument for a curriculum that involves individualization, flexible expansion or contraction, and stated goals that are task—analyzed as much as the present state of the art allows.

How to Use This Book

In this book the teacher will find components or areas of the curriculum. Within each component are modules that are units of learning. Each teacher must determine which component the children would do best to start with because there is no significance to the order of the components. Having selected a component, the teacher should decide which modules the children will do, and select a module with which to begin.

The teacher begins the module by reading the rationale then moves to the prerequisites to see what the teacher and/or children must do to get ready for this unit of learning.

Next, the teacher gives each child the preassessment, a series of behavioral tests corresponding to the module's objectives. These pretests show which children already have learned what is in the module and which children have little or no knowledge of what is in the module. Children passing the preassessment are not taken through the module because they are knowledgeable. Instead, they proceed to another module in the component. Children passing one part of the preassessment but not another part enter the module and proceed through the objectives with which they had difficulty. Those who did not pass any part of the preassessment begin with Objective 1 and proceed through all the objectives and the appropriate learning activities in the module.

For each objective in a module there is an activities section. The teacher must decide, depending on the learning style of each child, which of these activities the children will do. The teacher may choose one or all unless the activities for a particular skill must be accomplished in sequence.

Next the teacher proceeds to the alternate activities section found under each objective. Here there is a simple activities section for children having difficulty with the objective and a more advanced activities section for children who grasped the objective quickly. The teacher who decides that another activity is needed can design an activity to meet the needs of specific children.

Then the teacher gives the children the postassessment, which is the same series of tests as the preassessment. Those children passing the postassessment exit from the module and proceed to another module of the same component.

Those children who did not pass the postassessment go through the additional activities section with the teacher and retake the postassessment before exiting from the module and proceeding to another module within the same component.

Following is a flowchart diagramming the use of this book.

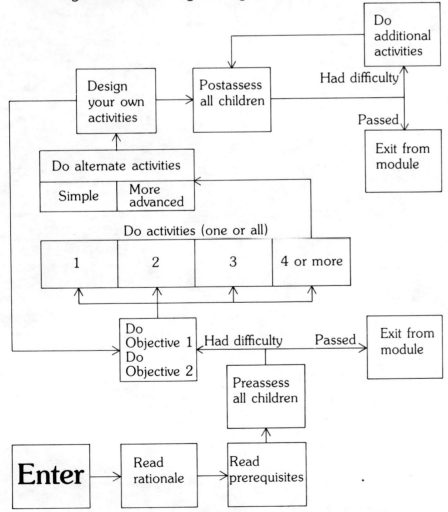

2
Economic Awareness in Family Living

Each child is a consumer from the day he/she is born, receiving the services of many producers including family, doctor, grocer, and many others. The child is a part of the economy, and very soon every child learns about some of the powers of money. Spending and saving habits, understanding of community services, and attitudes toward natural and capital resources shape the child's role in the economy. The young child needs to become aware of the economics in family living so that he/she can have a positive effect on the family budget as well as the general economy.

This chapter contains ten modules, or units of learning, designed to increase a young child's awareness of economics in family living. The modules are as follows:

2.1 Basic Needs of the Family
2.2 Family Members as Producers and Consumers
2.3 Medium of Exchange
2.4 Our Money
2.5 Human Resources—Public Services
2.6 Human Resources—Health Services
2.7 Natural Resources—The Farm
2.8 Natural Resources—Fishing
2.9 Capital Resources—Transportation
2.10 Capital Resources—Communication

2.1 Basic Needs of the Family

All children need to be aware that everyone has basic needs—food, shelter, and clothing. These needs are so basic and necessary to life that they are often taken for granted by the children, and little thought is given to them. Children should realize that all living things require food in order to survive and that food may be obtained from various sources. They need to be aware that people live in different types of shelters and that the type of shelter is often dependent upon

Rationale

2.7 Milking a glove—learning about the source of milk

2.1 Selecting from a "wants" and "needs" table

geography, family income, family size, and other factors.

Children are aware, of course, that they need clothing. They should become more aware of the purposes served by clothing and the differences in types of clothing worn by people in various occupations.

Prerequisites

Gather various books, pictures, and filmstrips about food, shelter, and clothing. Have pictures of various types of food, shelter, and clothing as well as many pictures of objects that are not basic needs. A collection of magazines from which the children can cut pictures of the basic needs would be helpful.

Preassessment

• To show an understanding of the basic needs of mankind, each child will select from a large group of pictures the things that are basic needs of the family and explain why they are so necessary.
• Each child will explain the need for three different types of shelter to show an understanding of this basic need. (Shelter can vary by size, function, and materials available foruse.)
• Each child will explain the importance of food and will identify by name four sources of food from an array of pictures to show an awareness and a knowledge of this basic need.
• Each child will select pictures of clothing appropriate to wear on five different occasions to demonstrate an understanding of the need for types of clothing. Given an array of clothing for paper dolls, each child will correctly dress the doll five times to match the occupation named by the teacher. (Examples: fireman, doctor, nurse, policeman, astronaut.)

After this preassessment, the child will exit from the module or proceed to the objectives.

The children will gain an understanding of the basic needs of mankind and an awareness that "needs" differ from "wants."

• The children will select from a large group of pictures examples of man's needs such as food, shelter, and clothing and give reasons for their selections to demonstrate their awareness of basic needs.
• On a bulletin board labeled "wants" and "needs" the children will classify pictures under the appropriate headings to show their understanding of the difference between wants and needs. This activity should be preceded by experiences in sorting objects or models into "wants" and "needs" boxes.
• To demonstrate their ability to discriminate between wants and needs, the children will identify, from given pictures, the things that are wants and the things that are needs.

Simple Activities
• *Going Shopping.* To demonstrate their comprehension of the difference in wants and needs, the children will select from a large array of objects the things that are "wants" and not "needs" and will put these in individual shopping bags to show the teacher.
• *Classifying.* To show their awareness and knowledge of the basic needs, the children will classify pictures on a bulletin board under the appropriate headings—Food, Shelter, Clothing.

More Advanced Activity
The children will show their awareness of the basic needs by role playing what mother needs, what a neighbor needs, what a brother or sister needs, and what a television personality needs.

Design your own activities to meet the needs of individual children.

The children will gain a better understanding of the need for different types of shelters.

• To increase their awareness of different kinds of shelters, the children will use crayons to draw pictures of their homes and will share these with the class.
• From pictures, the children will discuss the different kinds of houses that people live in to show their awareness of the need for different types of shelter.
• Using pictures of houses of different sizes and families of various sizes, the children will match the family with the appropriate dwelling to demonstrate their understanding of the need for different-sized dwellings.
• From pictures or models of shelters with different functions, the children will show their awareness that shelters vary in function by telling of experiences with such shelters. (Examples: picnic table shelters, garages, house, shopping mall, umbrella, car.)

Simple Activity
Using paint or crayons, the children will draw pictures of different types of dwellings to demonstrate their awareness of the need for different

9

types of shelter. (Prior to this, the teacher should arrange a tabletop display of various kinds of shelters.)

More Advanced Activities
After viewing pictures of shelters in different geographical locations, the children will state reasons for different types to show their understanding of the need for various types of shelters.

After hearing a series of stories read by the teacher about people and shelters from all over the world, the children will show their awareness of shelters varying in size, function, and materials by answering questions regarding the properties of shelters.

Design your own activities to meet the needs of individual children.

Objective 3

The children will realize the importance of food and some of the various sources of our food.

Activities

• The children will discuss the reasons people need food to show their awareness of why people need food. (Example: to stay alive.)
• On a bulletin board depicting various foods and sources of food, the children will use yarn to connect the food item with its source to demonstrate their knowledge of different food sources. (The length of the yarn serves as a self-checking device.)
• After visiting three local producers of foods, the children will name foods from these sources to show their understanding of the source of various foods. If food producers are scarce in the community, use films, filmstrips, television programs, or pictures.

Alternate Activities

Simple Activity (Cow Day)
The children will demonstrate their awareness of the importance of the cow as a food producer by cooking up a tasting party of items that come from the cow. (Examples: milk, cheese, cottage cheese, beef squares, and instant pudding.)

More Advanced Activity (Food Friends Day)
The children will demonstrate their awareness of various sources of food by preparing a table display in which the food source picture matches the food to be sampled. (Examples: farmer's picture with a series of vegetables; cow with milk products; pig with pork products; and chicken with eggs and other chicken products.)

Design your own activity to meet the needs of individual children.

Objective 4

The children will gain a better understanding of the need for clothing and the types of clothing needed by different groups of people.

Activities

• After a discussion with the teacher, the children will identify from pictures clothing worn for specific reasons. By doing so, they will show their awareness of the different purposes of clothing.
• The children will dress paper dolls appropriately for specific

10

occasions to demonstrate their understanding of the need for different types of clothing.

● After they have had several experiences dressing up as a fireman, a doctor, a nurse, an astronaut, or other professionals, the children will discuss clothing worn by people in various occupations to show their awareness of the need for various types of clothing.

Alternate Activities

Simple Activity
The children will show their awareness of the appropriate clothing for the different seasons by dressing up as Old Man (Woman) Winter; Hot, Hot Summer, etc.

More Advanced Activity
To demonstrate their understanding of the need for various clothing, the children will cut from magazines pictures depicting clothing worn during different seasons. The pictures can be categorized in a scrapbook by seasons with accompanying experience stories from the children.

Design your own activity to meet the needs of individual children.

Postassessment

The postassessment is the same as the preassessment. After the postassessment, exit from the module or proceed to additional activities.

Additional Activities

● To demonstrate their understanding of the basic needs of mankind, the children will on several occasions play "I need"—I need clothes to keep me warm, etc.
● After a baby has been brought to the class, the children will show their awareness of basic needs by discussing with the mother what the baby needs and how these needs are like or unlike their own.

Resources
Books

Department of Instruction. *Economics for the Primary School.* Oklahoma City Public Schools, 1964.
Economic Education. Minneapolis Public Schools, 1967.
Everyday Economics. Noble and Noble Publishers, Inc., 1967.
Families and Their Needs. Silver Burdett Co.
Green, Mary. *Everybody Eats.*
_____. *Everybody Has a House.*
Miles, Betty. *A House for Everyone.*
Parsons, Virginia. *Homes.*
Senesh, Lawrence. *Our Working World: Families at Work.* Science Research Associates, Inc., 1963.

Filmstrips

Encyclopedia Brittanica Films
Clothing
Shelter

2.2 Family Members as Producers and Consumers

Rationale
Children need to be aware that all human beings—even young children—are producers and consumers of goods and services. To become economically aware, the child must have many experiences in which he/she is conscious of acting as either a producer or a consumer. In addition, the child needs to be able to recognize when his/her family members are acting as producers or consumers. Inherent in these experiences is a growing awareness of the relationship of production to consumption and the child's role in this process.

Prerequisites
Gather books and filmstrips such as those listed in the resources section at the end of this module. Assemble a collection of pictures showing people consuming or producing goods and services. Introduce the terms *consumer, producer, goods,* and *services* by mounting pictures or charts on a bulletin board. Take photographs of the children, the teacher, and other people in their everyday roles as consumers or producers.

Preassessment
• To show an understanding of the role of family members as consumers of goods and services, each child will answer the following questions appropriately:
"Who are the consumers in your family?" (Child should name all family members, including himself/herself.) "What are some of the goods that your family consumes or uses?" (Acceptable answers would be foods, clothing, household objects, candy, cars, etc. The list must cover three consumer categories and should include at least ten items.) "What are some of the services that your family uses?" (An acceptable answer might be the telephone, Mother getting her hair fixed, going to the doctor, etc. Each child must name at least five services.)
• To show an understanding of family members as producers of goods and services, each child will answer the following question:
"Who are the members of your family who produce goods and services in the home?" (Child should name all the family members, including himself/herself.)
After this preassessment, exit from the module or proceed to the objectives.

Objective 1
The children will begin to understand the role of family members as consumers of goods and services.

Activities
• Using hand puppets, the children will display their awareness of family members as consumers by having the puppet say, "I am a consumer because I use _____."
• To demonstrate their understanding of the role of people as consumers, the children will cut from magazines pictures of people consuming goods.

12

• To indicate their awareness of the role of family members as consumers of services, the children will select from a group of pictures those showing people who provide a service to the family.
• To show their awareness of consumers of goods and services, the children will sort and discuss the photographs mentioned in the prerequisites according to whether they depict a producer or a consumer.

Alternate Activities

Simple Activity
To demonstrate their awareness of people as consumers of goods and services, the children will name some things they use each day and the people who provide them with particular services (postman, teacher, bus driver) in a game format, using tabletop models of people.

More Advanced Activities
• The children will mount pictures on a bulletin board under the appropriate headings—Consumer, Producer, Goods, Services—to demonstrate their understanding of these economic terms.
• The children will make cookies (as producers) and eat them (as consumers) to show their awareness of being a consumer.

Design your own activity to meet the needs of individual children.

The children will begin to understand the role of family members as producers of goods and services.

Objective 2

• Using hand puppets, the children will play, "I am a producer, I made _____, or I did _____," to indicate their understanding of the role of family members as producers.
• To demonstrate their role as producers, the children will (a) produce a sculpture using clay, (b) make a picture for Mother, (c) make room decorations, (d) produce music as a rhythm band, (e) grow lima beans in Dixie cups, (f) produce a play, etc.
• To illustrate their understanding of differences between goods and services, the children will discuss services that the family needs at home (ironing, running errands) while the teacher puts their ideas in words and pictures on experience charts or the flannel board.
• To show an awareness of family members as producers of goods and services, the child will tape record daily one way that Mother (or Father, Sister, Brother) was a producer. (She made cookies, cooked my food, made my bed, drove me to school, etc.) The child can replay the tape frequently so as to absorb the idea of the family as producers. As the tape recording increases in length, the child can be encouraged to add what services he/she provides in the home.

Activities

Simple Activity
As the teacher tells a story of a family member acting as a producer (Mother making beds, Father mowing the lawn), the children act out the parts illustrating their understanding of family members as producers.

Alternate Activities

More Advanced Activity
Given a consumable product, the children will demonstrate their understanding of producers by building a tabletop display of the process of changing the raw product into a consumable item. (A display of the story of milk from the cow to the table.)

Design your own activity to meet the needs of individual children.

Postassessment
The postassessment is the same as the preassessment. After the postassessment, exit from the module or proceed to additional activities.

Additional Activities
• The children will role play family members "consuming" and "producing" goods and services to demonstrate their understanding of family members as producers and consumers. The teacher can use familiar nursery rhymes and animal stories as part of the role-playing technique.
• After hearing a book like *The Little Family* by Lois Lenski, the children will identify the goods and services consumed and discuss the production required for each, indicating their understanding of these economic terms.

Resources
Books
Everyday Economics. Noble and Noble Publishers, Inc., 1967.
Just Like Father. Golden Press.
Just Like Mother. Golden Press.
"Our Home and the Family." *Economics Education of Enterprising Teachers,* vol. 11.

Filmstrips
Working Together in the Family. Encyclopedia Britannica Films.
Work Inside the Home. McGraw-Hill, Co.
Work Outside the Home. McGraw-Hill, Co.

2.3 Medium of Exchange

Rationale
Somewhere, sometime, somehow man invented money. We believe that some of the first money was shells, bones, stones, or some other objects easy to carry around. Although we are not sure what was used, we do understand the tremendous importance of the invention.

An early understanding of the inconvenience and limitations of these early monies will help the child appreciate the complex money system that civilization now enjoys.

Prerequisites
Have on hand stories and pictures of early money, clay dough or play dough with which to make primitive money, rocks, scrap materials for art, and unwanted or old toys and games to be used for bartering.

• Each child will be able to identify three pictures of early money and will be able to describe how the system worked, to show an understanding of early money. (Tests for objective)
• Given two tables, each child will demonstrate an understanding of bartering by making a good trade with the teacher who "owns" one table or box and wants to barter with the child. (Tests for objective)
After this preassessment, exit from the module or proceed to the objective.

The children will learn some early mediums of exchange and the process of trading and bartering.

• The children will develop an understanding of early mediums of exchange after seeing pictures, hearing stories, and making mediums from other countries in art. Examples: Yap Island—circle of stone carried on pole, Africa—lumps of salt, Indians—wampum.
• Using teacher-collected scrap materials, each child will demonstrate an understanding of trade, by creating a product to trade for another child's goods or products. (A good trade or barter is one that leaves both parties satisfied.)
• On a tabletop have the children convert the amount of one child's lunch money into Yap Island, African, and Indian monies discussed in the first activity of this section in order to increase their understanding of the problems with early mediums of exchange.

Simple Activity
Using old toys or games brought from home, the children will demonstrate their understanding of bartering by trading with friends several times until they get the toys or games that they want.

More Advanced Activity
After seeing pictures of several different kinds of money, the children will demonstrate their knowledge of the convenience of present-day money, by telling (in their own words) why we have changed from trade and barter to a monetary system.

Design your own activity to meet the needs of individual children.

The postassessment is the same as the preassessment. After the postassessment, exit from the module or proceed to additional activities.

• To increase the child's understanding of different mediums of exchange, the child will work with the teacher to change American money into Yap Island money and Yap Island money into African money.
• To increase the child's understanding of bartering and trading, the child will barter by using different objects in the room and choosing another child to trade with.

15

| Resources | Nitsche, Roland. *Money.* McGraw-Hill Co., 1970.
Wade, William. *From Barter to Banking: The Story of Money.* |

2.4 Our Money

Rationale	Heads have rolled, crimes been committed, and empires lost because of money. Money and other concepts of economics can be developed only through day-to-day learning and experience. Education about the value and uses of money will enable children to be better consumers and more knowledgeable about our economic structure.
Prerequisites	Have on hand real money, a teacher-made bank game, colored pencils, blank checks, books such as *I Know a Bank Teller*, by Barbara Williams, and a student-made city large enough to role play in.
Preassessment	• Given currency and checks, each child will show that he/she can recognize money by naming each piece of money correctly and telling what a check is for. (Currency used should be penny, nickel, dime, quarter, and fifty-cent piece and $1, $5, and $10 bills.) • Using 50¢ in change, each child will show an understanding of the values of different pieces of money by putting together enough of the change to exceed more than 25¢ and telling the teacher the value of each coin used. • Given 25¢ in change, the child will show a knowledge of money as a purchasing power by giving correct change for cookies or candy "sold" by the young ladies of the housekeeping area. After this preassessment, exit from the module or proceed to the objectives.
Objective 1	The children will recognize the different kinds of money up to ten dollars.
Activities	• After seeing a group of coins, the children will show their recognition of money by correctly classifying the coins according to denomination. (Example: pennies go in the penny box, nickels in the nickel box, etc.) • After inspecting $1, $5, and $10 bills, the children will show their recognition of money by pointing to the numbers that determine what amount each bill is for. • Using checks from several banks, the children will demonstrate their recognition of the different kinds of money by experimenting writing checks to each other.
Alternate Activities	*Simple Activity* Using appropriate colored pencils and white paper, each child will

place a coin under the paper and mark over it to show recognition of coin color and face as it develops. This activity should be repeated as often as necessary using different coins.

More Advanced Activity
After hearing stories and seeing pictures of the faces of money, each child will demonstrate an understanding by telling how he/she recognizes each piece of money.

Design your own activities to meet the needs of individual children.

The children will display beginning knowledge of the value of money.

Objective 2

Activities

• Given a group of pennies, each child will show beginning knowledge of the value of money by assembling stacks of five pennies and ten pennies. This activity should be experienced repeatedly for other coin denominations. For the ten pennies the child can exchange one dime, or for five stacks of five pennies, a quarter.
• Given three different bills, the children will demonstrate their knowledge of the value of money by putting the bills in appropriate order according to the number-value illustrated.

Simple Activity
Using pennies and nickels, the child will demonstrate an increased knowledge of the value of money by grouping values of 10¢. For each correct grouping, the child can have an item from among a "white elephant" collection that the class has assembled.

Alternate Activities

More Advanced Activity
Using a teacher-made piggy-bank game, the child will demonstrate an increased knowledge of size and value by collecting money for his bank each turn. At his turn, if the child can name the value of what he collects, he can put it in his piggy bank. The child with the most money wins the game.

Design your own activity to meet the needs of individual children.

The children will appreciate money as a purchasing power.

Objective 3

Activities

• Given a choice of jobs, the children will show an appreciation of money as a purchasing power by receiving a wage, paid by check, by the teacher, who role plays as employer.
• Using a student-made and -operated bank, the child will show an appreciation of money as a purchasing power by depositing part or all of his/her check. (Refer to the above activity.)
• After discussing wants and needs, each child will show an appreciation of money as a purchasing power by deciding where in the student-made city to spend his money. (Refer to the above two activities.)

Alternate Activities

Simple Activity
While visiting the school store, the child will display an appreciation of money as a purchasing power by asking what each coin will buy and interacting with the teacher (shopkeeper) about why some things cost more.

More Advanced Activity
To demonstrate appreciation of their snack money, the children will chart their deposits and help decide which snacks to buy.

Design your own activity to meet the needs of individual children.

Postassessment

The postassessment is the same as the preassessment. After the postassessment, exit from the module or proceed to the additional activity.

Additional Activity

After a field trip to the supermarket, the children will demonstrate their understanding of money by role playing a supermarket experience with paper money.

Resources

Arnold, Oren. *Marvels of the U.S. Mint.* Abelard-Schuman, 1972.
Elkin, Ben. *The True Book of Money.* Childcraft, vol. 7.

2.5 Human Resources in the Community— Public Services

Rationale

Each family has its needs and wants provided through public services. For safety and protection, people want many services also. Families want someone to direct and control traffic, enforce laws, help at accidents, put out fires, and rescue the lost. Some services, such as fire and police departments, are provided by the government because they are too expensive for a business to provide. Services produced by the government are used by all the people. The young child needs to become aware of some of the public services available to his family.

Prerequisites

Refer to the resources section for books, films, and filmstrips that will introduce the module to the children.

Preassessment

• Each child will demonstrate an understanding of the services rendered by the fire department by naming four of these services when asked. (Examples: puts out fires, rescues people or animals, runs ambulance services, gives first aid.)

18

• Each child will demonstrate an understanding of the services rendered by the police department by naming four of these services when asked. (Example: helps you get across the street, catches people who break laws, gives first aid, helps you if you are lost, and answers questions.)

• Each child will demonstrate an understanding of the services of the post office by naming four of these services when asked. (Examples: handles money orders, and registers aliens.)

After this preassessment, exit from the module or proceed to the objectives.

The children will learn what services the fire department provides for the community.

Objective 1

• Given a group of pictures, each child will demonstrate a knowledge of services performed by the fire department by choosing the pictures of services related to the fire department.

Activities

• Given a tape recorder and tape, each child will demonstrate skill in describing the equipment used by the fire department by telling a story about himself/herself as a fireman. Children work in twos and threes, listening to each other's tapes.

• After a visit to the fire department, the children will demonstrate their knowledge of services the fire department performs by constructing a mural of these services.

• After a discussion, each child will demonstrate a knowledge of four services of the fire department through role playing.

• Using various appropriate visual aids listed in the resources, the children will show their awareness of the services of the fire department by drawing the fireman engaged in his work. The drawings become a book called, "What the Fire Department Does for Us."

Simple Activity
After displaying pictures of various objects used by the fire department, each child will demonstrate an understanding of how they are used by role playing a fireman using them. (This can be done with hand puppets.)

Alternate Activities

More Advanced Activity
Given a certain situation, the children will show their knowledge of rescuing a pet by dramatizing every action the fire department would have to take in the rescue.

Design your own activity to meet the needs of individual children.

The children will understand what services the police department provides for the community.

Objective 2

• The children will demonstrate their knowledge of safety regulations taught by the police department by responding with the appropriate action (stop, slow, or go) when red, yellow, and green circles are held up by the teacher.

Activities

● After constructing a crosswalk, the children will demonstrate their knowledge of police service by showing how they cross the street on the way to school. Children will take turns playing the policeman.
● Given the situation of being lost, the children will demonstrate their knowledge of how to contact the police department by role playing the scene.
● Given bulletin-board materials, the children will demonstrate their knowledge of the different services of the police department by constructing their own bulletin board on this subject. (Variation: a tabletop display of services instead of the bulletin board.)

Alternate Activities

Simple Activity
Given paper and crayons, the children will draw a picture to demonstrate their knowledge of ways in which people are protected by the police department.

More Advanced Activity
After a visit to the classroom by a uniformed policeman and a plainclothes detective, the children will show their increased awareness of services by role playing or by constructing a puppet show about policemen and policewomen.

Design your own activity to meet the needs of individual children.

Objective 3
The children will learn some of the services that a post office performs for the community

Activities

● After a field trip to the post office, the children will demonstrate their knowledge of the functions of the post office by drawing pictures of the various things they saw going on.
● After listening to a story about mailing a letter, the children will demonstrate their understanding by supplying their own ending to the story. Each child will dictate a letter for the teacher. He will act as the mailman in delivering the letter.
● Given play money and stamps, the children will demonstrate their knowledge of postal service by buying and selling the stamps.
● Given a set of pictures, the children will demonstrate their knowledge of the postal functions by constructing a wall frieze showing the process of mailing and receiving a package.

Alternate Activities

Simple Activity
After drawing pictures, the children will demonstrate their skills in mailing by sending their picture through the mail to someone they know and asking that one be sent to them.

More Advanced Activity
The children will demonstrate their skills in postal functions by performing postal functions in a postal department setting they have constructed.

Design your own activities to meet the needs of individual children.

The postassessment is the same as the preassessment. After the postassessment, exit from the module or proceed to additional activities.

- After listening to the teacher read aloud from the books in the resources section, the children will retell what services were performed and how.
- Given the opportunity to play with doll-like models of personnel from the post office, the police department, and the fire department, the children will demonstrate their knowledge of services by telling the story of their play to the teacher.

Beim, Jerrold. *Country Fireman*.
Gramatky, Hardie. *Hercules: The Story of an Old-Fashioned Fire Engine*.
Henroid, Lorraine. *I Know a Postman*.
Leaf, Munro. *Safety Can Be Fun*.
Lenski, Lois. *The Little Fire Engine*.
Park, Dorothea. *Here Comes the Postman*.
Williams, Barbara. *I Know a Policeman*.

Encyclopedia Britannica Films
Our Community.
The Policeman.
Mailman.
The Fireman.
Street Safety.
Our Post Office.

Safety At School and At Play. Young American Films, Inc.
Fireman. Popular Science Publishing Co.
The Policemen. Popular Science Publishing Co.
The Postman. Encyclopedia Britannica Films.

2.6 Human Resources in the Community—Health Services

The special services produced by the doctors, nurses, pharmacists, and dentists are part of the interdependence of specialized services. Each family is dependent upon these specialists to provide for its needs. The family, in using these services, acts as the consumer. The interdependence between the home and the neighborhood in meeting the health needs of the family provides a good starting point for economic awareness in the young child.

Prerequisites Introduce the terms, *goods, services, producers, consumers*, and *specialists* to the children. Refer to the resources section for books, films, and picture sets that will introduce the module to the children. Gather materials listed in the activities below.

Preassessment Each child will demonstrate his knowledge of producers of health services by answering: Who helps us when we are sick? When you have a toothache, who would you call? Where would you go to get medicine when you are sick? What are three things you could use for cuts and scratches? What equipment do people who provide health services use? (The child should name three or more pieces of equipment for each health service person.)

After this preassessment, exit from the module or proceed to the objective.

Objective The children will become aware of the many goods and services they want or need in order to protect their health.

Activities
• Given a thermometer, a stethoscope, a toothbrush, and medicine bottles, the children will demonstrate their knowledge of who produces related health services by matching the person with the appropriate object. (Example: the pharmacist uses the medicine bottles.)
• Given cotton balls, tongue depressors, cotton swabs, adhesive bandages, white gauze, medical tape, and construction paper, the children will show their knowledge of health services by arranging the objects in any order, then drawing pictures of them in use in some aspect of health services. (Example: You can buy these items from a drugstore.)
• After several visits from producers of health services, the children will show their awareness of health services by role playing these services.
• Given paper and crayons, each child will demonstrate a knowledge of various health services by drawing pictures of at least one person who helps us protect our health.
• Given learning-center space, the children will display their awareness of health services by constructing a learning center that provides health services.

Alternate Activities
Simple Activity
After displaying pictures of various objects used by producers of health services, each child will demonstrate knowledge of how they are used by telling how they have value to the consumer.

More Advanced Activity
The children will demonstrate their knowledge of the hospital as a producer of services by dramatizing a child who goes to the hospital to have his/her tonsils removed.

Design your own activity to meet the needs of individual children.

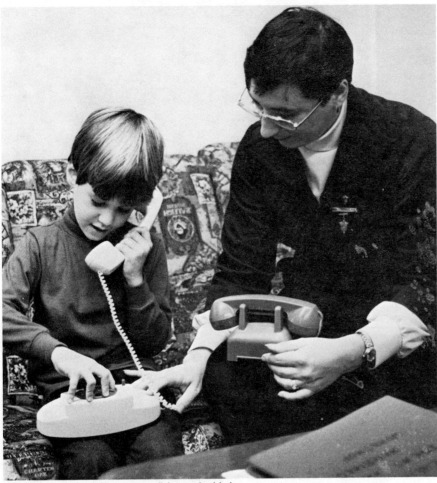
2.6 The nurse teaching how to call for medical help

The postassessment is the same as the preassessment. After the postassessment, exit from the module or proceed to the additional activities.

Postassessment

● After hearing a story about some aspect of health service (See resources section on books), the children will display their awareness of health services by acting out parts of the story.
● After constructing a drug store, the children will show their awareness of producers and consumers of health services by buying and selling products related to their health. (Cardboard boxes that patent medicines come in can be used.)
● Given a toy telephone, the children will show how to obtain health service when they are sick by making an appointment to see the doctor (telling him/her of their symptoms, etc.).

Additional Activities

Bolian, Polly. *I Know A Nurse.*
Greene, Carla. *I Want to Be A Nurse.*
_____. *Doctors and Nurses: What They Do.*
Economics Education. Minneapolis Public Schools.
Lakritz, Easter. *Randy Visits the Doctor.*

Resources
Books

23

songs such as "Old MacDonald's Farm."
● Shown pictures of large farm machinery, the child will demonstrate a knowledge of farm machinery by telling why these instead of a hoe and rake are used on large farms and why they are necessary tools for providing us with large amounts of vegetables.

Alternate Activities

Simple Activity
When given a sample of three or more cooked vegetables such as green beans, corn, and potatoes, the child will show a knowledge of different vegetables by tasting each vegetable and telling what it is and where it was grown.

More Advanced Activities
● The child will show an understanding of how vegetables can be grown by other means than seeds by placing a sweet potato partially in a jar of water and watching leaves, stems, and roots grow.
● Given an empty milk carton, popsicle sticks, colored coconut, and other art materials, the children will show their knowledge of the farm by constructing a model of a farm.

Design your own activity to meet the needs of individual children.

Objective 3

The children will learn that the farm and its machinery provide us with cotton, a product needed for making some clothing.

Activities

● After looking at and touching each other's clothes, the children will show their knowledge of clothing material by telling what products we get many of our clothes from. (Examples: cotton, wool.)
● After examining a boll of cotton, the children can show their knowledge of what cotton can be made into by pulling off a small quantity and twisting it in their fingers to make yarn.
● After taking a trip to a cotton field and picking cotton by hand, the children will show their knowledge of cotton picking by telling why we use cotton-picking machines instead of picking large quantities by hand.
● Following a trip to a cotton gin, the children will display their knowledge of the process involved in making cotton into cloth by describing the process.
● After seeing pictures of a cotton field, the children will display their knowledge of the process of making cotton into material by telling the things that must happen to it before it is wearing apparel.
● Given cloth samples of cotton, wool, linen, and silk, the children will demonstrate their recognition of cotton by picking out the cotton pieces from the other materials.
(If the last three activities are not practicable, use pictures or a film to help the child understand about cotton.)

Alternate Activities

Simple Activity
Given a paper sack, yarn for hair, and cotton material for clothing, the children will display their knowledge that clothes can be made out of

cotton by making a puppet for a puppet show. (Glue or staples can be used instead of thread for seams.)

More Advanced Activity
After examining different samples of materials, the children will show their understanding of cotton and other materials used for clothing by using the samples to dress paper dolls.

Design your own activities to meet the needs of individual children.

Postassessment

The postassessment is the same as the preassessment. After the postassessment, exit from the module or proceed to additional activities.

Additional Activities

• Given milk, chocolate, and sugar, the children will show their understanding of products made from milk by making hot chocolate and telling that it is a milk product.
• After planting and raising a garden, the children will show their understanding of vegetable soup as a product from the vegetable garden by making soup from their own vegetables and telling that this is a product we receive from the farmer.
• Given samples of cotton material, the children will show their understanding of cotton as a product by making a pin cushion of the material stuffed with cotton or by weaving a potholder with cotton loops.

Resources
Books

Economic Education. Minneapolis Public Schools, 1967.
Let's Go to the Dairy. Goodspeed, 1956.
Llewellen. *Tommy Learns to Drive a Tractor.* Crowell, 1958.
Floethe. *Farmer and His Cows.* Scribner, 1957.
Ipear. *Ten Big Farms.* Knopf, 1958.
The Social Sciences Concepts and Values. Harcourt, Brace and World, Inc. 1970.

Films

Uncle Jim's Dairy Farm.
Our Trip to a Dairy Plant.
Our Foster Mother, the Cow.

Poem

"The Harpers' Farm."

Songs

"The Farmer in the Dell."
"Old MacDonald Had a Farm."
"The Farmer and His Animals."

Other Resource

Flannel Kits about the Farm.

Design your own activities to meet the needs of individual children.

Objective 3 The child will understand that people help us get the food we want.

Activities
- Given a blank sheet of art paper, the child will show a knowledge of places we get food by drawing or describing some things they might eat if they lived near an apple orchard, a coconut grove, or a lake.
- Given hypothetical questions such as, "Suppose there were no farmers, would you have food? How?" "Suppose there were no fishermen, would you have fish? How?" the child will show an awareness of our dependence on other people for food by giving his own answers to the questions.
- As a way of showing that the child understands that people help us get food, the child will act out a skit pretending to help someone get food.

Alternate Activities

Simple Activity
Using a teacher-made game of cardboard people and objects, the children will show their understanding that people help us get food by matching the fisherman with a fish, the farmer with corn, etc.

More Advanced Activity
After a visit from a fish breeder, the children will show their awareness of people who help us get food by breeding goldfish or guppies in the classroom aquarium (or shrimp in salt water under a lamp).

Design your own activity to meet the needs of individual children.

Postassessment The postassessment is the same as the preassessment. After the postassessment, exit from the module or proceed to the additional activities.

Additional Activities
- Given water, a fishing pole, bait, and a plastic fish, the child will show a knowledge of the things needed to catch fish by fishing appropriately without assistance.
- To demonstrate their knowledge that many people depend on the fishing industry as means for a living, the children will take a trip to a fishing dock or harbor and question the people who work there about how they earn a living.

Resources Books
Lionni, L. *Swimmy.* 1963.
Meyers, G. *The Fishing Cat.* 1953.
Puccinellie, M. *Catch a Fish.* 1965.
Watts. *The First Book of Fishes.* 1965.

Films
Getting Food Ready for Market.
How Goods Come to Us.

30

2.9 Capital Resources—Transportation

By age five, a child should realize that different types of transportation are needed in the movement of goods between the producer and the consumer, and they should know some of these types. The child should be aware that types of transportation differ according to the distance the goods must travel and the type of goods being shipped.

Construct a large picture chart showing at least ten consumer goods; gather the books and filmstrips suggested in the resources section; collect paper, crayons, boxes of all sizes, glue, paint, brushes, scissors, and clay; and arrange for a field trip to the railroad yard.

• The child will show an awareness of the different vehicles of transportation by identifying pictures of a car, train, truck, airplane, boat, ship, space vehicle, submarine, bicycle, motorcycle, and bus.
• The child will demonstrate a knowledge of goods transported from far away by pointing out seven of those goods on a picture chart. After doing the preassessment, exit from the module or proceed to the objectives.

The child will gain awareness of different means of transportation.

• After making a bulletin board displaying different modes of transportation, the child will demonstrate a knowledge of these vehicles by attaching a yarn or string from the toy model of the vehicle to the picture and naming each vehicle. (The length of the yarn serves as a self-correcting device.)
• After hearing a story about trucks and a snowman, the child will demonstrate a knowledge of what kind of truck took the snowman by telling about the refrigerator truck and the kinds of goods it can carry. (The teacher makes up the story described.)
• After constructing a truck or a train from boxes, the child will demonstrate an awareness of trucks or trains as a means of transportation by telling what products the model truck or train could haul.
• During many experiences with vehicles in the sandbox, the child will show an awareness of different kinds of transportation by playing with many kinds of vehicles.

Simple Activity
After having a class discussion on loading train cars, the child will show a knowledge of freight-car loading by role playing the packing of a freight car.

More Advanced Activity
After dictating a story to the teacher about the types of transportation, the child will show an awareness of the means of transportation, by drawing pictures of the kinds of vehicles mentioned in the story.

Design your own activities to meet the needs of individual children.

Objective 2   The child will become aware of the ways communication helps in the buying and selling of goods.

Activities   • Given a play telephone, the children will demonstrate, by role playing the ordering of products for the play store, their knowledge of how the phone would be used for ordering products.
• After a field trip to a television station to see a commercial taped, the child will demonstrate a knowledge of how commercials on these instruments advertise products by making up a commercial and telling it to the other children.

Alternate Activities   *Simple Activity*
After watching television for thirty minutes, the child will show an awareness of commercials by telling what one commercial was selling during that thirty-minute period.

More Advanced Activity
Given hand puppets, the child will demonstrate a knowledge of commercials by using the puppet to do a commercial for selling a favorite toy.
Given a teacher-made telegraph set, each child will demonstrate a knowledge of buying and selling goods by sending the teacher a message about what he/she wants to buy or sell.

Design your own activities to meet the needs of individual children.

Postassessment   The postassessment is the same as the preassessment. After the postassessment, exit from the module or proceed to the additional activities.

Additional Activities   • After watching the filmstrip *How We Use Communication*, the child will show an awareness of types of communication by telling the type he/she likes best and why.
• After hearing the story, "Let's Take a Trip to the Newspaper," the child will show a knowledge of how a newspaper is used for communication by cutting out the picture advertisements in a newspaper.

Resources Books   Sootin, *Let's Take a Trip to the Newspaper.* 1956.
Tannebaum, *We Read about Television and How It Works.* 1960.
———. *Your Telephone and How it Works.* 1962.

Filmstrip   *How We Use Communication.*

3
Language Development

Language development continues from birth to death. The young child already has language when he comes to school. But he may need help in becoming a better listener so that he can become a better language receiver. In fact, many young children need help in communicating more effectively. Learning to discriminate in certain ways is the awareness process needed at this time as a preparation for reading or writing. A beginning awareness of the structure of the language is also necessary.

This chapter contains eighteen modules or units of learning designed to facilitate language development. There are no starting points in the chapter except for the modules on writing skills, which have prerequisites.

There is no complete curriculum in language development for young children. These eighteen modules are a comprehensive beginning toward a creative curriculum to be jointly developed by the classroom teacher.

The modules are as follows:

3.1   Listening Skills: Discrimination and Sequence
3.2   Listening Skills: Listening for a Purpose
3.3   Listening to Rhyming Sounds
3.4   Listening to Nature's Sounds
3.5   Visual Discrimination—Let's Look
3.6   Language Structure
3.7   Drama: The Voice
3.8   Communication and/or Conversation
3.9   Understanding Spoken Language
3.10   Vocabulary Building
3.11   Visual Discrimination: Sequential
3.12   Prewriting Visual—Motor Skills
3.13   Prewriting: Sensory Training
3.14   Beginning Premanuscript Writing
3.15   Manuscript Writing
3.16   Ask the Alphabet
3.17   Drama: The Gestures
3.18   Creative Dramatics

Design your own activities to meet the needs of individual children.

Postassessment

The postassessment is the same as the preassessment. After the postassessment, exit from the module or proceed to the additional activities.

Additional Activities

• After hearing a tape of local environmental sounds the children will show their ability to discriminate by naming the various sounds in the environment. The children will then show their awareness of these sounds and the ability to recognize them by identifying the various sounds while on a "listening walk" out-of-doors.
• The teacher will make up rhyming words by changing the end sounds of familiar words and say the words as well as give out pictures of the words. The children will show their ability to discriminate in terms of rhyming words by standing next to the child whose word now rhymes with theirs.
• The children will set out pictures of animals. One child will then name an animal by only saying the first part of its name. The other children will demonstrate their awareness of beginning word sounds by pointing to the picture that matches the sound.

Resources

Lambert, Hazel M. *Teaching the Kindergarten Child.* Harcourt, Brace and World, Inc., 1958.
Scott, L. B. *Learning Time With Language Experiences for Young Children.* Webster Division, McGraw-Hill Co., 1968.

3.2 Listening Skills:
Listening for a Purpose

Rationale

Children do not always know what to listen to or how to listen because they are subjected to endless numbers of sounds. Because of this inability, emphasis is being placed on the teaching of listening as a language skill requiring development.

Listening is an aid to language development. It is the most frequently used communication skill. It demands concentration and thinking. An effective method for improving listening skills is to have the children listen for a purpose.

Prerequisites

Have on hand the stories mentioned in the resources section.

Preassessment

The child will demonstrate an understanding of instructions by following five consecutive instructions correctly: "Pick up a box; put some crayons in it; take this to a particular table; do not sit down; draw a picture to surprise the teacher." The instructions are said after the teacher says, "Listen and do exactly as I say. I have something for you to do that's fun."

After doing this preassessment, exit from the module or proceed to the objective.

The children will learn to follow consecutive instructions by listening.

• Given three tasks consecutively, each child will demonstrate his ability to follow simple instructions such as "go get a book," "brush your hair," and "work on the puzzle."
• After a poem such as "The Sugar Plum Tree," by Eugene Field, each child will demonstrate an ability to understand simple instructions by listening to the poem and then drawing a picture showing two things the teacher asks him/her to draw from the poem.
• Given five different sounds (accelerate for go, cease for stop, simmer for slow down, reverse for go backwards, and rotate for turn around) each child will demonstrate an ability to follow simple instructions accurately by listening to the sounds and following the directions.

Simple Activity
Given two tasks consecutively, each child will demonstrate an ability to follow simple instructions such as "go get a puzzle" and "return it to the puzzle rack" by following the instructions accurately. Variation: "Go get a puzzle, put it together, check to see if all the pieces are in the box, put it back in the puzzle rack."

More Advanced Activity
Each child will demonstrate an ability to follow instructions by contracting with the teacher to do three activities and then doing them as was mutually agreed without having to be reminded of what they were.

Design your own activity to meet the needs of individual children.

The postassessment is the same as the preassessment. After the postassessment, exit from the module or proceed to additional activities.

• Given auditory discrimination games such as "Where Are My Reindeer?" "Will You Be My Valentine?" and "Bunny Wants a Home" (see resources section), each child will demonstrate an ability to follow oral directions by successfully playing the games.
• Upon hearing some "Where Am I?" stories, each child will demonstrate an ability to follow simple instructions by correctly identifying the locations.

Croft and Hess. *An Activities Handbook for Teachers of Young Children*. Houghton Mifflin Co., 1975.
"Gobble! Gobble!," "Circle Stoop," "Hunter," "Where are My Reindeer?," "Will You Be My Valentine?" and "Bunny Wants a Home." *Kindergarten: An Intuitive Approach*. Tulsa Public Schools.
Lorton, Mary. *Workjobs*. Addison-Wesley Co., 1972.
Scott, L. "The Cricket Who Didn't Listen." In *Learning Time With*

Language Experiences for Young Children. McGraw-Hill Co., 1968.
Smith, James A. *Creative Teaching of the Language Arts in the Elementary School*, 2d ed. Allyn and Bacon, Inc., 1973.

3.3 Listening to Rhyming Sounds

Rationale

Language development is a vital part of the school curriculum. One of the most important functions of the teacher of the young child is to plan and execute programs sensitive to the language needs of each individual.

The major goal of any auditory language program should be to develop a smooth flow of ideas and thoughts. The teacher who plans activities that facilitate these kinds of fluency can be assured of success.

The teacher should always keep in mind the importance of accepting the child's language. This language is a part of him/her, and to reject it is to reject the child himself/herself. To achieve fluency the child must have many opportunities to discriminate between sounds. The use of rhymes is an enjoyable way of learning to listen better.

Prerequisites

Read the following:
Dorsey, Mary E. *Reading Games and Activities*, Fearon Publishers, 1972.
Heyman, Marjorie Rowe. *Enriching Your Reading Program*, Fearon Publishers, 1972.

Preassessment

The children will demonstrate their ability to recognize a rhyming word by saying which two words rhyme when they hear three words presented. They should answer correctly four out of the five following instances:

    cat, rat, bear
    to, jump, who
    tick, lick, like
    bike, kite, mike
    running, funny, money

After the preassessment, exit from the module or proceed to the objective.

Objective

The children will learn to identify rhyming words.

Activities

• Given a word, the children will show that they perceive rhyming words by telling another word that rhymes with the original word. (Examples: I am thinking of a word that sounds like *big*. It goes oink, oink, oink! [Pig]. I am thinking of a word that sounds like *head* and it is a color [red].)

• After hearing a sentence, the children will complete the second

sentence with a word that rhymes with the last word of the first sentence to show their perception of rhyming words. (Example: You jump. I _____ [clump, dump, bump].)
● Given a picture of an object, the children will show their perception of rhyming words by holding up a second picture whose object name rhymes with the original.
● Using a series of jump-rope rhymes and a jump rope, each child will show an understanding of rhyming by jumping only on the rhyming words.

Alternate Activities

Simple Activity
To demonstrate their knowledge of rhyming words, the children will tell which pairs of words rhyme. (Examples: sat-stair, fat-sat, hair-stair, flip-flop, mother-brother.)

More Advanced Activity
Given a word, the children will demonstrate their understanding of rhyming words by saying a series of words that rhyme with the first one. (Example: *Love* rhymes with *shove, glove, above, dove.*)
(Variation: Draw pictures of words that rhyme with the teacher's.)

Design your own activities to meet the needs of individual children.

The postassessment is the same as the preassessment. After the postassessment, exit from the module or proceed to the additional activities.

Postassessment

● After listening to three sounds, the child will demonstrate a knowledge of rhyming words by telling which does not sound like the others. (Example: two taps of a spoon on a glass and one tap of the spoon on a plastic glass.)
● Each child will show an understanding of rhyming words by working with the teacher to think up one word for a line poem that rhymes with his/her or another's name. (Example: Glen bends ten men when Glen defends.)

Additional Activities

Baumer, Mary Phyllis. *Seasonal Kindergarten Units.* Fearon Publishers, 1972.
Dorsey, Mary E. *Reading Games and Activities.* Fearon Publishers, 1972.
Heyman, Marjorie Rowe. *Enriching Your Reading Program.* Fearon Publishers, 1972.
Kingsley, Bernard. *Reading Skills.* Fearon Publishers, 1972.

Resources

3.4 Listening to
Nature's Sounds

Rationale   Listening to nature's sounds sharpens listening skills and is fun. Nature is an inexhaustible materials resource for the teacher. It isn't just a matter of listening to sounds as they exist, but also of having the teacher simulate certain sounds and call attention to patterns that exist. This module should help the teacher to use nature in depth as a resource for learning.

Prerequisites   Have on hand recordings of regional animal sounds, stethoscopes for listening to heart beats, a faucet to drip water, rocks of different shapes, two metal buckets; a hamster, a mouse, and a parakeet; bean bags filled with different materials such as rice, feathers, small macaroni, sand, dried corn; a pillow, marbles, an aluminum picnic table, and materials to cover bean bags.

Preassessment   Each child will show his knowledge of nature's sounds by correctly answering all of the following questions:
* What sounds do each of these animals make? (Choose recordings of five regional animals.)
* I am going to drop a rock into something. Tell me what I dropped it into. (Drop it into an empty bucket, a bucket with water, a container of sand, and from one hand to another. All of this is out of sight of the children.)
* What sound does your heart make?
* I'll drop each of these bags (bean bags described in prerequisites) on the table. Tell me which has corn in it.
After doing the preassessment, exit from the module or proceed to the objective.

Objective   Each child will learn to discriminate between many of nature's sounds by carefully listening.

Activities   • After a walk around the neighborhood to listen to five of nature's sounds, the children will show their increased awareness of nature's sounds when hearing them replayed on tape by correctly identifying each. (This activity should be repeated several times, each time increasing the children's knowledge of different sounds.)
• After experimenting with dropping rocks into an empty bucket, into a water-filled bucket, onto a pillow, and onto sand, the children will demonstrate their ability to discriminate between these by playing Blindfold. (One child wears a blindfold while another drops a rock into one of the substances named above, asking the blindfold wearer to tell what he/she is doing.)
• After listening to his/her own heart beat and another child's using a stethoscope, each child will show an awareness of this natural sound by singing it, playing it on the drum, and by pounding the sound with fists on a table.

42

• After making bean bags of the materials described in the prerequisites of this module, the children will show their awareness of the sound of the different bean bag stuffings by putting the bags back in containers of those materials. (Example: all bean bags stuffed with feathers go back into a bowl of feathers for storage.) The children should use the bean bags daily in games such as ring-toss, and should also toss the bag onto a chalked square on the aluminum table for points.

Simple Activity
Given an aluminum table, some rocks and marbles, the children will show their knowledge of the differences in sounds by playing games with these objects. (Put a cardboard edge around the table with masking tape to keep objects from falling off.) Variation: Add sand to the tabletop to change sound.

More Advanced Activity
Given a bird, a hamster, a mouse, and time to listen to their sounds, the children will show that they can discriminate between sounds by tape recording these sounds and telling each other and the teacher which animal is making a particular sound on the playback.

Design your own activities to meet the needs of individual children.

Alternate Activities

The postassessment is the same as the preassessment. After the postassessment, exit from the module or proceed to the additional activities.

Postassessment

• After listening to a hamster's heartbeat and his/her own heartbeat with the stethoscope, the child will show an ability to discriminate between nature's sounds by describing how each sounded—which beat faster, which was louder, etc.
• After listening to a story tape by the teacher on ten regional animals, the children will show that they can discriminate between these sounds by following the taped instructions as to what to do on a prepared sheet. (Example: [taped] "I am a cardinal, a very fine bird. I make this sound [recorded sound]. Listen to me again [repeat sound]. Listen to me again [repeat sound]. My feathers come to a point on top of my head. Look for me as you walk to school. I am bright red. I say [repeat sound]. Color me red." And the child colors the cardinal red on the prepared paper.

Additional Activities

Karnes, Merle B. *Helping Young Children Develop Language Skills*. Arlington, Virginia: The Council of Exceptional Children, 1968.

Resource

3.5 Visual Discrimination—
Let's Look!

Rationale Observation is an aid to language development. A significant goal of the teacher is to help the child develop visual discrimination. When color concepts, puzzles, and designs are provided, the child sharpens his/her powers of observation by noting likenesses and differences and seeing how things are taken apart and put together. Many experiences in how to discriminate visually are needed as a prerequisite for reading and spelling.

Prerequisites The teacher should tell the story "The Gray Velvet Rabbit" (see resources section). This story, when told on the flannel board, provides a lesson which stresses discrimination of textures and colors.

Have on hand animal models (four of each) and wooden or heavy cardboard letters (four of each) for children to manipulate.

Preassessment The child will demonstrate an awareness of similarities and differences by pointing correctly, nine out of ten times, to identical objects on cards. Each card contains four pictures of the same object, but only two are alike in position. (Use pictures of animals and letters from the alphabet.)

After this preassessment, exit from the module or proceed to the objective.

Objective The child learns to become aware of visual similarities and differences in the environment.

Activities • Each child will demonstrate an awareness of visual similarities and differences by identifying animal shapes of same size lying in different positions.
• Each child will demonstrate an awareness of visual similarities and differences by identifying letters of different sizes lying in different positions.
• Given visual discrimination games such as Fruit Basket, Where's the Easter Egg?, and the Lollipop Game (see resources section), each child will demonstrate an awareness of visual similarities and differences by successfully playing the games.

Alternate Activities *Simple Activity*
Given simple puzzles, each child will demonstrate an awareness of visual similarities and differences by assembling the pieces using shape as a criterion. (The teacher aids by helping the child develop patterns for discriminating.)

More Advanced Activity
Given blocks, each child will demonstrate an awareness of similarities

44

and differences by correctly assembling the blocks to duplicate patterns, models, or pictures provided by the teacher.

Design your own activities to meet the needs of individual children.

The postassessment is the same as the preassessment. After the postassessment, exit from the module or proceed to additional activities.

• Given visual discrimination games such as Police and Lost Child, Finding a Friend, and Color on Color (see resources section), each child will demonstrate an awareness of visual similarities and differences by successfully playing the games.
• Each child will demonstrate an awareness of visual similarities and differences by successfully pointing to his/her name among three others on the blackboard.
• Given visual discrimination games such as What is Missing? (see resources section), each child will demonstrate an awareness of visual similarities and differences by successfully playing the game. (Teacher shows an array of five objects on a tray, then hides one.)
• Given an assortment of round and square objects, each child will demonstrate an awareness of visual similarities and differences by correctly sorting objects according to their shapes.

Croft and Hess. *An Activities Handbook for Teachers of Young Children*. Houghton Mifflin Co., 1975.
"Fruit Basket," "Where's the Easter Egg?" "Lollipop Game," "Policeman and Lost Child," "Finding a Friend," "Color on Color," and "What is Missing?," *Kindergarten: An Intuitive Approach*. Tulsa Public Schools.
"The Gray Velvet Rabbit." In *Learning Time with Language Experiences for Young Children*. McGraw-Hill Co., 1968.
Lorton, Mary. *Workjobs*. Addison-Wesley Co., 1972.
Schubert, Delwyn, ed. *Reading Games That Teach*. Creative Teaching Press, 1965.

3.6 Language Structure

Oral communication should be a real and successful experience for young children. The children must be able to speak freely. Good grammar habits are developed through usage and repetition. Presenting the children with good patterns to model their speech after, rather than constantly correcting poor speech, is a more positive and productive way of assisting them in improving their grammar. There is no good starting point for the young child, but two areas that usually meet with some success are simple verb forms and positional words.

Prerequisites	Have on hand flannel board, cutouts, suckers, books.
Preassessment	• After watching the teacher make movements with a hand puppet, each child will show a knowledge of verb forms by correctly answering questions asked in singular and plural form. (Example: Teacher: What am I saying to you? Child: You are saying "Hello" and "Good-bye." Using two puppets, the teacher has the gesture meaning "Come here" and then asks "What are they saying?" Child: They are saying "Come here.")
• The children will demonstrate their understanding of positional words by placing a sucker in correct relationship to a book or the teacher as directed: Put the sucker (a) on top of the book, (b) beside the book, (c) under the book, (d) inside the book, (e) between the book and me, (f) over the book, (g) next to the book, (h) behind me, (i) to the right of the book, and (j) to the left of the book.
After the preassessment, exit from the module or proceed to the objective.
Objective	The children will learn the correct usage of verb forms (singular and plural) and the meanings of positional words; on top of, over, next to, behind, to the right of, and to the left of.
Activities	• The children will demonstrate their knowledge of simple verb forms by answering questions asked by the teacher with the correct verb form. (Example: I was baking a cake yesterday, what were you doing yesterday, Gayle? Answer: I *was* making a doll dress.)
• The children will show their understanding of positional words by placing objects on the flannel board in correct relationship to other objects as the teacher specifies. (Example: Put the boy next to the wagon.)
Alternate Activities	*Simple Activity*
The children will demonstrate their understanding of positional words by correctly placing themselves in relationship to other children as directed by the teacher. (Example: Mary, please stand behind John.)

More Advanced Activity
The children will show their ability to use positional words by describing a mystery object in the room or by telling a story using these forms. Example: The strange bump (object) is sleeping under a blue thing with legs (table).

Design your own activities to meet the needs of individual children. |
| **Postassessment** | The postassessment is the same as the preassessment. After the postassessment, exit from the module or proceed to the additional activities. |
| **Additional Activities** | • The children will demonstrate their understanding of positional words by correctly playing a game of Simon Says. Every one of |

Simon's commands will contain a positional word. (Example: Simon says, "Put your hands over your eyes!")
● The children will show their ability to use singular and plural verb forms by making statements about themselves in sentence form. (Example: "I am five years old," or "My parents are much older.")

Dunn, L. M. *Peabody Language Kits Level #P.* American Guidance Service Inc., 1968.
Scott, Louise Binder. *Learning Time with Language Experiences for Young Children.* McGraw-Hill Co., 1968.

Resources

3.7 Dramatics: The Voice

Rationale

An added tool to language development is drama in the classroom. Through this medium the children learn effective methods with which to "color" their increasing vocabulary. With drama, children have the opportunity to become aware of voice inflection, pitch, and power.

Prerequisites

Have on hand: girl puppet, old lady puppet, three pigs puppets, wolf puppet, costumes for activities, materials for making puppets.

Preassessment

● Given puppets, the children will demonstrate their skill in high, medium, and low voice pitches by performing a puppet play and using the proper voice for each puppet. (Extemporaneously, such stories as "Little Red Riding Hood" or "The Three Pigs.")
● Given a word, the children will demonstrate their ability to use voice inflections to change the meaning of the word by presenting a "one word" play (Example: "Good-bye" said with different inflections has different meanings.)
● Given a character role, the children will demonstrate their ability to use "colorful" vocabulary by describing themselves as a character from one of the familiar nursery rhymes. (Example: The wolf is creepy, sneaky, mean, hungry, strong, ugly, etc.)
● Given an object, each child will demonstrate skill in persuasion by telling the teacher about his/her favorite toy and why the teacher should buy one, too.
After the preassessment, exit from the module or proceed to the objectives.

Objective 1

The children will learn the skill of matching high, medium, and low voice pitches to story characters.

Activities

● After making their own finger puppets and puppet stage, the children, two at a time, will demonstrate their skill in high, medium, and low voice pitch by presenting to the class a short play using spontaneous dialogue and proper voice pitch for their own particular puppet.

47

• After hearing a story in which the characters vary in the pitch of their voices, they will all demonstrate their skill in high, medium, and low voice pitch by portraying a character role of one of the two people in the following situations: The Lost Boy and The Policeman, A Visit to the Dentist, or Two of My Favorite Monsters.

Alternate Activities

Simple Activity
The child will show skill in high, medium, and low voice pitch by interacting with the teacher when asked "What would a daddy's voice sound like?" "a mother's?" "a baby brother's or sister's?"

More Advanced Activity
The child will show skill in using high, medium, and low voice pitch by presenting a "one man" act, and portraying no less than three different characters, each with a different voice pitch, changing hats as he/she changes voices.

Design your own activities to meet the needs of individual children.

Objective 2

The children will learn to use voice inflections.

Activities

• Given any single word, the children will demonstrate their ability to use voice inflections by pairing off and representing to the class a "one word" play. (Examples: "OH!" "OH?" "OH" or "HOW!" "HOW?" "HOW.")
• Given a single word, one child will demonstrate skill at voice inflection while the rest of the class will respond by trying to match voice inflections. The child coming closest to the right voice inflection will take the place of the first child and the game will continue.

Alternate Activities

Simple Activity
The child will demonstrate his skill in using voice inflections by responding correctly to the teacher's questions:
• "How would you say 'oh' if you fell and cut your knee?"
• "How would you say 'oh' if mother handed you an ice cream or a candy?"

More Advanced Activity
Two children will demonstrate their skill in voice inflections by interacting with one another, each with just one word. For example, one child uses the word *oh* and the other child uses the word *what*. They conduct a dialogue, trying to exchange meanings using just their one word and a variety of voice inflections.

Design your own activities to meet the needs of individual children.

Objective 3

The children will learn how to use colorful vocabulary.

Activities

• After being assigned to character roles taken from familiar nursery

48

rhymes, the children will demonstrate their ability to use colorful vocabulary by describing themselves, as that character appears in the rhyme, to the class. The first in the class to identify the character exchanges places with the describer and the game resumes. (Example: Mother Goose is loving, sparkling, funny, etc.)

• After each child in the class has been given a particular animal name, the child will describe his/her animal to the class until a classmate identifies the animal, thus demonstrating an ability to use colorful vocabulary.

Alternate Activities

Simple Activity
Given an object, the child will show an ability to use colorful vocabulary by describing that object in as vivid a vocabulary as possible.

More Advanced Activity
After the children are given object names, they will show their ability to use colorful vocabulary by describing what they look like, smell like, taste like and/or feel like, thus finding their match ups. (Examples: hot dog—bun; bat—ball; cup—saucer.)

Design your own activities to meet the needs of individual children.

The children will learn how to use persuasive language.

Objective 4

Activities

• After being given an item to "sell," a group of three children will demonstrate their skill in the use of persuasive language by presenting to the class a television commercial sequence to convince the audience to buy their item.
• After selecting their own scene, the children will demonstrate their ability to use persuasive language by (1) persuading Mother to let them have an ice cream cone, (2) persuading Dad to let them have a ride on the ferris wheel at the fair, etc.

Alternate Activities

Simple Activity
After being presented with a piece of candy, the child will demonstrate skill in the use of persuasive language by telling why he/she should keep the piece of candy.

More Advanced Activity
After being given an object, the child will show an ability to use persuasive language by persuading another classmate that he/she really needs that object. (Example: baseball, wooden building block, or a piece of blank paper.)

Design your own acitivities to meet the needs of individual children.

The postassessment is the same as the preassessment. After the postassessment, exit from the module or proceed to the additional activities.

Postassessment

Additional Activities

- The children will demonstrate their skill in high, medium, and low voice pitches by orally exhibiting several emotional situations (Examples: anger, sadness, surprise, fear) after a demonstration by the teacher using several different puppets.
- After choosing a classmate, the child will demonstrate an ability to use voice inflections by calling the classmate several different ways but using only the classmate's name. The classmate will make comments on what was meant such as: "He/she is angry with me" or "He/she is surprised."
- When the teacher names a familiar television character, the children will show their ability to use colorful language by describing the character. (Example: Wolf-Man on Electric Company—dances, is silly, is hairy, likes to sing, scares people, etc.)
- Each child will demonstrate his/her persuasiveness by trying to convince the teacher that they should take a trip to the fair, a farm, Disneyland, or another place that the child wants to visit.

3.8 Communication and/or Conversation

Rationale

In language development it is important that the teacher include opportunities, throughout the day, for the children to practice their oral language skills. If the children are to communicate effectively, they must learn to receive communications from others, express their own ideas, use language easily and appropriately, and select the right word with confidence. To speak intelligently and freely is a social skill that young children need to become aware of and, later, master.

Prerequisites

Read: Edith, Leonard, Dorothy VanDeman, and Lillian Miles. "Verbal Expression," *Foundations of Learning in Childhood Education.* 1963; Applegate, Mauree. *Easy in English.* Harper Brothers, 1960.

Have masks that the children can use to represent different feelings.

Preassessment

- Presented with items of common interest (toys), each child will demonstrate skill in verbalizing by speaking clearly and in a moderate tone when describing the toys to the teacher.
- Given properly simulated situations, the child will demonstrate a knowledge of good oral manners by responding properly to each situation. (Example: Making introductions, talking on the phone, using oral table manners.)
- Given familiar story characters, the children will demonstrate their skill in expressing their feelings and emotions by telling how they feel about story characters in relation to themselves.
- When the teacher presents new words in a sentence, the child will show an interest in enlarging his/her vocabulary by asking questions to gain the meaning of a word.

After the preassessment, exit from the module or proceed to the objectives.

The children will learn to verbalize in clear but moderate tones.

• By speaking clearly and using a moderate tone when discussing an item that interests the class, the children will demonstrate proper voice quality.
• After being presented a story sentence, the children will show their skill at proper voice quality as they develop their own stories from the teacher's sentence.
• The children will demonstrate that they can speak in clear but moderate tones by telling what they think might have happened before and after the event in a picture they are handed.
• The children will show their skill at using clear but moderate tones when presented with single words such as *lollipop, rhinoceros,* and *Gregory* by reproducing these words as spoken by the teacher. (Variation: Say "Gregory, the rhinoceros, has a lollipop.")
• The children will demonstrate clear but moderate tones when reciting familiar and unfamiliar nursery rhymes to show their knowledge of this skill.

Simple Activities
The child will show his skill in using a clear and moderate voice when he is appointed the "starter" in games and activities by saying: "Get ready, get set, go!" or "One, two, three, go!" or a similar phrase, so that *every* one understands him.

More Advanced Activity
The children will show skill in using moderate but clear voice tones when responding individually or in a small group to the teacher as he/she repeats the first five activities under Objective 1. The first two are advanced; the third may be simple or advanced—depending on the picture used; the fourth may be simple or advanced—depending on the choice of words; and the fifth may be simple or advanced—depending on the number of lines in the rhyme.

Design your own activities to meet the needs of individual children.

Each child will learn good oral manners.

• The children will exhibit good oral manners when introducing each other in role play, using such language as the following:
1. Hello, my name is _____.
2. Jane, may I present Don Jones?
    Don, this is Jane Kelly.
3. Mr. Smith (elder), I would like to introduce you to my friend, Laurie Henson.
4. How do you do? I'm pleased to make your acquaintance.
    It is a pleasure to meet you.
5. It was a pleasure meeting you.
    I enjoyed meeting you.
    It was nice to have met you.
• After being given toy phones, the children will show their knowledge of good oral manners when using the phone in role-playing situations such as the following:

1. John Doe residence, John speaking. May I help you?
2. Hello, this is John Doe. May I speak with Jane, please?
3. Hello, is this the Doe residence?
4. I'm sorry, you must have the wrong number.

• After being seated at the table in the playhouse, the children will demonstrate their knowledge of good oral table manners in a role-playing situation by using phrases such as these:
1. Would you pass the _____, please?
2. May I have the _____?
3. Thank you.
4. Please pass the _____.
5. Please excuse me.
6. May I be excused?

• After discussion of proper greetings the children will demonstrate their knowledge of good oral manners when greeting someone by role playing, one child being the guest and one the host (hostess), using such phrases as these:
1. Good morning.
2. Good afternoon.
3. Good evening.
4. Good day.
5. Hello.
6. How do you do?

• After discussion, the children will demonstrate their skill in choosing the proper oral manners of assistance, when presented different examples of situations. Responses might include the following:
1. May I help you?
2. Is there anything I can do to help you?
3. May I assist you?
4. Please, let me help you with that.

Alternate Activities

The children will show their skill in the proper use of oral manners when presented, individually or as a small group, with the same activities used previously. (Each of the five activities is simple but can be made more advanced.)

Design your own activity to meet the needs of individual children.

Objective 3

The children will learn to express their emotions orally as part of effective communication.

Activities

• After the class members have been presented with pictures depicting emotional situations, the children will demonstrate that they can communicate their emotions orally by telling just what is happening in the picture, what they think happened to cause the situation, and how the character feels.

• After an emotional or feeling situation has been "created," the children will express orally their emotions or feelings in response to a role-playing situation. (Examples: when you are lost, or when your brother hits you, or when your friend won't speak to you.)

• After listening to a particular type of music, the children will express orally their feelings in response to the music. (Types of music:

52

jazz, popular rock, discordant, happy, classical, sad, excited, etc.)
• When presented with words naming specific emotions and feelings, the children will orally describe those emotions and feelings, demonstrating their ability to communicate feelings effectively.
• After being read a story, the children will review orally the emotions and feelings of each character described in the story and tell how they (the children) would have responded or felt if they had been that character. This activity demonstrates that the children can communicate each character's feelings.

Using masks that indicate feelings, the children will show that they can express the feelings by selecting a mask and talking as the mask would indicate.

Design your own activities to meet the needs of individual children.

Alternate Activity

The children will show an interest in enlarging their vocabulary.

Objective 4

• The children will display an interest in enlarging their vocabulary by questioning the teacher for the meaning of an unfamiliar word presented in the story being read.
• After being introduced to a new word and its meaning, the children will show their interest in enlarging their vocabulary by using the word in a sentence or in an informal conversation.
• When encouraged by the teacher, the children will create fun words of their own, including definitions that go with them, to be compiled into a Fun Word Dictionary and thus exhibit their interest in vocabulary enlargement.
• After the children have cut out pictures depicting things they have never seen, they will discuss these pictures with the group, thus showing an interest in enlarging their vocabulary.

Activities

Repeat the above individually or in small groups. Each activity is simple in itself but can be made more advanced.

Design your own activities to meet the needs of individual children.

Alternate Activity

The postassessment is the same as the preassessment. After the postassessment, exit from the module or proceed to the additional activities.

Postassessment

• After painting pictures of animals at play, the children will demonstrate in group discussion that they can verbalize in clear and moderate tones by tape recording their picture description to review with the teacher.
• The children will exhibit their knowledge of good oral manners by giving a small room party for some guests with whom they can use their manners.

Additional Activities

- The children will show that they can express emotions orally and effectively by putting on a class play in which the parts rotate by performance so that each child has the opportunity to role play at least two characters.
- The children will demonstrate their interest in enlarging their vocabulary by using the New Word tapes (prepared by the teacher). Each tape discusses one new word in the following way: "A new word for you. How about *richer*? Would you like to be rich and have lots of money? I know a man who is so rich that he has two TVs in every room. Would you like to be richer than that? What would you have to have to be richer than that man?"

Resources

Applegate, Mauree. *Easy in English*. Harper Brothers, 1960.
Logan, Lillian M. *Teaching the Young Child*.

3.9 Understanding
Spoken Language

Rationale

The activities in this module are designed to aid the child who cannot listen, receive, understand, or respond to a spoken message. This module will also benefit any non-English speaking children. It will also benefit the child who has had little opportunity to be an important, contributing member of the family group. The module has been designed to strengthen the language ability of a child who appears to lack these crucial skills. It will also attempt to develop the child's ability to assimilate the events, characters, and details of a story.

Prerequisites

For the activities in Objective 1, you will need to gather several manipulative objects, a ball, and a cassette tape recorder.

For the activities in Objective 2 and the additional activities, you will need objects to see, feel, taste, smell, and hear. You will need a paper bag plus small, "feelable" objects. You will need the book *Brian Wildsmith's Circus*, a flannel board, flannel-board figures, and pictures of several familiar objects for identifying and labeling.

Preassessment

- Given a series of minor tasks, the child will show that he/she knows how to follow directions by performing these tasks correctly and in order. (Example: "Go to the chalkboard. Draw any animal you wish to draw. Then bring me your favorite toy.")
- After the teacher has told a story (using the flannel board and flannel-board characters), the child will demonstrate that he/she assimilates spoken language in story form by recreating the story using the flannel board and flannel-board figures.
After this preassessment, exit from the module or proceed to the objectives.

Objective 1

The child will understand spoken directions.

54

3.9 "Touch your nose."

● The children will demonstrate their understanding of spoken directions by playing the game "You Must" (variation of "Simon Says"): Form a circle. Leader stands in center and gives commands. Those who follow a command not preceded by the words *You must* are "out."

● The children will demonstrate their understanding of spoken directions by playing the game "Bring Me": Teacher asks children to bring him/her objects, including nonsense objects; i.e., the wall. The child called on remains seated if the task cannot be performed.

● The children will demonstrate their understanding of spoken directions by playing the game "Giants" correctly: Leader calls out one of the commands. If he/she says, "Giants," the children stand tall. If the command is "Boys and girls," the children stand naturally. If the leader says, "Dwarfs," the children stand low.

● The children will show that they understand spoken directions by playing the game "Touch" (for groups or individuals): Child responds to commands such as "Touch your hand to your ears" and "Touch your chair."

● The children will demonstrate their understanding of spoken directions by playing the game "Touch" at a more complex level: "Touch your left elbow to your right knee," "Touch your ear to your shoulder."

Simple Activity
Given a *short* sentence, the child will show that he/she understands spoken directions by echoing the teacher.

More Advanced Activity
Given a tape-recorded series of instructions, the child will demonstrate

an understanding of spoken directions by following the instructions in a learning-center situation.

Design your own activity to meet the needs of individual children.

Objective 2   The child will understand spoken language in story form.

Activities

- Given an allotted time for group discussion, each child will demonstrate an understanding of spoken language in story form by sharing an experience.
- Given a series of related pictures, each child will demonstrate an understanding of spoken language in story form by composing a story about the pictures (e.g., pictures from *Brian Wildsmith's Circus*).
- Given pictures of family members, each child will demonstrate an understanding of spoken language in story form by composing a story using family members as characters.
- Given puppets, the children will demonstrate their understanding of spoken language in story form by acting out a familiar story or fairy tale.

Alternate Activities

Simple Activity
Each child will demonstrate a knowledge of spoken language in story form by relating the story line of a favorite television show, movie, film, or other dramatization to the teacher.

More Advanced Activity
Given a series of pictures of the sequential development of a plant or animal, the child will demonstrate an understanding of spoken language in story form by telling what is happening in each picture.

Design your own activities to meet the needs of individual children.

Postassessment   The postassessment is the same as the preassessment. After the postassessment, exit from the module or proceed to additional activities.

Additional Activities

- Given a blank sheet of paper, each child will demonstrate an understanding of spoken directions by following the teacher's instructions: "Draw a black line across the top of your paper. Draw a yellow circle near the bottom," etc.
- Given a series of pictures taken by the teacher during a day's activities, each child will demonstrate an understanding of spoken language in story form by relating the day's events (with the pictures as aids).

Resources   Project Head Start. *Speech, Language and Hearing Program.* DHEW Pub. No. (OCD) 73-1025.

Quick, Alton, et al. *Project Memphis: Guides to Teaching Preacademic Skills.* Memphis State University, 1973.

Russell, D., and Russell, E. F. *Listening Aids Through the Grades*.
   Columbia University Teacher's College Press, 1959.
Tessel, Katherine Van, and Greimann, Millie. *Creative Dramatization*.
   Threshold Early Learning Library vol. 6. Macmillan, 1973.
Wildsmith, Brian. *Brian Wildsmith's Circus*. Franklin Watts, 1970.

3.10 Vocabulary Building

The best way to give breadth to a child's vocabulary is to provide opportunities for new, interesting and real experiences. Remember how Helen Keller's teacher, Anne Sullivan, taught her the word *water*? How How important it is to provide vivid, real experiences for young language learners. The actual number of words a young child should know is an extensively debated number. It is safer to say that an adequate vocabulary for any age is one that allows its owner effective communication in his/her environment.

Rationale

The teacher will need puppets; blocks; a well-stocked first-aid kit; manipulative objects; pictures of all kinds of objects, people, animals, and activities; objects to see, hear, feel, taste, and smell; a good picture book, such as one by Richard Scarry; a camera and film; and prints of paintings by old masters.

Prerequisites

Given a series of pictures of objects, the child will demonstrate a knowledge of words and their meanings by naming and defining the objects: farm animal, transportation vehicles, foods, community workers, zoo animals, actions, emotions revealed in facial expressions.
   After this preassessment, exit from the module or proceed to the objective.

Preassessment

The child will know an adequate number of words and their meanings.

Objective

• Given a number of objects to see, hear, feel, taste, and/or smell, the child will show that he/she knows the words associated with these objects by naming them as the teacher presents the objects.
• Given time adequate for interaction with objects in the preschool environment, the child will demonstrate a knowledge of words and their meanings by responding to questions posed by the teacher. (Examples: What is a kitchen? What do we do there? What things do we need for a kitchen? How do we use them?)
• Given a picture book (such as any by Richard Scarry), the child will demonstrate a knowledge of words and their meanings by naming objects found in the pictures and discussing their purposes or functions.
• Given a field trip to a place of interest, the child will demonstrate a knowledge of words and their meanings by identifying objects and their functions in pictures taken by the children at the visited place.

Activities

• After a field trip, the children will demonstrate with paints and white paper their knowledge of words and their meanings by creating pictures and by discussing the new parts of the experience.
• Given a series of reprints of paintings by the old masters, each child will demonstrate a knowledge of words and their meanings by identifying objects and discussing them in terms of then and now.
• Given an adequate amount of time (several weeks) to collect objects, each child will demonstrate a knowledge of words and their meanings by identifying his objects and developing an exhibit for classroom visitors. (The teacher should assist students in classifying and labeling.)

Alternate Activities

Simple Activities
• Given art materials, the child will demonstrate a knowledge of words and their meanings by drawing, labeling, and discussing objects and people.
• Given the task of naming objects they can see in the room, the children will demonstrate their knowledge of words and their meanings by having the teacher list these words and identifying their function as the teacher reviews the list orally.

More Advanced Activities
• Given objects such as books, the children will demonstrate their knowledge of words and their meanings by demonstrating the indefinite words (such as *some, several, most, few*) to unlock the mystery of these words.
• Given puppets and suitable objects, the children will demonstrate their knowledge of words and their meanings by demonstrating relationship words such as *over, under, among, between, across.*

Design your own activities to meet the needs of individual children.

Postassessment

The postassessment is the same as the preassessment. After the postassessment, exit from the module or proceed to additional activities.

Additional Activities

• Given a passage of prose read by the teacher, the children will demonstrate their knowledge of words and their meanings by discussing words that tell how characters felt, such as *happy, sad, gay, afraid, upset,* and *grouchy.*
• Given supplies found in a first-aid kit (i.e., bandages, cotton, burn ointment) each child will demonstrate a knowledge of words and their meanings by identifying the objects and participating in a mock emergency, such as the teacher's "skinned elbow." (Note: Do not include drugs—even aspirin—in the first-aid kit.)
• Given a series of sound words (i.e., *buzz, bang, crunch, hum, ping, tick, smack, chirp*), each child will demonstrate his knowledge of words and their meanings by identifying objects that would make these sounds.

Resources

Petty, Walter T., Petty, Dorothy C., and Becking, Marjorie F.

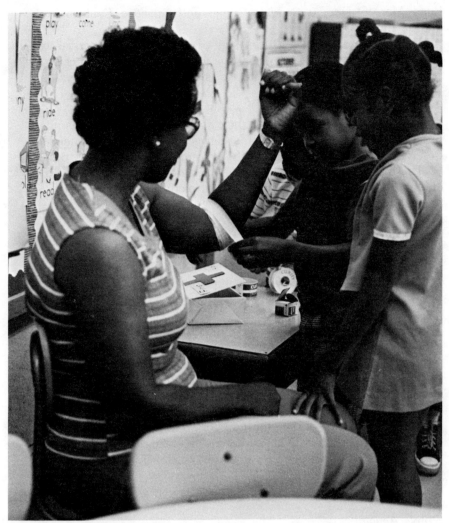
3.10 Fixing Teacher's skinned elbow

Experiences in Language: Tools and Techniques for Language Arts Methods. Allyn and Bacon, Inc. 1973.

Quick, Alton D., Little, Thomas L., and Campbell, A. Ann. *Project Memphis: Guides to Teaching Preacademic Skills.* Memphis State University, 1973.

3.11 Visual Discrimination: Sequential

The inability of children to read is one of the major areas of concern in today's school programs. It is a problem that must be approached with understanding and competence. Many teachers would agree that through the use of games, aids, and activities that stress visual discrimination, children who would otherwise fail to reach their potential can be helped. Sequential perception as a form of discrimination enables the child to gain meaning from symbols.

Rationale

59

Prerequisites

Read: Mary E. Dorsey, *Reading Games and Activities*. California: Fearon Publishers, 1972.

Have on hand sets of pictures, sets of letters and numbers, a wheel with numbers in mixed order and one with numbers in correct order, a set of color cards, a set of Bingo cards, and beans for markers.

Preassessment

• The children will demonstrate their ability to recognize sequential order by putting five number cards between 1 and 10 in sequential order and five alphabet letter cards between A and J in ABC order.
• The children will show their ability to perceive likenesses and differences by picking out, from a set of pictures, the ones which are alike and the ones which are different.

After this preassessment, exit from the module or proceed to the objectives.

Objective 1

The children will learn to perceive sequentially.

Activities

• Given a set of ten number cards, the children will demonstrate their knowledge of sequential perception, by putting the number cards in sequential order. (Example: 1-5, 2-6, 3-7, 4-8, 5-9, 6-10.)
• Given a set of alphabetical cards, the children will show their knowledge of sequential perception by putting the cards in order. (See ordering of the numbers above.)
• Given a wheel displaying the numbers one through ten in mixed order, with an attached movable hand, the children will demonstrate their knowledge of sequential perception by moving the hands to the numbers in the correct order.

Alternate Activities

Simple Activity
After viewing a set of animals in sequential order from largest to smallest and a set of animals of mixed size and order, the children will regroup the ones not in sequential order, showing their knowledge of sequential perception.

More Advanced Activity
After hearing a story and receiving a set of story pictures, the children will put the pictures in sequential order, to demonstrate their knowledge of sequential order. Begin with three story pictures and progress to a story sequenced in ten pictures.

Design your own activities to meet the needs of individual children.

Objective 2

The children will learn to perceive likenesses and differences.

Activities

• After hearing a story, the children will select the picture most like the story to demonstrate their knowledge of how to perceive likenesses.
• Given a set of toy cars, the children will demonstrate their knowledge of perceptual differences by picking the ones that are

60

different in terms of color, size, and make. They should park them in different lots depending on the classification used.

• Shown a picture card of a baby animal, the children will pick out an identical card to show their knowledge of perceptual likenesses. This can progress to perceiving other classifications about animal pictures.

Simple Activity
After seeing two sets of color cards, the children will point to the cards which are alike in each set to demonstrate their knowledge of perceptual likenesses.

More Advanced Activity
Given a bingo card, the children will demonstrate their perceptual knowledge of likenesses by placing a bean on the letter that the teacher shows them on a large card.

Design your own activities to meet the needs of individual children.

The postassessment is the same as the preassessment. After the postassessment, exit from the module or proceed to the additional activities.

• Given a set of ten alphabetical cards with pictures as well as letters, the children will demonstrate their knowledge of sequential order by putting the cards in sequential order.
• Given a set of six picture cards, four being alike, the children will show their perceptual knowledge of likenesses and differences by pointing to the two cards that are different. Example:

C	S	S	S	)	S

Dorsey, Mary E. *Reading Games and Activities*. Fearon Publishers, 1972.

3.12 Prewriting Visual Motor Skills

Children need many opportunities to practice the visual motor skills of top to bottom and left to right as a preparation for writing. This awareness module has been designed to give them some such opportunities.

61

Prerequisites	Teach children the proper way to hold a crayon or pencil. Materials: Mimeographed sheets with rows of dots. At the top place dots 1/2" apart one-quarter of the way across the page. Gradually increase distance between dots and lengthen row until they stretch across the page. Obtain large crayons (one for each child), a simple story book, ditto copies, record player, record ("The Hokey, Pokey"), flannel board, felt pictures of animals. (Pictures could be cut from magazines and mounted on felt or sandpaper. Pictures should represent a zoo, a circus, trees, wild animals, roads or paths leading to the right, one red box, one green box, and small toys or assorted nuts in the shell.)
Preassessment	• After a demonstration by the teacher, the child will demonstrate his/her preparation for writing by drawing four straight lines (without the aid of dots) from top to bottom on butcher paper with a large crayon. • After a demonstration by the teacher, each child will place pictures on a flannel board from left to right unaided to demonstrate skill and knowledge of moving from left to right. After the preassessment, either exit from the module or proceed to the objectives.
Objective 1	The children will show that they understand how to move from top to bottom.
Activities	• Given mimeographed sheets containing dots, the children will show their skill with top to bottom concepts by connecting the dots from top to bottom using a large crayon. (See Croft and Hess's book in resource section). • On the dittoed sheets the children will draw a line from the animal at the top of the page to the directly related object at the bottom of the page, demonstrating their skill in drawing lines from top to bottom. • Using body movement, the children will demonstrate their skill in top to bottom motion by moving their arms from high over head to the floor (bending knees) accompanied by descending music.
Alternate Activities	*Simple Activity* To show their knowledge of how to make straight lines, the children will carry out directions using *top*, *bottom*, *down*, and *up* until the concepts are well established. *More Advanced Activity* To show their knowledge of how to make straight lines, the children will draw lines to connect circles drawn at the top and the bottom of the chalkboard. *Design your own activities to meet the needs of individual children.*
Objective 2	The children will understand how to move from left to right.
Activities	• The children will do the actions according to the song, "The Hokey

Pokey," to show their knowledge of left to right.
● While playing "Simon Says," the children will show their skill in moving from left to right on commands involving these movements.
● After placing objects on a table, each child will demonstrate an awareness of left and right by picking up a series of objects on the left and placing them in a box on the right according to the directions of the teacher.
● After selecting an animal from the base of the flannel board, the children will show their knowledge of left to right movement by selecting a path leading from the left of the board to the zoo located to the right of the flannel board. (See Haynes and Russell's book in resources section.)

Simple Activity
Familiar classroom objects will be placed in a row on each pupil's desk top. The child will touch each object on his/her desk from left to right and tell about each as he/she moves from left to right to demonstrate an understanding of the movement.

More Advanced Activity
After placing different kinds of objects in a line on a table, the child will name each object from left to right to demonstrate an understanding of how to move in this direction.

Design your own activities to meet the needs of individual children.

Alternate Activities

The postassessment is the same as the preassessment. After the postassessment, exit from the module or proceed to additional activities.

Postassessment

● "Follow the Leader." The children will show their awareness of moving left to right by following the teacher as he/she goes through the movements of the game using left and right turns and slapping left and right thighs. (Variation: learning to slide with the feet from left side of room to the right side.)
● On art paper with large crayons, the pupils will demonstrate their awareness of down strokes by indicating the falling of rain with down strokes using both arms.

Additional Activities

Croft, Doreen J., and Hess, Robert D. *An Activities Handbook for Teachers of Young Children.* 2d ed. Houghton Mifflin Co., 1975.
Grant, Margaret. *School Methods with Young Children.* Evans Brothers Ltd., 1968.
Haynes, Grace B., and Russell, David H. *Games to Play.* Ginn and Co., 1964.
Osborn, Keith S., and Haupt, Dorothy. *Creative Activities for Young Children.* Merrill-Palmer Institute, 1964.

Resources

3.13 Prewriting Sensory Training

Rationale

In preparation for writing, pupils need many opportunities to develop the sense of feeling as an aid to symbol recognition.

Prerequisites

Do Module 3.12 "Prewriting Visual-Motor Skills" before this module. Materials: sand, boxes, sandpaper letters, felt letters, clay, art paper, paint, water and pan, toys (small and large), covered "feely box."

Preassessment

The children will demonstrate their skill in tactile writing by drawing four letters with their fingers correctly in a sandbox after feeling the sandpaper letters on a nearby table.

After the preassessment, exit from the module or proceed to the objective.

Objective

The children will understand how to draw letters by using the sense of feeling.

Activities

● After selecting a sandpaper letter from a "feely box," the children will demonstrate their knowledge of the formation of the letter by air-writing under the teacher's guidance.
● After a demonstration by the teacher, the child will demonstrate tactile writing skill by forming a familiar letter out of a ball of clay.
● In a sandbox, the children will show their skill with tactile writing by feeling alphabet letters made of felt and using the index finger to make the symbol in the sand. (Other children must guess the letter before the author erases it.)

Alternate Activities

Simple Activity
The children will demonstrate their skill in letter formation by using finger painting. The teacher guides, using an overhead projector.

More Advanced Activity
The child will observe large letters cut into two parts to form a puzzle. After being blindfolded, each child will show tactile writing skill by feeling out the correct parts to form a letter that matches the whole letter beside him/her.

Design your own activities to meet the needs of individual children.

Postassessment

The postassessment is the same as the preassessment. After the postassessment, exit from the module or proceed to additional activities.

Additional Activities

● After being paired with another child in the classroom, each child

64

will take turns using his/her index finger to write on the other child's back. The other child will then show his/her skill of feeling by naming the alphabet letter made on his/her back.
● After selecting an object (toy or alphabet letter) from a covered table, each child will demonstrate his/her sense of touch writing by naming the object he/she has selected under the cover on the table.

Braley, William T. *Daily Sensory Motor Training*. Educational Activities, Inc., 1968.
Hackett, Layne C., and Jenson, Robert G. *A Guide to Movement Exploration*. Peek Publications, 1967.

Resources

3.14 Beginning (Premanuscript) Writing

Children need many opportunities to practice premanuscript writing skills, such as making vertical strokes, slant lines, and circles. This module has been designed to give them some of these opportunities.

Rationale

Do Modules 3.12 and 3.13 before doing this module. See Freeman's *Starting to Write* for guided instruction (in resources section). Before commencing each activity, give a short exercise on air-writing.
　　Materials needed: butcher paper, large crayon, newsprint, and art paper.

Prerequisites

● Given art paper and a large crayon, each child will show that he/she can make three straight vertical strokes in a row and three slanted lines in a row by performing these operations correctly after a demonstration by the teacher.
● Given art paper and crayon, each child will show skill in drawing circles by drawing three circles of approximately the same size in a counterclockwise motion after a demonstration by the teacher.
After the preassessment, exit from the module or proceed to the objectives.

Preassessment

The children will learn how to make rows of vertical strokes and rows of slant lines as a preparation for writing.

Objective 1

● Given mimeographed sheets containing dots, the children will connect dots to form vertical strokes, demonstrating their skill in making these kinds of strokes.
● Given large sheets of butcher paper and large crayons, the children will draw tepees to demonstrate their skill in making slanted lines.
● The children will show their knowledge and skill in making slanted lines by drawing their interpretation of snow falling (on newsprint with a large crayon).

Activities

3.14 Forming a circle

Alternate Activities

Simple Activity
Using body movements, the children will show their awareness of slanted lines by pretending that they are paddling about through the water using the paddle only on the left side of the boat as the teacher says "stroke."

More Advanced Activity
Using crayons and art paper, the children will show their skill in drawing slanted lines by drawing a picture of a house with a fence and tree—all of which are leaning to the right.

Design your own activities to meet the needs of individual children.

Objective 2   The children will understand and demonstrate how circles are formed.

Activities   • Given newsprint and one crayon per child, the children will show their awareness of circles by scribbling spontaneously as they sing "Here We Go 'round the Mulberry Bush."
• Given newsprint and crayon, children will show their awareness of circles by drawing circles to "Pop Goes the Weasel" as the teacher demonstrates on the chalkboard.

66

Simple Activity
Using body movements, the children will show their awareness of circles by circling with their peers in a counterclockwise motion after a demonstration by the teacher. (Variation: Do a simple circle dance moving counterclockwise.)

More Advanced Activity
Using crayons and newsprint, the children will show their skill in drawing circles by drawing a snowman with a circular head, body, and feet. (Begin all circles at top and move counterclockwise.)

Design your own activities to meet the needs of individual children.

The postassessment is the same as the preassessment. After the postassessment, exit from the module or proceed to additional activities.

Postassessment

● Given art papers containing large dots, the children will connect dots to form vertical strokes, slant lines, and circles after a review of each by the teacher.
● Given art paper and crayon, each child will show skill in drawing circles in the air, or on paper, to the rhythm game "Farmer in the Dell" or "Here We Go Looby Lou."

Additional Activities

Dallmann, Martha. *Teaching the Language Arts in the Elementary School.* Wm. C. Brown Co., 1970.
Freeman, Frank N. *Starting to Write.* Zaner-Bloser Co., 1969.
_____. *Ready Set Go.* Zaner-Bloser Co., 1969.

Resources

3.15 Manuscript Writing

Children need many opportunities to practice manuscript writing skills, such as making half-circles, circles, vertical lines, and drawing the lowercase letters *b, p, d, l,* and *q.* The module has been designed to give them some of these opportunities.

Rationale

Do Modules 3.12, 3.13, 3.14 before doing this module. See Freeman's *Starting to Write* for guided instruction (in resources section). Before beginning each activity, give a show exercise on air writing or body movements for writing.
   Material needed: art paper, sandpaper letters, masking tape, crayons, chalkboard, chalk.

Prerequisites

● Given art paper and a crayon, each child will show that he/she can make five rows of circles and half circles of approximately the same length or size after a demonstration by the teacher.

Preassessment

• Given large sheets of paper and a crayon, each child will demonstrate his/her skill in making five of the lowercase letters (*b, p, l, d, q*), using straight lines and half circles, after a demonstration by the teacher.
After the preassessment, exit from the module or proceed to the objectives.

Objective 1   The children will learn to make half circles and circles.

Activities   • Given large sheets of paper containing dots of half circles, the children will connect the dots to form half circles.
• Children will show their knowledge of making circles by drawing a large design of circles on the chalkboard after a demonstration by the teacher.
• Given crayons, shapes of half circles and circles, and large sheets of paper, the children will demonstrate their skill in tracing over the shapes to form half circles and circles after a demonstration by the teacher.

Alternate Activities   *Simple Activity*
Using body movements, the children will show their awareness of half circles by curving their bodies to form a half circle after a demonstration by the teacher. (Variation: The children will lie in the shapes of whole circles down on the floor.)

More Advanced Activity
Using crayons and art paper, the children will show their ability to draw circles by drawing pictures of big balloons floating in the air.

Design your own activities to meet the needs of individual children.

Objective 2   The children will learn how *b, d, l, p,* and *q* are formed.

Activities   • Given art paper and crayons, the children will show their knowledge of how to make one part of each letter (*b, d, l, p, q*) at a time. (Example: *l, o,* then *b.*)
• Given crayon and art paper containing dotted letters (*b, d, l, p,* and *q*), the children will show their skill by tracing the dotted lines.
• Given mimeographed sheets containing partial dots of letters (*b, d, l, p,* and *q*), the children will demonstrate their skill in drawing the letters by completing the letters.

Alternate Activities   *Simple Activity*
Using their bodies, the children will demonstrate their skill in forming the letters *b, d, l, p,* and *q* by lying on the floor and, with a partner, forming these letters.

More Advanced Activity
Using crayon and newsprint, each child will show skill in writing by

68

tracing the outline of the felt letters *b, d, l, p,* and *q* to make accurate letters.

Design your own activities to meet the needs of individual children.

The postassessment is the same as the preassessment. After the postassessment, exit from the module or proceed to additional activities.

Postassessment

- Using a sandbox, the children will demonstrate their skill in making the letters *b, d, l, p,* and *q* with their fingers, after a demonstration by the teacher.
- Given a large box containing lowercase letters, each child will show a recognition of the letters *b, d, l, p,* and *q* by picking out the letters and placing them on a flannel board, where he/she will match these same letters already placed at the top of the board by the teacher.

Additional Activities

Croft, Doreen J., and Hess, Robert D. *An Activities Handbook for Teachers of Young Children.* 2d ed. Houghton Mifflin Co., 1975.
Freeman, Frank N. *Starting to Write.* Zaner-Bloser Co., 1969.
Monroe, Marion. *Learn to Listen, Speak and Write.* Scott Foresman and Co., 1960.

Resources

3.16 Ask the Alphabet

Children learn the alphabet as a decoding process for reading. Asking the alphabet to unlock its mysteries is an exciting game for some young children, a puzzling paradox for others, and for some a bore. Those children "turned off" by the preassessment in this module are probably not ready to ask the alphabet anything. The teacher should not force these children to take this first step in reading. It would be better for them to come back to this module in a few weeks or months. However, for those children who are interested in but puzzled by the pretesting experience, the time has come for them to ask the alphabet. Learning the alphabet involves learning the names of the letters and the sounds the letters make alone and in concert with others.

Rationale

Have on hand alphabet letters sized for use on the desk as well as for large-group demonstrations, (flannel board letters covered with velveteen, sandpaper, or dotted swiss), eight cardboard boxes of the same size, tagboard, star seals, a cardboard box large enough for two children to crawl into, stickum paper, tape recorders and blank tapes, a camera and film, colored paper for making scrapbooks, several sets of toy cars, paper bags, blocks of different sizes and shapes, a collection of Dr. Seuss books, M. W. Brown's book *Shhhhhh Bang,* a flannel board, a magnetic board and magnetic letters, six teacher-made fishing poles, two yards of oilcloth, and a play store with boxes and cans.

Prerequisites

Preassessment

- Upon seeing all the letters of the alphabet, each child will be able to say the letter names correctly when the teacher points to the letters in order.
- Upon hearing the following questions concerning the letter sounds, each child will demonstrate a knowledge of these sounds by correctly answering these questions: (1) What is the sound of "a" in *hay* in *I lay in the hay?* (2) What is the sound of "a" in *bat* in *The bat in my hat is fat?* (3) What is the sound of "e" in *he* in *He sees the bees?* (4) What is the sound of "e" in *let* in *Let the jello set?* (Continue these questions concerning the rest of the vowels and all the consonants.)
- Tell me the sound that "bl" makes in *blue blouse?* (Continue through the consonant blends and the diphthongs.)

If a child is having trouble with each of these areas, ask only five questions under each. Otherwise, continue to find out which he/she does not know and keep a record on each child. (The record is used for planning activities.)

After the preassessment, exit from the module or proceed to the objectives.

Objective 1

The children will learn to say the letters of the alphabet when they see them.

Activities

- After the teacher shows and tells the names of the letters *A, B, C,* and *D* (ten inches tall in the same colored tagboard) seen as a series, each child will show that he/she knows the letter names by closing his/her eyes while the teacher removes one letter from the sequence and then telling which one the teacher removed. (Variation: Do the same at another time with the following series: *EFGH, IJKL, MNOP, QRST, UVW, XYZ.*)
- After the teacher has shown and named *A, B, C,* and *D,* each child will demonstrate a knowledge of their names by feeling each letter (each child has a set covered with velveteen, sandpaper, or dotted swiss) and calling out each letter's name as he/she feels it. (Variation: Do the same at another time with the other letter series mentioned in the first activity.)
- After a visual review of *A, B, C,* and *D* in which the teacher mentions the letter names, the children will indicate that they know these letters by saying the letter names and working together to join the cardboard boxes so they form each letter in order.

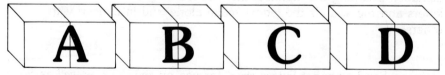

(Variation: Redo the boxes for each letter series of the alphabet.)
- Given all the letters of the alphabet in cardboard or wood, each child will show an understanding of the letters and their names by picking out and putting in order the series of letters (example: *ABCD*) that the teacher calls for. (Variation: The teacher puts the letter series *ABCD, EFGH,* etc., on cards, and each child selects a card then tries to find letters to match the card.)
- After the teacher has explained that *A* and *a* are partners or cousins, the children will show their awareness of this association by

finding *A a, B b, C c, D d* (always in alphabetic order) and calling them "big A," "little a," etc.

● After dictating a story for the teacher to print, each child will show an understanding of *A a* by pasting a star above each of those letters in his/her story. (Variation: Do the same with other such combinations in the alphabet.)

Simple Activity
While playing in the ABCD box (that two children can crawl into and that has cave paintings of the outlines of ABCD throughout), the children will demonstrate their knowledge of an alphabet series by putting the colored letters (backed with stickum) in the right places in the letter outlines on the box walls.) Variation: Remove stickum letters and put in new series outlines and stickum letters.

If stickum letters are a problem, let the children color the outlines.

More Advanced Activity
Using Bingo-type cards containing letters from the alphabet, each child will demonstrate a knowledge of the alphabet by picking and naming a letter from a coffee can and covering the same letter on his/her card if he/she has it. If the child doesn't, he/she puts it back in the can and the next child takes a turn. (Play in groups of four or five.) A tagboard card with the following letter arrangement can serve as an example:

b	o	u	s	l
i	k	e	t	o
e	a	t	c	a
n	d	y	i	n
m	w	r	c	n

Design your own activities to meet the needs of individual children.

The children will learn the sounds that the letters make in words.

● The children listen to a teacher-prepared tape. (The tape is about the "A" train: "I am the 'A' train. I go to *a* far away place called 'A'-ville. I make **a** puff, **a** puff, **a** toot, **a** toot, **a** bang, **a** crash because I am the 'A' train. The sound I like best is A," etc.). Each child shows an understanding of one of the sounds by wearing a sign that says " 'A' train" and jumping forward when he/she hears the *a* sound.

(Four children wear signs and play the part of the train. One child operates the tape and acts as a referee as to which train got the farthest by the end of the tape.) Variations: Tapes can be made about the "E" wheel, the "I" kite, the "O" boat, and the "U" ukelele—all utilizing a long vowel sound.

● *Camera Game.* During the game "Camera," each child will show that he/she knows the short vowel sounds by acting out what the camera sees. The teacher pretends to be the camera or uses a camera and says, "I am the camera. I take pictures of 'A' when it says 'ă'.

    Bat, click-click
    Rat, click-click
    Mat, click-click
    Gnat, click-click"
          etc.

(Variations: The camera can also be used to take pictures of the children acting out words that have other short vowel sounds. The teacher can put these pictures in scrapbooks with the letter name on the cover and the words under the pictures inside.)

● *Scary Game.* While playing the "Scary Game," each child will show that he/she understands the sound of the letter "B" by acting afraid of only those words that begin with that letter. Teacher says: "Old Benny Botch is afraid of words beginning with *b* because he was once bitten by a bonk. He acts very brave when he hears words beginning with other letters."

You can be Benny Botch for a few minutes and show how scary "b" words are for him. "Catsup, claw, bang [act scared], toothbrush, monster, beetle [act scared]," etc. (Variations: The Laughing Game— Children laugh when they hear words beginning with a certain letter. The Singing Game—Children sing when they hear words beginning with a certain consonant letter. Also, try the Smiling Game, the Frowning Game, and the Make-a-Face Game.)

● *Alliteration Game.* While playing the "Alliteration Game," the children show their knowledge of letter sounds by telling the teacher the one letter that all his/her words begin with. (Example: "Benny Botch built benches" [b], or "Annie asks, Andy answers" [a]).

● *New Cars Game.* While playing the "New Cars Game," the children indicate that they know letter sounds by suggesting names for cars beginning with a particular letter sound. The teacher says, "The boss has told me that all our new cars must have names beginning with *m*. John, can you give this car a name (hands John a toy car) beginning with *m*?" Some possibilities are *Matador, Maxi, Mini, Monster, Mickey Mouse, Master,* and *Mercedes.* (Variations: Change the letter that the new cars must begin with.)

Alternate Activities

Simple Activity
Using paper-bag hand puppets (with a letter from the alphabet on each), each child will show an understanding of the sounds that letters make by creating a puppet show in which the puppets make only the letter sounds for dialogue. Examples:

    A! (angry)   A?
    bbbb   M m m m m
    Eee?   Eee! (happy)
    bbbb

More Advanced Activity
Who Am I? Game. While playing this game, the children say "My name begins with a *C*. I am an animal. I walk like this. Who am I?" Answer: Camel.

Design your own activities to meet the needs of individual children.

The children will learn consonant blends and vowel diphthongs.

- *Noisy Words Game.* While playing the "Noisy Word Game" the children will show that they know the consonant blends *bl, cr,* and *dr* by creating a machine (made of blocks) and sharing its noises with the other children and the teacher. (Appropriate machine noises would be *blast, blickedy, crunch, crash, bring-a-ling, blong, blonk, crinkle, cringle.*) The teacher shares her machine noises first and introduces the blends to be used. (Variations: Use such words as *chug, choo, drip, drop, frip, frap, great, growl, glong, prune, plonk, skoosh, scat, trub, thunk, thwack.*)
- *Body Chants Game.* While playing this game, the children will demonstrate their knowledge of consonant blends by acting out the parts of the chant that is the day's consonant blend. (Example: "*Br—* bring breakfast [act out]; call the cat; bring bricks [act out]; clap your hands; break the bridge [act out]; stamp the paper.") (Variation: Develop other chants for the other blends.)
- *Some-Rain-in-Spain Game.* While playing this game, the children show their understanding of vowel diphthongs by helping the teacher develop new lines to the song. (Words are sung to tune of "A Partridge in a Pear Tree.") Teacher begins, "On the First Day of Christmas [Easter] my true love gave to me some rain in Spain and a chain. On the Second Day of Christmas my true love gave to me [here the children help to think up words containing *ai*]." (Variation: Play the game with other diphthongs such as: Boy with a toy, Beater for the meat, Bee you couldn't see.)
- *A Dr. Seuss Hunt.* While playing the "Hunt," the children will show their knowledge of consonant blends or diphthongs (whichever is under study at the moment) by listening to the teacher read a *Seuss* passage heavy with the blend or diphthong and telling what it is.
- After hearing Margaret Wise Brown's *Shhhhhh Bang* (Harper and Row, 1943), the children create their own story using *shhhhhh bang* frequently in it to indicate their understanding of the *sh* blend. (The stories can be tape recorded by the children and later transcribed by the teacher for them to read.) (Variation: Read the story again, calling it *Swoosh Bong* for the *sw* sound or use another consonant blend.)
- *Story Telling With a Flannel Board.* While the teacher tells a diphthong story using the flannel board, the children show their understanding of vowel blends by helping him/her put a consonant in front of the blend to make the needed story word. (Example: "Today I will tell you about *ai*, pronounced 'ā'. As the story begins, an old man is snoring. It sounds like [whistle] 'ai', [whistle] 'ai'. He snores funny. Outside, the rain is coming down [Teacher moves an *r* and *n* into place beside the *ai* to spell rain.] But the old man snores on: [whistle] 'ai', [whistle] 'ai'. [During this line, teacher removes the *r* and the *n*.] A little girl walks by the window pulling a chain. Mary and Bob, can you

make it spell chain? [They come up and put the *ch* and *n* into place.] But the old man sleeps on. He snores on [whistle] 'ai', [whistle] 'ai'. (The teacher removes the letters so that just *ai* appears again on the board. The story can continue indefinitely.) (Variation: Story telling on the flannel board with other diphthongs, the story created by the teacher. This is a small-group activity so that each child gets a turn. As the teacher creates the stories, he/she can put them on tape for the other children.)

Alternate Activities

Simple Activity
Using teacher-prepared playing cards (tagboard with consonant blends laminated on) the children demonstrate their knowledge of blends by matching three cards and pronouncing the name of the blend. The game is a simple form of Rummy. Each of four players is dealt seven cards. At his turn, a child may pick up from the pile and must discard. In the deck are four sets of each consonant blend. The first player to get rid of all his/her cards wins. (Variation: Cards with diphthongs.)

More Advanced Activity
While building new words, each child will indicate an understanding of consonant blends by putting the right consonant blend in front of other letters shown to match the pictures. (A magnetic board with magnetic letters is helpful.) (Examples: *cl, ch, st*)
    ick (picture of a chick)
    ock (picture of a clock)
    op (picture of a red stop sign)

Design your own activities to meet the needs of individual children.

Postassessment

The postassessment is the same as the preassessment. After the postassessment, exit from the module or proceed to additional activities.

Additional Activities

• *For Objective 1.* As children fish for letters in a pool (box), each child will demonstrate an understanding of the letters in the alphabet by placing "caught" letters under the same letter fastened to an oilcloth lying nearby on the floor. The child says the letter aloud for the teacher, then recites all the letters at the end of fishing. (Should be a group of about six children.)
• *For Objective 2.* After the children have shopped at the play store, they will show that they know the sounds that letters make in words by giving the cashier (teacher) the items they have that begin with the letter sounds that he/she names.
• *For Objective 3.* Each child completes the missing part of a riddle to show a knowledge of blends posed by the teacher, who gives only the beginning blend sound. (Example: "I have a ch_____ that is small, round, and sweet to eat." [cherry].)
    "How Are They Alike?" Game. After the teacher shows two words that are alike because both contain the same diphthongs, the children demonstrate their understanding of diphthongs by telling the teacher what is in the two words. (Example: r*ai*n and cl*ai*m)

Croft, Doreen J., and Hess., Robert D. *An Activities Handbook for Teachers of Young Children.* 2d ed. Houghton Mifflin Co., 1975.

Hennings, Dorothy G. *Smiles, Nods and Pauses: Activities to Enrich Children's Communication Skills.* Citation Press, 1974.

Holland, Bernice C. *How to Individualize Kindergarten Teaching.* Parker Publishing Co., 1974.

3.17 Drama: The Gestures

Another module in this component deals with the *voice* in drama. However, much of the language with which we communicate is nonverbal. We rely heavily on a language of gestures and facial expressions. Young children are in the process of learning and understanding gestures to make language more meaningful to them. Drama has the facility to enable the young child to become a better sender and receiver of gestural language.

Rationale

Have on hand a cardboard box taller than children, handkerchiefs or veils, paper with blank faces on it, crayons, Eleanor Schick's book *Andy*, tapes with short pieces of music of various moods, and famous works of art expressing moods.

Prerequisites

Preassessment

• Each child will show an understanding of how to communicate with meaningful gestures by using hands, face, and body appropriately when asked to show how Daddy or Mother would act if one of them were (1) angry at a child for spilling milk, (2) happy because the child has cleaned his/her plate, and (3) upset because he/she thinks the child is lost.

Note: The more body parts the child uses, the better. Using several gestures to express one of the above actions is better than using only one. The child who uses only one facial expression per emotion, and only one gesture or body part in communications definitely needs to go through this module.

• Each child will show that he/she can effectively recognize the gestures of others by watching the teacher communicate the following nonverbally and telling the teacher what he/she is saying: (1) Good-bye, (2) Come here, (3) Don't do that, (4) I don't understand, (5) Hurry up, (6) I don't want to hear any more, (7) Please continue, (8) I don't know, (9) Bring it here, (10) I'm afraid, (11) Don't hurt me, (12) Let's be friends, (13) I just love this, (14) I can't see, (15) Hello, and (16) I don't want to do it.

After the preassessment, exit from the module or proceed to the objective.

Each child will learn to communicate with meaningful gestures and to receive nonverbal communication accurately.

Objective

Activities

- The children will demonstrate that they know how to make a variety of greeting gestures by expressing these in body language while playing the "Birthday Party Game." In the game, two children act as host and hostess. A third child acts as the one having the birthday. The other children act as guests. None can speak during the game except through facial expressions, gestures, and body postures. Prior to playing the game, the teacher helps the children to express nonverbally in several different ways the following: "Hello," "Good-bye," "Come in," "Sit here," "Would you like some cake." He/she covers ways to greet the dear friend, the friend you haven't seen for a long time, the child with the biggest present, and other arrivals. (Variations: "Lost-in-the-Woods Game": gestures of fear, surprise, and relief at being found; "Mask Game": facial expressions and body postures to express "Don't do that," "Hurry up," "I won't listen to you," "I don't know," "Don't hurt me," and "I don't understand.")

- *Watch-My-Walk Game.* While playing this game the children will show their understanding of how walking conveys a mood by changing their styles of walking to fit the mood to be expressed. (Example: People walk fast to show they are in a hurry; they walk slowly when thinking or showing interest in something they see; they run because they are afraid or very happy; they stamp their feet or walk heavily when they are angry, etc.) (Variation: Watch-My-Hands Game. Use a cardboard box tall enough that a child can stand behind it and put both arms through holes. The other children will see only his/her arms. As the teacher reads a story about a child going through several moods, the child behind the box expresses these moods with his/her hands. [Example: Wringing hands indicates anxiety and clapping hands expresses joy.]

- The children will demonstrate their knowledge of eyes as a means of communicating by playing the "Eyes Game." Half the children wear veils or handkerchiefs covering their noses and mouths. These children try to send messages with their eyes to the unveiled children. They communicate such ideas as "I am frightened [amused, shy, sleepy, interested]," "There's a fly on my nose," and, "It's over there." The children exchange roles in a few minutes.

Alternate Activities

Simple Activity
Given crayons and paper with blank faces on it, the children will show their understanding of facial expressions by filling in the faces to match the puzzled, upset, happy, and sad expressions on the teacher's face.

More Advanced Activity
After the teacher reads Eleanor Schick's book *Andy*, the children show that they can communicate with gestures by reenacting nonverbally all the people that Andy pretends to be as the story is reread.

Design your own activities to meet the needs of individual children.

Postassessment

The postassessment is the same as the preassessment. After the postassessment, exit from the module or proceed to additional activities.

76

• While music that changes in mood several times is played, the children indicate their understanding of these changes by communicating them nonverbally. (Better than using one record is taping several distinctly different short pieces.) (Variation: Use pictures instead of music.)
• Given three pictures (one of a character, one of an action, and one of a place such as the bathtub), each child will show that he/she can communicate nonverbally what it is he/she has seen in the picture by successfully pantomiming before other children.

Resources

Fast, Julius. *Body Language*. Pocket Books, 1971.
Hennings, Dorothy G. *Smiles, Nods and Pauses: Activities to Enrich Children's Communication Skills*. Citation Press, 1974.
Porter, Lorena. *Movement Education for Children*. American Association of Elementary, Kindergarten, and Nursery Educators.
Schick, Eleanor. *Andy*. Macmillan, 1971.

3.18 Creative Dramatics

Rationale

In day-to-day living we often get bogged down with habitual tasks and problems. Children feel this exasperation also. A fantastic way to escape to a different world for a little while is to indulge in creative dramatics. In this module many forms of literature are used to stimulate creative expression in children. The imagination, when the child is guided to use it, can be self-stimulating as a method of enriching language development. No child who has been to the Land of Make-Believe has ever returned quite the same.

Prerequisites

The teacher should have on hand some copies of stories, poems, and fairy tales, rewritten in play form on small note cards; old clothing, and props of miscellaneous articles and cardboard boxes; art material such as paint, glue, tape, and scissors; and a stapler.

Preassessment

After hearing a simple piece of literature, the children will demonstrate their interpretation of that piece of literature by presenting it in play form to a small group or an entire class. (Those who can make-believe are those most involved and caught up in their assumed role playing.)
   After the preassessment, exit from the module or proceed to the objective.

Objective

Each child will be able to separate himself/herself from daily activities to *enjoy* a new experience in some type of creative dramatics.

Activities

• After hearing a poem like "Bubbles," by Margaret Hillert, the children should express themselves as a nonliving object such as a bubble.

77

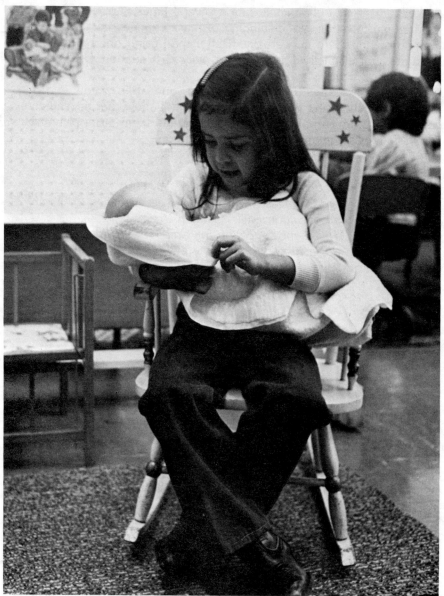

3.18 Playing mother

They may dramatize being inside a bubble, and what happens when they are caught.

• Have children pair off and play "Follow the Leader" (in their pair formation). To express themselves creatively, the children should face their partners and take time being a "mirror" to the actions of their partners.

• After a demonstration of how carpentry tools are used, the children pretend they are carpentry tools and use their *entire* bodies to imitate the work each tool may do.

• After hearing a poem like "Skating," by Billie M. Phillips, the children should pantomime the described action while accompanied by an instrumental selection appropriate for skating. If the children want to learn the poem, they can recite it aloud as they act it out.

• To develop their imaginations and ability to express themselves creatively, children should pretend they are walking in the rain. Then they should pretend it's raining ice cream cones and exaggerate their

acting to accommodate this ridiculous but delightful concept.
• After viewing a movie on wild or domesticated animals, children may imitate an animal that is hungry, on the prowl, being chased, or performing tricks.
• Pick a simple-to-read animal story for children, such as "The Three Little Pigs" or "Little Red Riding Hood." After they have read the story, let them design their own costumes and rehearse the story to express themselves creatively for invited guests.
• After the teacher reads a fairy tale, have the children discuss a character's action and how this action could be expressed creatively in shadow plays (using hands and arms) on a suspended sheet lighted from behind.

Simple Activity
Provide time for children to do research on New Year celebrations that take place at different times of the year (e.g., Chinese and Jewish New Years). After they have a knowledge of the basic customs, have the class act out some of the customs performed at such occasions to express themselves creatively in the roles of peoples of other countries.

More Advanced Activity
After acquainting the children with the basic plot of a fairy tale, allow them to dictate their own favorite fairy tale. Follow up with the children acting out their fairy tale, making costumes and scenery to express themselves creatively. (Variation: Puppets could be used instead of people.)

Design your own activities to meet the needs of individual children.

The postassessment is the same as the preassessment. After the postassessment, exit from the module or proceed to the additional activities.

Postassessment

• After hearing a familiar fairy tale or legend, the children will make up a new ending for the tale, then act it out as a way of expressing themselves creatively.
• After a study of different countries (this may be in conjunction with Social Living), have the children pick a favorite custom from each country and share it at a party as a way of expressing their new understanding creatively.

Additional Activities

Abell, Kathleen. *King Orville and the Bullfrogs.* Little, 1974.
Ambrus, Victor, reteller. *The Three Poor Tailors.* Harcourt, 1966.
Bishop, Claire H. *The Five Chinese Brothers.* Coward, 1938.
Bodeker, N. M. *It's Raining Said John Twaining.* Atheneum, 1973.
Bright, Robert. *Georgie.* Doubleday, 1959.
Brown, Marcia. *The Bun: A Tale from Russia.* Harcourt, 1973.
Carle, Eric. *Do You Want to Be My Friend?* Crowell, 1971.
Childcraft. Books 1, 2, and 3.

Resources

Croft, Doreen J., and Hess, Robert D. Section on Creative Activities. *An Activities Handbook for Teachers of Young Children.* 2d ed. Houghton Mifflin Co., 1975.

Freeman, Don. *Cordoy.* Viking, 1968.

Goodall, John S. *Midnight Adventures of Kelly, Dot and Esmerelda.* Atheneum, 1973.

Livermore, Elaine. *Find the Cat.* Houghton, 1973.

McCloskey, Robert. *Time for Wonder.* Viking, 1957.

McDermott, Gerald. *Anansi the Spider—A Tale from the Ashanti.* Holt, 1972.

Mosel, Arlene, reteller. *Tikki Tipki Tembo.* Dutton, 1968.

Mother Goose. *Book of Nursery and Mother Goose Rhymes.* Doubleday, 1954.

Paterson, A. B. *Cinderella, or the Little Glass Slipper.* Holt, 1970.

Ryan, Cheli D. *Hildilid's Night.* MacMillan, 1971.

Sauer, Julia L. *Mike's House.* Viking, 1954.

Sawyer, Ruth. *Journey Cake, Ho!* Viking, 1953.

Sendak, Maurice. *Where the Wild Things Are.* Harper, 1963.

Seuss, Dr. *And to Think I Saw It on Mulberry Street.* Vanguard, 1937.

Shulevitz, Uri. *One Monday Morning.* Scribner, 1967.

Steig, William. *Sylvester and the Magic Pebble.* Windmill Books, 1969.

Teacher Magazine, any edition. (See green pages in back of book.)

Wildsmith, Brian. *Brian Wildsmith's Circus.* Watts, 1970.

Yeoman, John. *Sixes and Sevens.* MacMillan, 1971.

4
Social
Living

To experience success in social living, the young child must understand himself/herself in relation to other people and his/her environment. This group of modules deals with some of the aspects basic to successful social living. To be successful in school, the child needs to be trusting and cooperative. He/she needs to be aware of his/her dependence upon others for such basic needs as food, clothing, shelter, and transportation. The quality of his/her social living depends upon his/her appreciation of the people in the past and present who, in the community and beyond, have enriched his/her culture.

Young children are at the threshold of awareness of social living with their knowledge of family living and what they see on television. The teacher must build upon their past experiences while extending their horizons. This is not easy. In fact, it is one of the most difficult areas of the curriculum, especially in a world of many societies. However, the teacher must build upon the foundation begun by the parents, broadening it where needed. For example, because the module on environmental awareness deals with only one form of pollution, air pollution, the teacher will need to extend understanding of this problem by creating modules on other types of pollution.

Similarly, the component dealing with the problem of what a child needs to learn about himself/herself in relation to others examines only cooperation and trust. The teacher needs to think about what else is involved in a successful social relationship. Modules need to be written in these areas, too. Unfortunately, very little is available to the teacher in this area of curriculum. An excellent beginning reference section follows the module Trusting Others. This should help the creative teacher who wishes to expand the curriculum.

The modules in the component on social living are as follows:

4.1 My Community
4.2 Our Traveling Nation
4.3 Awareness of Environmental Problems
4.4 Recreation
4.5 Man's Basic Needs Yesterday and Today
4.6 It's a Small World: Mexico

4.1 My Community

Rationale

The young child comes to school with some knowledge about the community in which he/she lives. He/She may be able to recognize the policeman, the doctor, or others with whom he/she has had contact. Many times the young child knows policemen, doctors, or others from television alone and may have some fears about each. Giving the child simple background information about what really goes on in a community, and where some of the services are performed, helps the child overcome these fears and begin to see the community and its members as a large group of which he/she is a part.

Prerequisites

Invite various community members to visit the class; set up an interest area of books, records, (see resources section) community helper puppets, uniforms, and life-sized props; have pictures of community members and community situations displayed in the room; gather large boxes, paint, milk cartons, clothespins, magazines, material scraps, and newsprint.

Preassessment

• Using pictures displayed by the teacher, each child will indicate knowledge of people in community service by naming and correctly acting out the jobs of the following: policeman, postman, dentist, doctor, fireman, nurse, farmer, carpenter, plumber, and clergyman.
• The child will take a stack of community-helper pictures and sort them into three stacks labeled "safety," "comfort," and "well-being" to demonstrate a knowledge of the services performed in the community.
• Each child will demonstrate that he/she can live, work, and play with other children cooperatively by his/her day-to-day behavior in school. After the preassessment, exit from the module or proceed to the objectives.

Objective 1

Each child will learn the names of different people who offer services to the community.

Activities

• After hearing visitors from the community talk about their jobs, each child will indicate knowledge of community members by naming the jobs and telling about what people in these jobs do. On various occasions invite the following: a policeman, a postman, a dentist, a doctor, a fireman, a nurse, a farmer, a carpenter, a plumber, and a clergyman.
• Given community-helper puppets, uniforms, tools and life-sized props, the children will show their knowledge of community helpers by

82

saying who they are and role playing the parts.
• Given materials, the children will make community-helper booklets to demonstrate their knowledge of the people who service the community.
• The child will show he/she can recognize community helpers by playing a game: "On the way to school I saw Mr. Fireman [Mr. Policeman, etc.]." (The child dons part of the costumes of each during the game.)

Simple Activity
The child will play a community-helper game by matching pictures of helpers with appropriate objects of their jobs (such as a mailman and a letter) to indicate knowledge of community members.

More Advanced Activity
To demonstrate knowledge of community helpers, the class will play charades, with one child acting and the rest guessing the name of the community helper whose role is being acted out.

Design your own activities to meet the needs of individual children.

Each child will learn some of the services rendered by people in the community for our safety, comfort, and well-being.

Objective 2

Activities

• After touring such places in the community as the post office and the fire station, the child will show knowledge of the services rendered by people in the community by telling the teacher three ways the community is served by these people.
• To indicate knowledge of the ways community members serve the community, each child will be a certain member of the community and tell how this community helper might solve a problem that the teacher has posed.
• Given large boxes the children will make community-helper vehicles such as police cars, fire trucks, and mailcarts to demonstrate their knowledge of ways the community is served by these people.

Alternate Activities

Simple Activity
After being taught the melody, the children will sing "Here We Go Round the Community" to the tune of "Here We Go Round the Mulberry Bush," acting out community-helper jobs to show their knowledge of the kinds of jobs done by community helpers.

More Advanced Activity
After making puppets, the children will demonstrate their knowledge of community jobs by creating their own puppet show dramatizing how each community person helps.

Design your own activities to meet the needs of individual children.

The young child will learn to live, work, and play with other children.

Objective 3

Activities
- Given milk cartons and art supplies, the children will demonstrate they can work together cooperatively in a group by building a table model of their community. (Appropriate behavior will be taught by the teacher prior to the activity.)
- The children will demonstrate they can work together constructively by cutting community helpers and situations out of magazines and pasting them on a large box as a collage. (Appropriate behavior will be taught by the teacher prior to the activity.)
- The children will show they can play together as a group by playing a team game in which winning depends on helping each other. (Appropriate behavior will be taught by the teacher prior to the activity.)

Alternate Activities

Simple Activity
After hearing a story about family life, the children will show their understanding of group cooperation by retelling the story in terms of their own family doing the same thing. (Use flannel-board characters.)

More Advanced Activity
To indicate that they can work together cooperatively, the children will make a large mural of what community living together should look like.

Design your own activities to meet the needs of individual children.

Postassessment
The postassessment is the same as the preassessment. After the postassessment, exit from the module or proceed to additional activities.

Additional Activities
- After hearing music or a story about a community helper and being given art paper, glue, and scissors, the children will make nurse hats, postman bags, police badges, fireman hats, or other accoutrements of community helpers, to demonstrate their knowledge of those who serve the community.
- To demonstrate knowledge of how community members make the community a safer or better place to live, each child will make up and tell a story about his/her favorite community helper.
- Given brooms, rags, and cleaning materials, the children will indicate they can work together effectively by cleaning a portion of the classroom.

Resources
Books
Horwick. *A Day Downtown with Daddy.*
Lenoke. *Davey Goes Places.*
————. *Policeman Small.*
McGinley. *All Around the Town.*
Thomas. *Your Town and Mine.*
Tippett. *I Live in the City.*
Witty. *The Fireman.*
————. *The Mailman.*

Encyclopedia Britannica Films
Our Community.
Good Citizens.
The Fireman.
The Policeman.
The Doctor.
Our Post Office.

Coronet Films
Helpers in Our Community.
Stores in Our Community.
Jimmy Visits the City.

"At the Little Corner Store" and "The Gas Station Man." In *Music Round the Town.*
"Taxis" and "My Policeman." In *Music in Our Town.*

"Shop Windows," "The Postman," "The Dentist," and "My Policeman." In *Time for Poetry.* Arbuthnot, May H., and Root, Shelton L., Jr., 3d ed. Scott Foresman and Co. 1968.

Community Workers and Helpers, Group 1, SVE., Singer Education and Training Products.

Films

Songs

Poetry

Record

4.2 Our Traveling Nation

Because transportation is so important in the lives of all people, it has a vital place in the learning of the child. No matter where the child lives, he/she and his/her family are dependent upon some type of transportation. When the child comes to school it is time for him/her to learn not only about the transportation of his "small" world, but about the transportation of a larger world.

Rationale

Plan a trip using some mode of transportation that will be a new experience for most of the children; set up a learning center with books, records, films, pictures, and favorite transportation toys brought from home by the children; gather boxes of various sizes, clay, crayons, paint, scissors, string, kites, art paper, blocks, and construction toys.

Prerequisites

• Each child will demonstrate that he/she knows why transportation is important to him/her by naming three ways transportation has made his/her life better.

Preassessment

• From pictures displayed by the teacher, each child will tell whether the picture illustrates land or water transportation.
• To demonstrate knowledge of air and space travel, each child will identify by name pictures of at least four kinds of vehicles used in air and space travel.

After the preassessment, exit from the module or proceed to the objectives.

Objective 1 Each child will learn the importance of transportation in his/her own everyday life.

Activities • Each child will demonstrate knowledge of the importance of transportation in his/her life by reviewing community helpers and drawing the kinds of transportation each helper uses.
• After taking a bus ride through the community to see how people and things are transported, each child will show an understanding of vehicles in his/her life by discussing how and when he/she could use them.

Alternate Activities *Simple Activity*
Given art supplies, the child will indicate an awareness of the different vehicles by drawing his/her favorite for (a) visiting his grandmother, (b) going to the store, (c) going to the doctor, (d) fishing on the lake, and (e) looking at the bottom of the lake.

More Advanced Activity
After listening to a recording of the different sounds made by land and water vehicles, the child will show a knowledge of transportation by recognizing and imitating the different sounds. (What the teacher can't get recordings of, he/she should tape live, so that the children can hear a broad variety of vehicle sounds.)

Design your own activity to meet the needs of individual children.

Objective 2 Each child will learn the modes of transportation used in air and space.

Activities • After hearing a story about air and space travel, the child will model air and space vehicles in clay.
• The children will demonstrate their knowledge of space travel by dramatizing a trip into outer space, given some boxes, blocks, and pictures of space ships.
• After visiting the airport, the children will show their knowledge of air travel by setting up a table model of the airport.

Alternate Activities *Simple Activity*
After flying kites, the children will show their knowledge of air and space travel by describing the differences between how a kite behaves on the ground and how it behaves in the air. (They may need to experiment with real kites.)

4.2 Experimenting with a kite

More Advanced Activity
The children will demonstrate their knowledge of air and space travel
by building mobiles of vehicles that travel in air and space.

Design your own activities to meet the needs of individual children.

The postassessment is the same as the preassessment. After the
postassessment, exit from the module or proceed to additional
activities.

Postassessment

• The children will show they have an understanding of transportation
in their lives by making a mural of community transportation of the
future.
• Each child will demonstrate an understanding of travel vehicles by
building large models in which he/she can role play.
• Each child will demonstrate a knowledge of transportation by playing
with land, sea, and air block-vehicle sets.

Additional Activities

Bate. *Who Built the Highway?* 1953.
Bendick. *First Book of Airplanes.* 1952.

**Resources
Books**

Bragg. *The Little Engine That Could.* 1930.
Flack. *Boats on the River.* 1946.
Horwick. *A Big Coal Truck.* 1953.
Lenski. *Little Airplane.* 1948.
_____. *Little Auto.* 1937.
_____. *Little Train.* 1942.
Nale, Creekmore, Harris, and Greenman. *Curriculum Kindergarten Keys.* Economy Co., 1970.

Films   Encyclopedia Britannica Films
The Passenger Train.
Boats and Ships.
The Truck Driver.

Coronet Films
The Big Wide Highway.
What Do We See in the Sky?
Our Class Explores the Moon.

4.3 Awareness of Environmental Problems

Rationale   Air is an inexhaustible resource, but pure air—air fit to breathe, air that does not irritate our eyes, air that does not damage plant life, air that does not soil and corrode the materials that we use—is becoming scarcer. Most Americans today have not acted very responsibly and sensibly in taking care of our natural resources. The problems we have created cannot be solved in our lifetime. Therefore, we must educate today's children to these problems. Responsibility must become the sustaining theme of the primary years. Children must learn to take responsibility for themselves and their environment.

Prerequisites   The following materials are needed for a display table: books, pictures, models of polluting machinery (cars, trucks, airplanes), gas mask, spray gun, and other desired items.

The following materials are needed for teaching activities: a big poster showing a city scene (*World Book Encyclopedia* has an excellent one entitled *City Picture,* copyright 1965), a white saucer, a candle, pieces of cardboard, an electric fan, pictures of volcanoes and forest fires, a household sprayer, resource people (doctor, nurse, or health official), two geranium plants, and vaseline. Arrange for a field trip.

The following books are needed for the children: a pamphlet entitled *A Story of Air Pollution and Cars,* by General Motors Corporation; *An Introduction to Pollution,* by Harold E. Schlicting, Jr., and Mary Southworth Schlicting; *Who Cares? I Do,* by Munro Leaf; *The Lorax,* by Dr. Seuss; and *Clean Air—Sparkling Water,* by Dorothy E. Shuttlesworth.

This article is a prerequisite for the teacher: Dorothy Needham, "Pollution—A Teaching and Action Program," in the October 1970 issue of *Grade Teacher*.

<table>
<tr><td>

• Each child will demonstrate a knowledge of air pollutants by telling what an air pollutant does to the air.
• Each child will show that he/she knows the causes of air pollution by naming four things that cause air pollution and by telling whether each cause is man-made or natural.
• Each child will show that he/she understands the results of air pollution by naming three ways that air pollution causes harm.
After the preassessment, exit from the module or proceed to the objectives.

</td><td>

Preassessment

</td></tr>
<tr><td>

Each child will learn about air pollutants—what some of them are and what they are called.

</td><td>

Objective 1

</td></tr>
<tr><td>

• After hearing that pollutants are the things that make air dirty and after seeing a picture of a city, each child will show that he/she understands what an air pollutant is by naming the things that are making the air dirty.
• The children will demonstrate an understanding that nature also pollutes the air: observing pictures of volcanoes and forest fires, each child will tell what is coming from the fire or volcano and making the air dirty.
• While taking a walk around the neighborhood with the teacher, the children will show their understanding of what pollutes by pointing out pollutants.

</td><td>

Activities

</td></tr>
<tr><td>

Simple Activity
The children will learn that crop dusting and garden spraying are man-made causes of air pollution by demonstrating and operating a household sprayer in the classroom. (Use water with vegetable dye.)

More Advanced Activity
Each child will develop a better understanding of the causes of air pollution by drawing a picture of something that causes air pollution, by explaining to the class how it pollutes the air, and by telling whether it is a man-made or a natural cause of pollution. (This would occur after the teacher reads one of the books from the resources section.)

Design your own activities to meet the needs of individual children.

</td><td>

Alternate Activities

</td></tr>
<tr><td>

Each child will discover the results of air pollution.

</td><td>

Objective 2

</td></tr>
<tr><td>

• After a doctor talks to the children, each child will demonstrate a knowledge of the results of air pollution by naming three ways that air pollution affects health.

</td><td>

Activities

</td></tr>
</table>

89

• After explaining to the children that plants need air just as we do and that plants have tiny openings on the leaves for air to enter, children will discover that plants are affected by air pollution by coating the leaves of one plant with vaseline, by observing what happens to the leaves, by telling why they think the leaves withered, and by telling how air pollution could also make the leaves wither.

Alternate Activities

Simple Activity
After reading *The Lorax* by Dr. Seuss, the children will discover the results of air pollution by discussing the pictures and the story.

More Advanced Activity
The children will discover some results of air pollution by touring a fire station and seeing equipment, such as masks and oxygen tanks, used by firemen to keep from being overcome by polluted air.

Design your own activities to meet the needs of individual children.

Postassessment

The postassessment is the same as the preassessment. After the postassessment, exit from the module or proceed to additional activities.

Additional Activities

• The children will understand more about air pollutants by observing the school incinerator while it is in operation. (Other incinerators available in the neighborhood should also be studied.)
• By smelling the exhaust fumes in the air coming from the buses as they arrive to take the children home, the children will learn that school buses produce air pollutants.
• By inspecting the outside of the school building and by naming the places that are dirtier than others, places where the paint has peeled, where the stones have eroded, or where the steel has corroded, the children will learn that air pollution soils and corrodes buildings.

Resources

Arkansas Department of Education. *Early Childhood Curriculum Handbook Of Minimum Skills and Concepts.* 1973.
Blough, Glenn O., and Schwartz, Julius. *Elementary School Science and How to Teach It.* Holt, Rinehart, and Winston, 1964.
General Motors Corporation. *A Story of Air Pollution and Cars.* 1973.
Mitzumura, Kazue. *If I Built a Village.* Crowell, 1971.
Munro, Leaf. *Who Cares? I Do.* J. B. Lippincott Co., 1971.
Needham, Dorothy. "Pollution—A Teaching and Action Program." *Grade Teacher* (October, 1970).
Schlichting, Harold E., Jr., and Schlichting, Mary Southworth. *An Introduction to Pollution.* Steck-Vaugh Co., 1971.
Seuss, Dr. *The Lorax.* Random House, 1971.

4.4 Recreation

Rationale

Recreation is any type of activity that not only gives us pleasure but helps to renew the mind and body. It is carried on in leisure time. Americans today have more leisure time than ever before but we seem unable to use it wisely. A leading economist has estimated that our nation will have 660 billion more leisure hours in the year 2000 than it had in 1950. Recreation is essential to the mental, physical, and social well-being of each individual. Considering the increase in the amount of leisure time and the importance of recreation to each individual, education for recreation is imperative. Leisure time is not something for adults only. Children, too, need guidance in the wise use of leisure time.

Prerequisites

The following materials are needed: one group of pictures showing people working at their daily jobs, another group of pictures showing people involved in a recreational activity, one group of pictures showing winter recreational activities and another group of pictures showing summer recreational activities. Arrange for a field trip, obtain a neighborhood map or group of pictures showing recreational areas and related activities. (Example: lake-boat, zoo-monkey, park-baseball player.) From *Compton's Young Children's Precyclopedia,* volume 7, show pictures of the Wright Brothers' airplane and Eli Whitney's cotton gin. Ask resource people to visit the classroom. (people in the community, teachers, and other students who have hobbies and would bring them and discuss them.) Have bird song records available for the children to hear.

Collect books for children. See resource section for a list of possible books to use; *Nothing To Do* by Russell Hoban is a very good book to teach the children about the wise use of leisure time.

Article for the teacher: "All Work and No Play Makes...." *Instructor* (1974), p. 62.

Preassessment

• Each child will demonstrate knowledge of four recreational activities by naming them and by picking from an array of pictures the picture that correctly matches a recreational activity that the teacher calls out. (The teacher should call out activities not named by the child in this part of the assessment.)
• Each child will show that he/she knows the recreational and cultural centers in the immediate community by naming five centers and one activity conducted at each center.
• Each child will demonstrate a knowledge of five hobbies by naming them.
After the preassessment, exit from the module or proceed to the objectives.

Objective 1

Each child will demonstrate an increased awareness of various types of recreational activities.

Activities	• Following a class discussion of what is meant by recreation and work, each child will demonstrate knowledge of recreational activities by selecting from two groups of pictures those that show a recreational activity. (The other group of pictures shows work activities). • Each child will show knowledge of recreational activities by pantomiming a recreational activity until the class guesses the activity. • After distinguishing between winter and summer recreational activities, the child will show an understanding of summer recreational activities by using scraps of colored construction paper to make a poster illustrating summer fun. (Variation: same activity showing fall, winter, or spring fun.)
Alternate Activities	*Simple Activity* Given a description of a recreational activity, each child will show an understanding of the activity by selecting from a group of pictures the picture of the activity being described and by putting those described in a pile. *More Advanced Activity* In addition to performing the first activity under Objective 1, the child will further demonstrate knowledge of recreational activities by telling where this particular activity could take place (i.e., in the back yard, at the golf course, etc.). *Design your own activities to meet the needs of individual children.*
Objective 2	Each child will learn about recreational and cultural activities in his community.
Activities	• Following a field trip to a recreational center, the child will show what he/she learned by drawing a picture of the center and by drawing a picture of a recreational activity carried on in the center. (While there, each child should have the opportunity to participate in one or more recreational activities.) • Using a neighborhood map the child will locate each recreational and cultural center by pointing to each center, naming the center, and naming one activity conducted at the center. (It helps if, as the child visits each center, the teacher draws its shape on the map.)
Alternate Activities	*Simple Activity* Given a resource person from each of the recreational centers in the community, the child will demonstrate knowledge of recreational centers by choosing to participate in activities from more than one center. *More Advanced Activity* By using clay, sticks, or other desired media, the child can further his concept of recreational centers in the community by creating a model of a park showing play areas, picnic tables, etc. (Encourage innovative ideas.) *Design your own activities to meet the needs of individual children.*
Objective 3	Each child will learn about hobbies as a recreation.

• After hearing some of "Collecting Things" in *Compton's Young Children's Precyclopedia*, each child will learn about hobbies by choosing a hobby of his/her own to do as a project at school.
• Each child will learn more about hobbies by displaying and telling about his/her hobby at an "Outdoor Hobby Fair," by looking at other hobbies displayed, and by listening to other people tell about their hobbies.
• After hearing other children (third to sixth grade) describe their hobbies, each child will show that he/she has learned about hobbies by describing one that he/she would like to undertake. (The older children can serve as teachers of hobbies for the younger children.)

Alternate Activities

Simple Activity
Each child will develop an understanding of gardening as a hobby by planting seeds and by watching and caring for the plants in the classroom.

More Advanced Activity
Each child will learn that some people's hobbies have resulted in inventions by looking at pictures of the Wright Brothers' first airplane and Eli Whitney's cotton gin. Using parts from simple machines (i.e., old clocks, speedometers, etc.), screwdrivers, nails, wood, and a hammer, each child will experiment with inventing as a hobby.

Design your own activities to meet the needs of individual children.

Postassessment

The postassessment is the same as the preassessment. After the postassessment, exit from the module or proceed to additional activities.

Additional Activities

• Each child will show an understanding of recreational acrivities by drawing a picture of himself/herself engaged in a recreational activity on the weekend.
• With the aid of the teacher, each child will learn more about the recreational and cultural centers in his community by visiting these areas several times.
• Each child will become familiar with bird watching as a hobby by observing birds and naming them while taking a Bird Walk. Have records of bird songs for them to hear.

Resources

"All Work and No Play Makes. . . ." *Instructor*, April 1974.
"Collecting Things." *Compton's Young Children's Precyclopedia*, vol. 7, pp. 114-119.
Fisher, Aileen. *Up, Up the Mountain*. Thomas Y. Crowell Press, 1964.
Harmer, Mabel. *The True Book of the Circus*. Childrens Press, 1964.
Hoban, Russell. *Nothing To Do*. Harper and Row, 1964.
Kraus, Richard. *Recreation Today*. Appleton-Century Crofts, 1966.
McCloskey, Robert. *Time of Wonder*. The Viking Press, 1957.
Munari, Bruno. *Bruno Manari's Zoo*. The World Publishing Co., 1963.

Ray, Bert. *We Live in the City*. Childrens Press, 1963.
Shick, Eleanor. *Katie Goes to Camp*. MacMillan Co., 1968.
Staats, Sara Radar. *Big City ABC*. Follett Publishing Co., 1963.
Zolotow, Charlotte, *The Park Book*. Harper Brothers, 1944.

4.5 Man's Basic Needs
Yesterday and Today

Rationale

Most children are fascinated by the colorful costumes and daring feats of the people who settled America. Children need to develop an appreciation and respect for these early people whose values and customs have been blended to form our American heritage. All these early explorers from many continents helped to create the multicultured society that is America today. Each culture has shared the same basic needs—food, clothing, and shelter.

Prerequisites

Assemble as many picture books from the library as possible on American Indians, Pilgrims, Colonials, and other ethnic groups in America; pictures of American Indians, Pilgrims, and other ethnic groups; pointed paper cups, paints, brushes, scissors, drawing paper, crayolas, Lincoln logs, oatmeal boxes, coffee cans, light bulbs, papier-mache, old broom sticks (or dowel pins), mural paper, inexpensive brown or tan cloth, and construction paper (in bright colors.)

   Also needed are several globes of the world; popcorn, squash, melons, beans, marshmallows, "weenies"; large, colored plastic beads and laces; pieces of elastic, colored real feathers, or construction paper feathers.

Preassessment

• Given an Indian tepee, a log cabin, and a house from modern times, each child will demonstrate knowledge of man's need for shelter by telling how each is needed.
• Each child will indicate a knowledge of man's basic need for clothing by identifying and discussing the function of clothing worn in the summer and winter by Indians, Pilgrim children, and today's children.
• By selecting and interpreting pictures from an array that shows Indians, Pilgrims, and people today raising crops, each child will show a knowledge of man's basic need for food after the teacher asks what is happening in each picture and why.
• The children will demonstrate their knowledge of the contributions made by more than one ethnic group by naming two of the contributions of Pilgrims, Indians, Blacks, Orientals, or Mexican-Americans to our culture.
After the preassessment, exit from the module or proceed to the objectives.

Each child will learn of man's basic need for shelter in the early days of our country as well as today.

• After hearing picture-book stories about the Indians and the Pilgrims and their need for shelter, the children will show their knowledge of man's need for shelter by naming this need and discussing its importance. (Variation: Play "Suppose Game": Suppose we didn't have houses or schools; what would we do if it rained, snowed, or became very hot?)
• To show a knowledge of man's basic need of shelter, each child will select a picture to sculpt in clay from a display of pictures of Indian, early Mexican-American, and Pilgrim shelters. All the shelters should be displayed on a tabletop. (See prerequisites section for materials needed.)
• To show an understanding of man's need of shelter, each child will select a picture from a picture display of shelters used in the past and describe the picture, telling why man needs the shelter. (Variation: Have the children determine how all the shelters are alike.)

Simple Activity
From the large selection of books on display in the library corner, the child will pick out a book to use for telling the group about what it would be like to live in the shelter, displaying knowledge about the basic need for shelter.

More Advanced Activity
The child will demonstrate a knowledge of man's basic need for shelter by visiting an outdoor museum of old houses, churches, and schools from the past and comparing these with today's buildings nearby.

Design your own activities to meet the needs of individual children.

Each child will learn of man's basic need for clothing in the early years of our country as well as today.

• To show their knowledge of man's need for clothing, the children will dramatize a scene of early Americans using clothing made from animals or plants. (Variation: Children dress up in today's clothes and talk about how they are different from early Americans.)
• To show their knowledge of man's basic need of clothing, the children will draw pictures of Indian and early American winter clothing. (Variation: Compare these with clothing of today.)
• After a discussion of why we wear clothes today (covering at least three reasons), the children will show their understanding of the need for clothing by examining stories and pictures of early Americans to see if they wore clothes for the same reasons.

Alternate Activities   *Simple Activity*
The children will string colored plastic beads on laces as part of their costumes to show their knowledge of man's need of ornamental clothing yesterday and today. (The teacher can display necklaces worn today.)

More Advanced Activity
Given a precut material, the children will make Pilgrim bonnets, aprons, collars, and hats to show their knowledge of man's need for clothing yesterday. They will also discuss with the teacher why these are worn or not worn today.

Design your own activities to meet the needs of individual children.

Objective 3   Each child will learn that man's basic need for food existed in the early years of our country as well as today.

Activities   • To show knowledge of man's basic need for food, the children will dramatize a scene showing the Indians teaching the Pilgrims about the animals of the forest and how each one could be used for food.
• To show their knowledge of man's basic need for food, the children will prepare and eat the food Indians, Pilgrims, and Mexican-Americans ate in the early days of our country. Discussion should center around whether we still eat any of these foods today. Why?

Alternate Activities   *Simple Activity*
To show their knowledge of man's basic need for food, the children will pick from a large array of pictures of farm animals, those depicting animals that the Pilgrims brought.

More Advanced Activity
To show their knowledge of man's basic need for food, the children will tell some of the problems the Pilgrims encountered in this new country while raising the farm animals shown in the previous picture array.

Design your own activities to meet the needs of individual children.

Objective 4   Each child will demonstrate a knowledge of several ethnic contributions made to our American culture.

Activities   • The children will sing Indian and Pilgrim songs ("Ten Little Indians," "I Am an American," or others) to show their understanding of the contributions of both these ethnic groups to our country. (The Pilgrims represent the White ethnic group in early America.)
• The children will make Indian musical instruments (see resources section) to show their knowledge of the contribution of this ethnic group to our culture.
• The children will learn and do Indian dances with Indian music to

4.5 Looking at shelters

demonstrate their knowledge of the Indian's contribution to our
country.
● Using *Coyote Goes Hunting for Fire* (see resources section), the
children will show their understanding of Indian contributions to our
culture by discussing the stories that Indians made up.
● The children will demonstrate their understanding of Indian
contributions by researching and gathering Indian foods (see resources
section of this module) with the teacher and preparing several meals
or snacks.
● The teacher will use the resources section of this module to redo
the above activities substituting colonial Americans, Blacks, and
Mexican-Americans for Indians.

Alternate Activities

Simple Activity
After the children have visited in a Black, Mexican-American, Oriental,
or Indian home, they will show their understanding of a minority
group's contribution by talking about what was similar or dissimilar to
the way they live.

More Advanced Activity
To demonstrate their understanding of what minorities have
contributed, the children will work in small groups with tape recorders
to record "A Day in the Life of _____ [a minority group]" to share
with the class. The teacher should help each group cover music,

97

dance, food, family customs, or whatever would help to make the account authentic. (Older children of these minority groups should act as resource people.)

Design your own activities to meet the needs of individual children.

Postassessment

The postassessment is the same as the preassessment. After the postassessment, exit from the module or proceed to additional activities.

Additional Activities

• After the teacher tells the story "The Emperor's New Clothes", by Hans Christian Anderson, each child will show that he/she understands why we need clothes by discussing at least three reasons.
• Repeat the first activity with shelter as the subject and using the Mother Goose rhyme "The House That Jack Built."
• Repeat the first activity using Marcia Brown's retelling of *Stone Soup; An Old Tale* (Scribner, 1947) to discuss why we need food.

Resources

Amon, Aline. *Talking Hands: Indian Sign Language.* Doubleday, 1968.
Armer, Laura. *Waterless Mountain.* McKay, 1931.
Baker, Betty. *Little Runner of the Long House.* Harper, 1962.
Baylon, Byrd. *Before you Came This Way.* Dutton, 1969.
Bealer, A. W. *Only the Names Remain: The Cherokees and the Trail of Tears.* Little, 1972.
Beatty, H. *Little Owl Indian.* Houghton-Mifflin Co., 1951.
Benchley, Nathaniel. *Only Earth and Sky Last Forever.* Harper, 1973.
_____. *Small Wolf.* Harper, 1972.
Bernstein, M., and Kobrin, J., (retellers). *Coyote Goes Hunting for Fire.* Scribner, 1974.
Bierhorst, John (ed.) *In the Trail of the Wind: American Indian Poems and Ritual Orations.* Farrar, 1971.
Bontemps, Arna. *Story of the Negro.* 5th ed., Knopf, 1969.
Bulla, C. R. *Squanto, Friend of the Pilgrims.* Crowell, 1954.
Clapp, Patricia. *Constance: A Story of Early Plymouth.* Lothrop, 1968.
Clemens. *Invitation of Rhythm.*
Clifton, Lucille. *Some of the Days of Everett Anderson.* Holt, 1970. (About a young Black boy.)
Colby, Jean. *Plymouth Plantation Then and Now.* Hastings, 1970.
Dalgliesh, Alice. *The Courage of Sarah Noble.* Scribner, 1954.
Earle, A. M. *Home and Child Life in Colonial Days.* MacMillan, 1969.
Elisofon, Eliot. *Zaire: A Week in Joseph's World.* Crowell-Collier, 1973.
Encyclopedias: two or three different series for basic facts about Pilgrims, Indians, and other ethnic groups.
Erdoes, Richard. *The Sun Dance People: The Plains Indians, etc.* Knopf, 1972.
Green, Mary M. *Everybody Has a House and Everybody Eats.* William R. Scott, 1965.
Harris, J., and Hobson, J. W. *Black Pride: A People's Struggle.* McGraw, 1969.
Hays, W., and Vernon, R. *Foods the Indians Gave Us.* Washburn, 1973.

Jones, Hettie, (comp.) *The Trees Stand Shining: Poetry of North American Indians.* Dial Press, 1971.

Jones, Wayman. *Edge of Two Worlds.* Dial Press, 1968.

Krementz, Jill. *Sweet Pea: A Black Girl Growing Up in the Rural South.* Harcourt, 1969.

Krumgold, Joseph. *. . . And Now Miguel.* Crowell, 1953.

Lester, Julius. *Long Journey Home.* Dial Press, 1972.

Meltzer, Milton. *Langston Hughes: Biography.* Crowell, 1969.

Monjo, F. *The Secret of the Sachem Tree.* Coward, 1972.

Montgomery, J. *The Wrath of Coyote.* Morrow, 1968.

Nale, N. Creekmore, M., Harris, T., and Geenmen, M. *Kindergarten Keys.* Economy Co., 1970.

Politi, Leo. *A Boat for Peppe.* RJC, NU., 1950.

———. *Angel of Oliveria Street.* RJC, NU., 1946.

Preito, Mariana (comp.) *Play It in Spanish etc.* Day, ' 1973, (Games and folklore)

Reynolds, C. R., Jr. *American Indian Portraits From the Wanamaker Expedition of 1913.* Greene, 1971.

Rounds, Glen. *The Treeless Plains.* Holiday, 1967. (Settlers' houses)

Shapp, Charles and Martha. *Let's Find Out About Houses.* Franklin Watts, 1962.

Speare, E. G. *Life in Colonial America.* Random, 1963.

Wildsmith, Brian. *Fishes.* New York: Franklin Watts, Inc., 1968.

Wolf, Bernard. *Tinker and the Medicine Man.* Random, 1969.

Wonderriski, William. *The Stop.* Holt, 1972.

Wood, L. *Singing Fun.* Webster Division of McGraw-Hill, 1961.

———. *More Singing Fun.* Webster Division of McGraw-Hill, 1961.

4.6 It's a Small World: Mexico

Rationale

This module will provide an opportunity for children to gain a better understanding of our southern neighbor, Mexico. The educational and cultural patterns of Mexico differ greatly from those of the United States. Unfortunately, the average citizen of the United States knows far too little about this Central American nation. At an early age, children should develop attitudes of tolerance and friendship toward their neighbor, Mexico.

Prerequisites

The teacher will need a variety of books, films, and records (see resources section). Have on hand a variety of musical instruments typical of Mexico.

Preassessment

• Each child will demonstrate knowledge of the music of Mexico by naming two of three Mexican songs played and by doing the correct

steps to a Mexican dance after he has experienced the dance twice.
● Each child will demonstrate knowledge of the customs of Mexico by naming three customs and describing how each is practiced.

After the preassessment, exit from the module or proceed to the objectives.

Objective 1   The children will learn the culture of Mexico through the music of the country.

Activities   ● After listening to the record, "Uy Tara La La," the children will demonstrate their knowledge of Mexican music by singing this song of Mexico with the record. (The children will need to experience this many times.)
● Following a listening activity and demonstration of two rhythms by the teacher, the children will indicate their knowledge of Mexican rhythms correctly several times.
● Following a discussion and show-and-tell demonstration by the teacher, each child will demonstrate knowledge of musical instruments of Mexico by identifying two instruments among a group of instruments used in Mexico. (The show-and-tell demonstration should include only two instruments each time the activity is done.)
● Following a "Let's Listen, Sing, and Move" session and a demonstration of the dance by the teacher, each child will demonstrate knowledge of Mexican music by correctly performing the Mexican Hat Dance. (See resources section for record.) (Limit the variations in dance steps to three.)

Alternate Activities   *Simple Activity*
Given a bongo drum, each child will indicate knowledge of Mexican music by correctly beating a Mexican rhythm two times after several demonstrations by the teacher.

More Advanced Activity
Following a film on Mexico, the children will demonstrate their increased knowledge of Mexican culture by role playing dancing from the films.

Design your own activities to meet the needs of individual children.

Objective 2   The children will learn about the culture of Mexico through the customs of the people.

Activities   ● After listening to a story and seeing pictures of family life in Mexico, the children will demonstrate their understanding of Mexico by identifying each member of the family.
● After viewing a film on "Art in Mexico" and seeing a demonstration by the teacher on Mexican art, the children will draw a picture of Mexican life to demonstrate their knowledge of Mexican customs.
● Invite a person who has traveled in Mexico to talk with the class and show some articles purchased in Mexico. Following this visit, the children will demonstrate their knowledge of Mexican culture by

selecting and identifying two articles from the display table and telling how and why they are used.

Simple Activity
Given construction paper and crayons, each child will demonstrate knowledge of customs in Mexico by accurately drawing a picture of a house and family in Mexico.

More Advanced Activity
The children will demonstrate their knowledge of Mexican life by role playing and pantomiming the roles of different people in Mexico. (Examples: the policeman, fireman, mother, father, grandmother.)

Design your own activities to meet the needs of individual children.

Alternate Activities

The postassessment is the same as the preassessment. After the postassessment, exit from the module or proceed to additional activity.

Postassessment

Following lunch at a local Mexican restaurant, the children will demonstrate their knowledge of Mexican food by correctly matching the name with the food (tortilla, tamales, etc.). (Suggestion: Upon completion of this activity, any problem encountered should be treated on an individual basis focusing on the child's needs.)

Additional activity

Dodge, David. *Fly Down, Drive Mexico*. Macmillan, 1968.
Ervin, Russell C. *Six Faces of Mexico*. University of Arizona Press, 1966.
Ross, Patricia Fent. *Mexico*. Information Classroom Picture Pub., 1958.

Resources
Books

Boy of Mexico: Juan and His Donkey.
Hand Industries of Mexico.
Adobe Village (Mexico).

Films

Raspa, La Mexico, LPM 1623, RCA Records, 1974.
Folk Songs of Mexico, Alfonso Cruz Jiminez, Educational Records.
Mexican Hat Dance, Mantovani and His Orchestra, London Label.

Records

4.7 Africa: People and Customs

Africa affects our imagination like no other place on earth. It is rich in details of human history with a record number of fascinating animals

Rationale

101

4.7 Bongo drums

and landscapes. Going through this module should facilitate children's development cognitively, affectively, and interpersonally as well as delight them. The Afro-American culture represents the second largest ethnic group in America today. This module should serve as a stimulus to better understanding of culturally different children.

Prerequisites

The teacher will need large pictures of African animals and African people, a variety of books, films and records. (See resources section at end of this module.) Have on hand pieces of wood from a lumber yard and musical instruments typical of Africa.

Preassessment

• Each child will demonstrate knowledge of African people by correctly identifying three pictures as to who the people are (mother, father, brothers, sisters) and by pairing each of these pictures with the corresponding picture of a member of a white family.
• From a group of twelve animal pictures, each child will demonstrate knowledge of African animals by correctly selecting eight animals, typical of Africa, as the teacher calls out the animal names.
After this preassessment, exit from the module or proceed to the objectives.

The children will gain a general idea of African people, their culture, and their similarities to other peoples.

Objective 1

• Following the film *Kenya: Land and People*, each child will demonstrate his knowledge of African people by correctly identifying the members of the family as mother, father, baby, just as he would when talking about his own family.
• After listening to the record "Mambo," and seeing a demonstration of the rhythm by the teacher, each child will demonstrate his knowledge of African culture by correctly repeating the rhythm several times.
• After the teacher reads the book, *Manda La* aloud, each child will show his understanding of African culture by building a tabletop village and reenacting the story with models each time the teacher rereads the story.

Activities

Simple Activity
After listening to the story "Congo Boy" the children, given coffee cans and cardboard, will demonstrate their knowledge of African culture by correctly making bongo drums and playing them.

Alternate Activities

More Advanced Activity
Following a demonstration of the rhythm and dance to an African folk-music selection by the teacher, each child will demonstrate knowledge of African culture by correctly repeating the demonstration several times.

Design your own activities to meet the needs of individual children.

The children will learn about the variety of animals in Africa.

Objective 2

• Following a field trip to the museum and a visit to the African jungle display, each child will demonstrate knowledge of African animals by correctly naming and identifying animals of Africa when the teacher shows him/her table models of them in the classroom. (If your museum does not have this, use storybooks about African animals.)
• Given construction paper, crayon, and a group of pictures to choose from, each child will demonstrate knowledge of animals of Africa by drawing his/her favorite animal. (Variation: clay modeling of animals.)
• Given a group of animal puzzles, the children will indicate their knowledge of African animals by correctly assembling the puzzles. (All the puzzles should be of animals found in Africa.)

Activities

Simple Activity
Following a demonstration by the teacher and given paper plates, scissors, glue, and a pattern, each child will demonstrate knowledge of African animals by making an elephant.

Alternate Activities

More Advanced Activity
After the teacher reads a teacher-made book to them introducing African animals who talk to children telling them what they eat, how they hide, or other habits, the children, given modeling clay, will demonstrate their knowledge of animals of Africa by correctly modeling two animals of Africa and what they eat.

Design your own activities to meet the needs of individual children.

Postassessment

The postassessment is the same as the preassessment. After the postassessment, exit from the module or proceed to additional activities.

Additional Activities

• Following a visit by a person who has traveled in Africa and after a show-and-tell session, each child wll indicate knowledge of African culture by selecting and correctly identifying two articles from the display table.
• Given tempera, pieces of wood, and a brush, each child will demonstrate knowledge of African culture by painting an African picture on the wood. (The pictures will be the child's concept of an African picture.)
• Following a demonstration by the teacher the children will indicate their knowledge of African culture by correctly playing each of the games demonstrated: (1) Let's Go For a Jungle Walk, (2) Monkey See, Monkey Do, and (3) Animals in My Cage. (Each of these games should be taught at different times.)
(Suggestion: Upon completion of additional activities, any problem should be treated on an individual basis.)

Resources
Books

Adoff, Arnold. *Manda La.* Harper, 1971.
Clarke, Mollie. *Congo Boy.* Scholastic Book Service, 1972.
Coughlan, Robert. *Tropical Africa.* Time Incorporated, 1962.
Fielder, Jean. *My Special House.* Whitman Publishing Co., 1966.
Ingalls, Leonard. *Getting to Know Kenya.* Coward-McCann, Inc., 1963.
Olderogge, Dmitry. *The Art of African Negro Art.* The Hamlyn Co., 1962.

Films

Kenya: Land and People. Eye Gate Instructional Materials.
Life along the Congo River. EBF Films.

Records

African Folk Music. Educational Records.
Mambo, D-105. Educational Records.

4.8 Trusting Others

The young child needs to trust others, especially the grown-ups in his/ her life. Trust is most often based on being honest with each other. This is something a child this age can understand. Part of trusting others is knowing when you need their help or their companionship and being able to ask them for these things. Young children may not be able to make this choice. Trusting others is a developmental step toward a higher level of social living and functioning.

Rationale

The teacher needs to read Eda Le Shan's article, "The Most Important Things Parents Can Teach a Little Child," *Woman's Day*. (April, 1973).

Prerequisites

After observing the child, remembering past experiences with him/her, and checking with the parents and the child, the teacher will determine whether each child trusts others by using the following checklist:

Preassessment

• Accepts babysitter without being upset
• Accepts teacher's absence from room without becoming upset with a substitute
• Accepts teacher as a significant adult; accepts teacher as a class leader
• Asks teacher for help when needed
• Accepts teacher's suggestions
• Is willing to go with another adult at the teacher's request
• Accepts authority of mother at home
• Accepts authority of father at home
• Accepts authority of parent substitute at home (if there is no mother or father in the home)
• Will lend another child something that the child requests
• Expresses feelings (e.g., anger, happiness, fear) to others without apparent fear of losing their friendship
• When asked, "What is your favorite toy? Who would you trust enough to let hold it for a day?" Mentions (make note of answer) teacher, mother, father, sibling, friend(s) not in his class, friend(s) in his class, grandparent or other relative, TV character or other imaginary character, nobody, or other (specify _____).
The most trusting child is the one who would entrust his favorite toy to his teacher, parents, friends, older relatives, and (perhaps) sibling. A child who is not trusting chooses imaginary characters or no one as an answer.
After the preassessment, exit from the module or proceed to the objective.

Each child will learn to trust others more.

Objective

• *Helping Game.* While each child plays, he/she will demonstrate trust in others by allowing the teacher to lead him/her blindfolded around the room, stepping over and ducking under obstacles when told to do so.

Activities

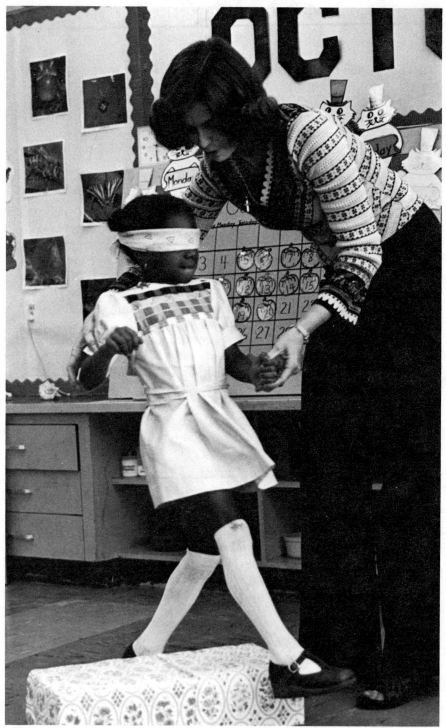

4.8 "I trust you."

● *Mother's Day Game.* (Tape-recorded by each mother for the teacher, who writes part of the script.) "Hello, Timmy, this is Mama. Hope you are having a good day in school today. Sometimes I forget to tell you how proud I am of you. You know how mothers are. They get tired and fuss, or they have to cook dinner. What I really wanted to do was listen to you for a while. I wanted to ask you about what you wanted for your next birthday?" (Here the parent pays the child a compliment on some aspect of his/her behavior, etc.)

While playing the tape, each child learns to trust others more by interacting with the tape and with the parent about the tape when he/she gets home. (Variations: A tape to the child from his/her father or principal for him/her to listen to often in school.)

• *I-Trust Game.* While playing this game, each child demonstrates an ability to trust others by trusting the child he/she
picks out to do what he/she asks. (Example: Sam says, "I trust you to hit my hand, but not too hard, John." John, who was selected, must say the same thing to Sam who picked him. John next says, "Mark, I trust you to say something good about me." Mark responds by saying something good about John. Other *I-Trust* situations: "Pinch my arm,

Simple Activity
After each child has picked out a toy to play with, the child demonstrates that he/she trusts others by trading it to another child whom the teacher has selected, saying, "I trust you to give it back to me in one minute." When the teacher says that one minute is up, each child gives back the toy.

More Advanced Activity
Children work in pairs to show that they are learning to trust others (the children helping each other and the teacher coordinating) by preparing something to eat for the whole class. Examples: instant pudding (2 children per mixing bowl), Kool-Aid, Jello, and lemonade.

Design your own activities to meet the needs of individual children.

Alternate Activities

The postassessment is the same as the preassessment. After the postassessment, exit from the module or proceed to additional activities.

Postassessment

• While singing the song, "Trust Your Partner," to the tune of "Yankee Doodle," the children will indicate they trust others by doing what the song says.
   If you trust us
   All the time
   Shake your partner's hand.
   Lead him to and
   Lead him back
   And do it very grandly.
   Chorus:
   You trust him
   And he trusts you
   Together you turn around.
   Stamp your feet
   One, two, three
   And walk him back to town.
• After an informal visit with a policeman, the children will demonstrate that they trust others by telling the policeman how he can help them. (Variation: Use fireman, postman, doctor, nurse, etc.)

Additional Activities

Resources

Axline, U. *Play Therapy*. Ballantine Books, 1969.

Blatz, W. E. *Human Security*. University of Toronto Press, 1966.

Caplan, G. *Emotional Problems of Early Childhood*. Basic Books, 1955.

Dawson, M. *Are There Unwelcome Guests in Your Classroom?* Association for Childhood Education, International, 1974.

Developing Understanding of Self and Others. DUSO Kit D-1. American Guidance Service, Inc.

Doll, E. *Vineland Social Maturity Scale*. American Guidance Service, Inc.

Goldstein, H. *The Social Learning Curriculum*. Columbus, Ohio: Charles E. Merrill Co., 1974.

Goodman, M. E. *Race Awareness in Young Children*. Collier Books., 1964.

Greene, J. *Discipline As Self-Direction*. Department of Elementary/Kinder-garten/Nursery Educators.

Hymes, J. L., Jr. *Behavior and Misbehavior: A Teacher's Guide to Action*. Prentice-Hall, Inc., 1955.

LeShan, I. *The Conspiracy Against Childhood*. Atheneum Press, 1968.

Multi-Age Grouping: Enriching the Learning Environment. Department of Elementary/Kindergarten/Nursery Educators, 1968.

Paton, C. "Patterns of Family Organization: An Approach to Child Study," *Young Children*. Dec. 1970.

Read, K. *The Nursery School: A Human Relationships Laboratory*. W. B. Saunders, 1971.

Soltys, J. *When the Child is Angry*. American Association of Elementary, Kindergarten, and Nursery Educators.

4.9 There's Nobody Exactly Like Me!

Rationale

Billions of people live in the world, and yet no two people are exactly alike. At times, children feel very insecure about themselves, even though each is unique. Each should be proud to be "me." The purpose of this module is to help the child see himself/herself in a unique and positive sense.

Prerequisites

Have on hand an ink pad and paper, individual hand mirrors, a full-length mirror, a blindfold, baby pictures of each child, current pictures of each child, a tape recorder, index cards, magic markers, a magnifying glass, scissors, paper, pictures of several children taken by the photographer and developed so that they have two right sides and two left sides facing each other as if they had grown that way, pictures that the children have drawn or painted during free time, the book *I Like to Be Me* by Barbara Bel Geddes, the poem "Mr. Tall and Mr. Small" by Bernice Wells Carlson.

Preassessment

Given current pictures of each child in the group, the child will show that he/she knows that people are different by finding three pictures

108

that are exactly alike. (The response should be that no two pictures are exactly alike.)

After the preassessment, exit from the module or proceed to the objective.

Each child will understand that people are different and that there's nobody exactly like him/her.

• After looking at themselves in a hand mirror, the children will understand that people are different by trying to find someone among their classmates whose face looks like theirs.

• After looking at themselves in a full-length mirror, the children will understand that people are different by trying to find someone among their classmates whose whole appearance looks like theirs.

• Same as preceding activity, except that they will try to find someone among their classmates dressed in every detail exactly like themselves.

• Given baby pictures of the class, the children will understand that people are different by trying to find baby pictures that are exactly alike.

• After writing their first names on index cards, the children will understand that people are different by comparing the index cards to find two that have formed the letters exactly alike.

• Given paper and ink pad to fingerprint themselves, the children will understand that people are different by comparing with a magnifying glass all the children's fingerprints to find out if they are alike.

• Same as preceding activity, except use footprints.

• After the teacher blindfolds the children, they will understand that people are different by feeling the faces and hair of their classmates to find that the faces and hair do not feel the same. (Variation: feeling someone else's face and then your own.)

• After hearing some children discuss dreams they have, the child will understand that people are different by acting out through pantomime some of his/her dreams.

• After hearing the children discuss some new clothes they are wearing, the child will understand that people are different by having a fashion show with the other children in the class.

• Using pictures the children have painted, the child will understand that people are different by comparing the paintings to see the differences in ideas and uses of colors.

• Using the picture halves that are matching right and left sides as well as the current uncut picture, the child will understand that people are different by seeing that if the two left halves of the face were to grow side by side and the two right halves of the face grew side by side you would have two pictures different from the uncut picture.

• After hearing a poem like "Mr. Tall and Mr. Small," by Bernice Wells Carlson, the children will understand that people are different by acting out the poem and playing the parts of Mr. Tall and Mr. Small.

Simple Activity
Given paper and magic marker, children will draw around the left and right foot and cut them out. The child will then understand that people are different by comparing the size and shape of the left foot with

109

those of the right foot. (Variation: Compare your right foot with someone else's to see how they differ.)

More Advanced Activity
After the teacher has recorded the children's voices during an activity period, the children will understand that people are different by listening to the tape for the differences in the sounds of their voices.

Design your own activities to meet the needs of individual children.

Postassessment

The postassessment is the same as the preassessment. After the postassessment, exit from the module or proceed to additional activities.

Additional Activities

• After hearing the book *I Like to Be Me*, the children will understand that people are different by telling why they like being who they are.
• After role playing stories about differences in people, the children will understand that people are different by using an art medium of their choosing to make a picture showing differences in people.

Resources

"About Me." *Childcraft Annual*. Field Enterprises Educational Corporation, 1969.
Bel Geddes, Barbara. *I Like to Be Me*. Viking Press, 1963.
Bishop, Claire, and Weise, Kurt. *The Five Chinese Brothers*. Coward-McCann, Inc., 1938.
Leaf, Munro. *Ferdinand*. Viking Press, 1936.
Lionni, Leo. *Frederick*. Pantheon Books, 1967.
May, Julian. *Do You Have Your Father's Nose?*

5
Science
through Cooking

Although science can be learned many ways, young children like to learn science by cooking food and eating it. This component of modules uses the preparation and cooking of foods as a method of teaching science concepts that can be understood by children of this age. It is fun even for the teacher.

Since science at this level is an awareness process, the teacher should be prepared to have the children experience ingredients through the senses before cooking. This can get quite messy at times. Children need to feel and taste flour and sugar, for example, before mixing. Their first attempt at scrubbing raw vegetables might be unsanitary in terms of adult standards, but it is important that they experience the materials with as many senses as relevant to the science of the moment.

Chapter 6 of this book treats science in a more conventional manner. These two chapters combined will enable the teacher to be more comprehensive in approaching science as a part of the young child's curriculum.

This cooking component could be expanded to cover such things as seasonal foods, more on measuring, how spices change the taste and smell of food, portions of food, and spreading as in snacks. Care should be taken in creating modules, because some concepts such as colloidal suspensions could be mistaken by the teacher for changes in states of matter. Teachers need either a college chemistry background or advice from an expert friend to be sure that the science concepts they are teaching through cooking are valid and appropriate for young children.   The modules in the component on science through cooking are as follows:

5.1   Measuring and Stirring
5.2   Stone to Bone Soup
5.3   A Puff of Magic
5.4   A Slice of Bread
5.5   An Egg by Any Other Name
5.6   Heat Can Travel

5.1 Measuring and Stirring

Rationale Measuring and stirring are a part of science as well as of cooking. The success of the science often involves how well measuring and stirring are understood and used. Is a pinch of salt the same as a tablespoon of salt? Do you stir with a fork or a spoon? Is a cup of flour the same amount as a cup of milk? Children wonder about these things when they see grown-ups cooking. The teacher's role is to give them the experiences to answer some of these questions themselves.

Prerequisites Collect utensils and ingredients necessary to the recipe given at the end of this module. Provide pictures for children to read that demonstrate the ingredients and steps for following the recipe.

Preassessment

- Provided with the ingredients to be used in the recipe, the child will show that he/she can identify each correctly by naming them after having had an opportunity to see, smell, taste, and/or feel each of the ingredients.
- Provided with a bowl of sand, a set of measuring spoons, a set of nested measuring cups and a big spoon, each child will demonstrate knowledge of measurement by accurately measuring one cup, three cups, one-fourth cup, one-half cup, and one teaspoon.
- Starting with a partially-filled bowl of sand and a large spoon, each child will demonstrate knowledge of how to stir by grasping the spoon in the appropriate manner and by stirring in one direction.

After the preassessment, exit from the module or proceed to the objectives.

Objective 1 The children will show that they can identify each of the ingredients of the recipe by using several of the five senses.

Activities

- Given flour and sugar, each child will name them correctly by using one or more of his/her five senses.
- Same as first activity, using vanilla and sour milk.
- Same as first activity, using baking soda and egg.

Alternate Activities

Simple Activity
Given an apple and an orange while blindfolded, each child will show how he/she can identify each by naming it correctly, using the senses of smell, taste, and touch. The child checks his/her conclusions by opening his/her eyes. (Variations: Same, using pear and apple, lemon and orange, tomato and plum.)

More Advanced Activity
Same as above, using salt and sugar, sand and brown sugar, brown sugar and white sugar, baking soda and flour.

Design your own activities to meet the needs of individual children.

112

5.1 Measuring to make a Jack-o'-lantern

The children will show that they can measure accurately.

● Given sand and water, the child will show that he/she can measure by accurately measuring one cup, three cups, and one teaspoon after he/she has had several opportunities to practice this under the teacher's direction.
● Same as above, using one-fourth and one-half cup.
● Using pictures mentioned in prerequisites to this module, the children will read and follow the recipe as to measuring ingredients for cookies.

Activities

Simple Activity
Provided with flour, water, and food coloring, the children will make pies using a measuring cup and a teaspoon.

More Advanced Activity
Provided with ingredients, the child will make play dough, measuring his own flour, salt, water, oil, and flavoring as directed by picture recipe cards provided by the teacher.

Alternate Activities

113

5.1 Measuring and stirring

Design your own activities to meet the needs of individual children.

Objective 3

The children will show that they have learned to stir.

Activities

• Given a bowl of sand and a large spoon, the child will show that he/she can hold the spoon appropriately and stir in one direction in the sand after a demonstration by the teacher.
• Same as first activity, using sand and water.
• Using pictures mentioned in prerequisites of this module, the children will read and follow the recipe as to stirring in the ingredients.

Alternate Activities

Simple Activity
Given ingredients, the child will show that he/she can stir by mixing instant pudding with a partner. (They take turns.)

More Advanced Activity
Given other ingredients, the child will demonstrate that he/she can stir by folding and beating after a demonstration by the teacher.

Design your own activities to meet the needs of individual children.

Postassessment

The postassessment is the same as the preassessment. After the postassessment, exit from the module or proceed to additional activities.

Additional Activities

• With a sandbox and plenty of measuring utensils, the child will demonstrate that he/she can measure "on his/her own" by doing so

114

with different utensils. (A rice table can be used, also, containing uncooked rice.)
- Same as above, using water in a large container.
- Using the recipe pictures mentioned in the prerequisites of this module, the children will read and complete the recipe for baking cookies. (The teacher will handle the very hot parts.)

Recipe: Sugar Cookies

1¼ cups sugar	1 egg
1½ sticks margarine or	1 teaspoon vanilla
	1 teaspoon soda in
¼ cup sour milk	3½ cups sifted flour

Mix together sugar and margarine. Add egg and stir. Add sour milk and vanilla. Stir well. Add sifted dry ingredients, several spoonsful at a time. Spoon onto a well-greased cookie sheet. Flatten with bottom of a glass that has been greased and dipped in colored sugar. Bake at 350 degrees, 10 to 12 minutes or until done.

Resources

Croft, Doreen J., and Hess, Robert D. *An Activities Handbook for Teachers of Young Children.* 2d ed. Houghton Mifflin, 1975.
Hoban, Lillian. *Arthur's Christmas Cookies.* Harper and Row, 1972.
James, Jean R. "When Kids Take Over the Kitchen," *Dimensions* (March 1974).
Winslow, Marjorie. *Mud Pies and Other Recipes.* Collier Books, 1961.

5.2 Stone to Bone Soup

Rationale

Through a group cooking experience such as making soup, the child learns that he/she is one of many contributors, just as each vegetable is, to the final, varied taste of the soup. He/she learns that soup doesn't just come in a can or a dehydrated package. Many different ingredients are often needed to make it tasty. The child learns that even after vegetables are washed, peeled, cut, and cooked, you can still recognize them by sight, smell, and taste. The soup has changed the vegetables a little but not completely.

Prerequisites

Read *Stone Soup* (see resources section) to the children. Prepare a picture recipe using children's suggestions as a guide for selecting vegetables for soup. Collect utensils, a soup bone, vegetables, and spices for making vegetable soup. Choose an appropriate recipe using children's suggestions and any good cookbook. Also have four boxes of jello, vanilla pudding, grapes, bananas, ice-cream ingredients, cherries, bouillon cubes, and cooked mushrooms.

Preassessment

Given water, dirt, grass, and gravel, each child will demonstrate an understanding of a mixture by identifying the ingredients and telling what would happen if they were mixed together. (Appropriate answer:

115

You would still have dirt, grass, gravel, and water unless the water has evaporated.)

After the preassessment, either exit from the module or proceed to the objective.

Objective   Each child will learn what a mixture is by making soup.

Activities
- Each child will demonstrate an understanding of a mixture by following the first recipe picture card about washing vegetables.
- Same as first activity, except that the recipe picture card says to peel potatoes, scrape carrots, etc.
- Same as first activity, except cut and/or dice vegetables.
- Same as first activity, but children pretaste before cooking each vegetable.
- Same as first activity, but continuing step by step through the preparation steps of the recipe, measuring water, putting in spices and bones, and boiling on the stove, adding vegetables and simmering until done.
- Each child will show that he/she understands a mixture by tasting different cooked vegetables in a bowl of soup and telling how he/she can tell that a potato is a potato, a carrot a carrot, etc.

Alternate Activities

Simple Activity
After making vanilla pudding with whole seedless grapes, the children will indicate that they understand a mixture by finding and tasting the grapes that did not mix with the pudding as they eat.

More Advanced Activity
After making four flavors of jello with banana slices (with the teacher pouring one flavor on top of the other so that each forms a separate layer), the children will show that they understand what a mixture is by commenting on how the colors, flavors, and bananas are still separate parts of the whole.

Design your own activities to meet the needs of individual children.

Postassessment   The postassessment is the same as the preassessment. After the postassessment, exit from the module or proceed to additional activities.

Additional Activities
- After making freezer ice cream (see *Cooking and Children Mix Well* in the resources section) and adding pitted whole cherries, each child will demonstrate an understanding of a mixture by finding the cherries have not mixed. (Use cherry juice instead of cherries to see if children can tell what happened.)
- After making soup with bouillon cubes and cooked mushrooms, the children will indicate that they know a mixture by finding the mushrooms in their soup and eating them separately.

Linguist, Willia. *Stone Soup*. Western Press, 1970.
Steinsiek, Ruth and Clark, Jean. *Cooking and Children Mix Well*. Head Start Center at Arkansas State University, August 1971.

Resources

5.3 A Puff of Magic

Children often watch and listen to the action of corn popping, thinking that it just happens, or that it is a puff of magic. Experimenting with corn (and other seeds) will enable children to be more knowledgeable about the popular snack, "popcorn."

Rationale

Have on hand popped corn, a container of unpopped corn, water, cooking oil, popcorn poppers with glass lids, straight pins, lima bean seeds, radish seeds, other vegetable seeds, white cotton balls, and balloons.

Prerequisites

• While viewing containers of popped corn, lima beans, carrot seeds, seed corn, navy bean seeds, radish seeds, and small white cotton balls, each child will show hiw knowledge of the fact that you have to start with corn to get popped corn by correctly answering the following question: "Which seeds do we start with to get this (the popped corn)?"
• While examining the container of popped corn, each child will demonstrate an understanding of the process by correctly answering the following questions: (1) What makes the corn pop? (Acceptable answer: The heat caused the water in the corn to swell up and burst.) (2) How has popping the corn changed it? (Acceptable answer: It has changed its color, its shape, its taste, and its size.)
After the preassessment, exit from the module or proceed to the objective.

Preassessment

Each child will learn that
• popcorn is made from corn,
• what makes corn pop is the action of heat on water, and
• popping corn changes it in at least four ways.

Objective

• After the teacher has put unpopped corn and oil into each popcorn popper (turning only one popper on), the children will express their understanding of the process by holding one hand over each popper and telling what they feel (heat) over the popper in which the corn pops. (Following this activity, the children eat the popcorn.)
• The next time that the teacher pops corn, the children will demonstrate that they understand that heat is necessary to corn popping by singing "Popcorn in a Pot" (to the tune of "I'm a Little Teapot.")

Activities

I'm a little popcorn in a pot.
Heat me up and watch me pop.
When I get all fat and white, I'm done.
Popping corn is lots of fun!

(Following this activity, the children can make necklaces and wrist chains with the popcorn.)
• Prior to this activity the teacher and the children have hypothesized that water is trapped inside the corn's waterproof shell. When heated the water swells up and bursts the shell.) After the children have used pins to prick the shells of half their corn, the children will show that they understand the process by predicting that only the unpricked corn, (in one popper) will burst becoming popped corn. (Following this demonstration and discussion the children can help the teacher make popcorn balls.)
• Repeat the third activity with balloons instead of corn, and air instead of heat
• At the next corn-popping session, the children will demonstrate their understanding that heat leads to bursting by role playing a seed of popcorn dancing over a red spot (fire), swelling up with bent arms and puffed face, and jumping to show popping.
• After other seeds have been tried in one popper (one kind of seed at a time) while corn is popped in the other popper, the children will show, by drawing and commenting on what happens in each popper, their understanding that corn alone pops. (Following this activity, the children can make rattles using unpopped corn.)
• After a tasting party of uncooked corn, popcorn, corn on the cob, and creamed corn, the children will express their understanding that corn changes its taste when popped by making a chart of the descriptive words they use to describe the differences. (Following this activity, the children can make caramel corn with the teacher to explore another taste difference.)
• After making pictures (of their own choosing) using uncooked corn, popper corn, and paste, the children will show that they understand color, size, and shape changes by describing these attributes as part of their art work. The teacher can help by asking questions such as: Which corn would I use to make something round? Would a straight line of four pieces of uncooked corn be longer than a line of four pieces of popped corn? Why? If I wanted a white tail for my rabbit, which should I use? If I want a yellow nose, which should I use?
• After hearing the story, "Mr. Picklepaw's Popcorn," the children will show their knowledge of the popcorn process by telling how the seed changes into popcorn.

Alternate Activities

Simple Activity
After placing seed and popped corn in separate pans, the children will demonstrate their knowledge that these two are different by running their fingers through each, commenting into a tape recorder as to what they are doing (making roads, castles, words, numbers, etc.) and how the material feels and looks.

More Advanced Activity
Using the two popcorn poppers, each child will show, by experimenting

5.3 Tasting corn in different forms

with other seeds such as sesame, poppy, soybean, and celery seeds, an understanding that popcorn pops.

Design your own activities to meet the needs of individual children.

Postassessment

The postassessment is the same as the preassessment. After the postassessment, exit from the module or proceed to additional activities.

Additional Activities

● After listening to the poem "What Makes Popcorn Pop?" (from "How Things Work," *Childcraft* vol. 8, the child will show understanding of what makes popcorn pop by comparing, through discussion and role playing, the rhythm in the poem and the rhythm of corn popping.
● After learning the song "Pop My Corn," the child will show that he/she knows that corn changes shape by singing and acting out the song.

Pop My Corn
(to the tune of Row, Row, Row Your Boat)

Pop, pop, pop my corn,
Pop it big and white,
Popping, popping, popping, popping,
Until it is just right.

Resources
Books

Adams, Ruth. "Mr. Picklepaw's Popcorn." In *Rewards*. Houghton-Mifflin Co., 1971.
Childcraft, "How Things Work," vol. 8; "Make and Do," vol. 9; Scientists and Inventors," vol. 11. Field Enterprises Corp., 1968.
Dolana, Roberts W. *Musically Speaking*. Word Making Productions.

Activities

"The Popcorn Game."
"Popcorn Rhymes."

5.4 A Slice of Bread

Rationale

Bread is a food that most children have seen and tasted but know very little about. They may think of it as always white and bought at the store. This module will enable them to learn about the processes from the grain to the slice as they experience the ingredients and the making of bread.

Prerequisites

Have on hand ingredients used in making bread, several recipes for making bread besides the one given at the end of this module (varying the grain you start with), utensils for measuring and stirring ingredients, facilities for baking, and process pictures on bread.

Preassessment

• After viewing, smelling, and tasting ingredients on a table, each child will show knowledge of what is needed to make bread by pointing to the correct ingredients. (Acceptable answer: yeast, water, milk, flour, sugar, salt, and soft shortening.) Include on the table other ingredients not used in the making of bread.
• After viewing a series of scrambled pictures of the processes of bread making (from field to table) and sugar (from field to table), each child will select only those pictures relating to the process of bread, and put them in the order in which the process occurs to demonstrate an understanding of the bread process.
After the preassessment, exit from the module or proceed to the objective.

Objective

Each child will learn that certain ingredients are used in the making of bread and that bread goes through a number of stages (changes) from the grain in the field before it becomes a slice of bread on the table.

5.4 Slicing and eating bread

• After hearing the story, "The Little Red Hen," the children will indicate that they know which ingredients are needed for making bread by recounting these with the teacher.
• Same as first activity, except that they role play the process including in the drama those who wouldn't help the hen.
• After learning the song "The Farmer Grows Wheat" (found at the end of this module), the children will show their understanding of the bread process by doing the movements indicated to the song.
• After seeing the film *Bread* (see resources section at end of this module), the children will demonstrate their understanding of the bread process by making a picture list with the teacher.
• After making bread (each action or stage photographed by the teacher or an aide), the children will show their knowledge of the ingredients and the process by putting the photographs in order. The pictures should be taken as follows: one picture for each ingredient, several pictures of the children feeling and tasting the ingredients, a separate picture for each ingredient measured, watching the yeast action (several pictures showing the yeast action), mixing each ingredient according to the recipe, several pictures of the dough rising, several pictures of kneading the dough, several pictures of the dough rising some more, a picture of the pans being greased, several pictures of the dough being shaped for pans, a picture of the bread pans being placed in the oven, and several pictures through the oven door showing the baking process.
• During a tasting party, each child will show his understanding of the ingredients that make bread by responding appropriately to most of the

Activities

121

following questions: (1) Put your finger in the flour and taste it. Now taste the bread. Can you taste the flour in it? (2) Repeat with each ingredient.

• While at a commercial bakery, the children will demonstrate their understanding of bread ingredients by helping the teacher name the ingredients they see being used.

• After interacting with a resource person visiting the classroom (farmer, mill operator, baker, man who delivers bread to store or homes), the children will show their knowledge of the resource person's role in the process by role playing what the resource person does.

• After the next session of bread making, each child will indicate an understanding of the ingredients used in making bread by choosing the ingredient(s) for use in painting or pasting a picture.

Alternate Activities

Simple Activity
During a puppet show of "The Little Red Hen," each child will show that he/she understands the bread process by performing his/her part correctly and in the right sequence.

More Advanced Activity
During a bread-tasting party, the children will demonstrate their knowledge that bread can be made from many grains by identifying the grains with the bread each is made from, using sight, taste, touch, and smell. (Try rye bread, corn bread, whole-wheat bread, and oatmeal bread.)

Design your own activities to meet the needs of individual children.

Postassessment

The postassessment is the same as the preassessment. After the postassessment, exit from the module or proceed to additional activities.

Additional Activities

• Using tabletop models of farmers growing wheat, a mill, a bakery, and other steps in the process, each child will show that he/she understands the process of bread making by playing with the items appropriately.

• While experimenting with the materials used for making bread, each child will tell the teacher, by talking into a tape recorder, how certain things taste and feel, what they are called, and what happens when they are mixed together, thus indicating an awareness of how to make bread. (Later the child and the teacher listen to the tape, and the teacher asks questions that will aid the child in better understanding the process.)

Resources
Books

Better Homes and Gardens New Cookbook. Des Moines, Iowa, 1971.
Betty Crocker Cookbook. McGraw-Hill, 1961.
Betty Crocker Cookbook for Boys and Girls. McGraw-Hill, 1963.
Buchheimer, Naomi. *Let's Go to the Bakery.* G. E. Putnam and Sons, 1956.

Hollow, Clara. *Story of Our Bread.* International Publishers of N.Y., 1959.
"The Little Red Hen," Golden Press.

Bread. Encyclopedia Britannica Films, 1970.

Song: "The Farmer Grows the Wheat" (to the tune of "The Farmer in the Dell"):

Words
The farmer grows the wheat, etc.
The millers grind the flour, etc.
The baker makes the dough, etc.
The truck goes to the store, etc.
The grocer sells the bread, etc.
The child eats the slice, etc.

Pantomime
Digging, planting, cutting, threshing.
Windmill turning, grinding, sifting, filling flour bags.
Mixing, kneading, dough rising, putting in oven.
Putting loaves on the truck, driving to the store, unloading.
Putting on shelves, pricing with stamper, operating cash register, putting in sack.
Carrying the package home, opening it, spreading something on bread slice, eating.

Recipe: Enriched White Bread

2 pkg. dry yeast	3 tbsp. sugar
½ cup warm water	1 teas. salt
1¾ cups scalded milk	2 tbsp.
7-7¼ cups flour	soft shortening

In a large bowl dissolve yeast in water. Measure flour. Add milk, half the flour, and all the sugar, salt, and shortening to the yeast mixture in the bowl. Beat until smooth. Mix in the remaining flour. Turn onto a lightly floured board or surface. Cover with a wet cloth and let rest ten to fifteen minutes. Knead ten minutes until smooth. Place in greased bowl. Bring greased side up. Cover with cloth. Let rise in warm place until double in size (1 to 2 hours). Punch down and cover. Let rise again until almost double in size (45 minutes).

Divide into two or more parts and shape each into loaves. Place in greased loaf pans (or smaller pans). Cover with cloth and let rise until sides reach top of pan (50 to 60 minutes for larger pans, less for smaller ones). Bake in oven at 425° for 25 to 30 minutes or until deep golden brown in color. Place on wire cooling racks for a few minutes before slicing and eating. (Makes enough for two home-baked loaves of bread.)

5.5 An Egg by
Any Other Name

Rationale   Eggs are consumed in many forms: raw, fried, scrambled, soft-boiled, hard-boiled, poached, and as a part of many recipes. Although the egg is always on the scene, children may be unaware that a chemical change can be seen (color differences), felt (consistency changes), tasted, and even smelled. Heat can produce these interesting changes. An egg by any other name, cooked or uncooked, is still an egg, and yet it is different. Beating the egg can change what it looks like (a physical rather than a chemical change). This module will enable children to be more aware of how to detect changes in matter through a study of eggs.

Prerequisites   Have on hand uncooked eggs, cooked eggs, cooking utensils, a heating unit, recipes for eggnog, French toast, and the materials for the egg cookies recipe mentioned under More Advanced Activity later in this module.

Preassessment   Upon seeing an uncracked egg, each child will show knowledge of the differences between cooked and uncooked, beaten and unbeaten eggs by answering the following questions correctly.
- What is this? (Acceptable answer: an egg)
- If I break it and it is raw (uncooked egg), what will I see? (Acceptable answer: a soft orange part and a watery part that has no color)
- If it is a soft-boiled egg and I break it, what will it look like? (Acceptable answer: a runny white part and a runny orange part)
- If it is a hard-boiled egg, what will I see? (Acceptable answer: a hard white part and a hard orange part)
- Look at these two bowls and tell me what happened? (One bowl contains a raw egg unbeaten and the second bowl contains a raw, beaten egg.) (Acceptable answer: This one has a beaten egg, and this one hasn't been beaten.)
- When I cook a raw egg, will it taste different? (Answer: Yes)
- When I cook a raw egg, will it smell different? (Answer: Yes)
- How does a cooked egg feel different from a raw one? (Acceptable answer: The cooked one is not runny, while the raw one runs through your fingers.

After the preassessment, exit from the module or proceed to the objective.

Objective   Each child will become aware of the differences in taste, smell, color, and consistency between cooked and uncooked eggs. Each child will learn that beating an egg produces a change in terms of color.

Activities   • Given two raw eggs, the children, after witnessing one of the eggs being cooked in a Teflon pan, will show their understanding of color change by drawing the raw egg and the fried egg. (Don't use oil.)

• Same as first activity, except that the children discuss the differences in taste between the raw and the cooked eggs.
• After the teacher has cooked one egg in a pan and put an uncooked egg in an identical, unheated pan, the children will indicate their awareness that heat has produced a chemical change by telling how the pans were different and why the teacher can pour the uncooked egg but not the cooked one.
• After a tasting party of raw, soft-boiled, and hard-boiled eggs, the children will show their awareness of change by developing with the teacher descriptive words for the differences noted in taste and consistency. (The raw eggs can be used for making eggnog.)
• After a tasting party of uncooked egg and scrambled egg, the children will show their awareness of change by making thumb print pictures using the uncooked and cooked eggs.
• After experimenting by spinning raw eggs as compared to boiled eggs, each child will demonstrate his knowledge of the differences by predicting correctly from the test of the spin which egg is raw and which is boiled. (After marking their predictions on the egg, the children should crack them open to see if they were correct.)
• Each child will indicate an awareness of chemical change by blowing out the material from an uncooked egg containing two holes and by being unable to blow out the material from a hard-boiled egg, commenting on his observations throughout the activity.
• After breaking open an uncooked egg, a soft-boiled egg, and a hard-boiled egg, the children will show that they understand the color, taste, and chemical differences by sampling each and discussing how eggs taste, feel, and look, as well as by drawing or painting these changes.

Alternate Activities

Simple Activity
After the children have pierced the yolks of raw and fried eggs, they will show their understanding of change by describing what happened to the yolks when they were cooked.

More Advanced Activity
Using the following recipe, the children will show that they understand how eggs can be used to make other things (further chemical changes) by making cookies as follows:

Recipe: Egg Cookies

1½ cups brown sugar	3 eggs
¾ cup white sugar	2¼ cups flour
½ cup shortening	1 tsp. vanilla
2 tbsp. milk	1 tsp. baking powder
1 tsp. salt	1 sm. pkg. chocolate chips

Cream shortening and sugar. Add egg, milk, vanilla. Add dry ingredients and stir in chocolate chips. Bake in 9"-by-13" pan for 35 minutes at 350°. Cut into bars.

Design your own activities to meet the needs of individual children.

Postassessment
The postassessment is the same as the preassessment. After the postassessment, exit from the module or proceed to additional activities.

Additional Activities
• With the teacher's help, the children will plan and prepare a meal centered around eggs so that they can become more aware of the changes that occur between the raw egg and the cooked one.
• After collecting many magazine pictures showing eggs, the children will show their awareness of change by pasting the pictures in a scrapbook under an appropriate egg classification.

Resources
Bigger and Better. John C. Winston Co., 1954.
Experiences in Homemaking. Ginn & Co., 1964, pp. 207-10.
Health and Growth. Book 2. Scott, Foresman and Co., 1971.
Just Like Me. Scott, Foresman and Co., 57.
Nutrition and Physical Fitness. 9th ed. Philadelphia: W. B. Saunders Co., pp. 393–94.

5.6 Heat Can Travel

Rationale
Without heat transfer, food would not cook in pots and pans. Heat transfer occurs differently in a glass dish, an iron skillet, and an aluminum pan. Children need to be aware of these differences in their environment. They need to realize that handles on many pans are made of materials that reduce heat transfer so that hands won't be burned.

Prerequisites
Have on hand candle, matches, metal utensils, glass and metal pans, cooking sources, ingredients for hot chocolate and chicken bouillon, measuring cup, food for cookout, two metal containers, cooking implements made out of different materials, metal spoons with and without wooden handles, metal potato prongs, potatoes.

Preassessment
After each child has held a metal spoon and a metal spoon with wooden handle over a candle flame, he/she will show an understanding of heat transfer by answering correctly the following questions:
• What do you feel in this hand (one with metal spoon)? (Acceptable answer: heat)
• Why does it feel this way? (Acceptable answer: because the heat from the flame has moved along or through the spoon to my hand)
• What about your other hand, what do you feel? (Acceptable answer: nothing *or* no heat)
• How can you feel heat in one hand and not the other? (Acceptable answer: The heat from the flame moves through the metal spoon but not the wood-handled one, *or* Metal is a better conductor of heat than wood.)

After the preassessment, exit from the module or proceed to the objectives.

Through cooking experiences and sensory observation, each child will learn the concept of heat transfer.

Objective 1

• After warming the milk for hot chocolate, the children, stirring with metal spoons, will show their understanding of heat transfer by telling how the spoon and the milk get hot. (Add chocolate *after* discussion, so as not to confuse the children.)
• After watching a container of ice cubes melt and feeling the metal pan as well as the warm water from the melted ice cubes, the children will show their understanding of heat transfer by describing accurately what happened.
• After cooking chicken bouillon, the children, stirring with metal spoons, will show their understanding of heat transfer by telling how the heat went from the stove, through the pan, the bouillon, and the spoons, to their hands.
• After cooking three potatoes on the oven rack and three potatoes on an upright set of prongs (metal), the children will show their understanding of heat transfer by explaining why the potatoes on the prongs cooked faster, especially in the centers, than did the other potatoes.

Activities

Simple Activity
The children will demonstrate their understanding of heat transfer by telling what they felt and why when touching the hood of the teacher's car after it had been sitting idle in cool weather for some time and after the teacher has run the motor for few minutes.

More Advanced Activity
Given a variety of cooking containers (iron, pyrex glass, aluminum, and steel), the children will show that they understand heat transfer by cooking a chicken leg in each (using two tablespoons of oil in each container) simultaneously to see which container cooks the chicken first (which is the best heat conductor).

Design your own activities to meet the needs of individual children.

Alternate Activities

The postassessment is the same as the preassessment. After the postassessment, exit from the module or proceed to additional activities.

Postassessment

During a cookout in a park, the children will indicate their understanding of heat transfer by commenting on what happened when cooking hot dogs on a grill, potatoes with butter in the centers in aluminum foil, marshmallows on a stick and on long metal forks.

Additional Activities

6
Science through the Senses

Kindergarten and the primary grades are a period in which children learn to use their senses in more directed ways to discover the science of their environment. Wherever possible the teacher should encourage the child to use as many senses as are appropriate to the situation. Science is not just a matter of watching the teacher do an experiment or a demonstration. Science happens in the classroom when the child personally looks, smells, tastes, feels, listens, and interprets those sensations. Science is not simply discovery. It is *guided* discovery through the senses and the sensitivity of the teacher.

This chapter should be considered with Chapter 5 as a larger component in the area of science. Thinking of the two components as one whole will enable the teacher to be more comprehensive in approaching science as a part of the kindergarten curriculum. Consider, too, that this sensory component could be expanded to cover other science topics such as modules on air, plants, rocks, and animal babies, for example.

The component Science through the Senses includes the following modules:

6.1 Farm Animals,
6.2 Zoo Animals,
6.3 Machines Work for Us,
6.4 Magnets Attract?
6.5 Day and Night, and
6.6 Weather.

6.1 Farm Animals

This module on farm animals offers many opportunities to create in children awareness of animal life and habits. This module covers recognizing the farm animals, their habits, habitats, coverings, movements, their growth patterns, their sounds, their means of protection, and their usefulness.

Rationale

64 Removing hair pins with a magnet

Prerequisites Gather numerous library books listed in the resources section or make substitutes as needed; also, use library filmstrips and pictures that will be useful. You might also have students bring in farm-animal stories and pictures they own. Records and suitable songs should be on hand. Have a film projector and record player available. Various art supplies will also be needed.

Preassessment
- The children will show their recognition of farm animals by naming ten farm animals, either domestic or wild, and by saying the appropriate animal names that match the pictures of ten animals.
- The children will demonstrate that they know ten farm animal sounds by reproducing appropriate sounds for each animal picture.
- The children will show their knowledge of which animals are protected and which are beneficial to man by naming three that are protected and three that are beneficial.

After the preassessment, exit from the module or proceed to the objectives.

Objective 1 The children will learn to recognize and name ten farm animals.

Activities
- While on a field trip to a farm, the child will relate the names of animals he/she sees to show a recognition of farm animals and their names.
- Given a sheet with pictures of ten animals, the child will demonstrate a knowledge of farm animals by following the teacher's directions. (Example: Find the cow; color her spots. Do you see the pig? Make his tail curly.)
- Using paints or crayons of his choice, the child will demonstrate a recognition of farm animals by painting or coloring his/her impression of an animal after the teacher has read a story. (See resources section.)
- After viewing animal movements, either real or on film, children will imitate these to show that they can recognize them.
- After hearing an animal riddle, a child can answer correctly with the animal's name to show a recognition of farm animals and their names. (Example: This animal looks fat and makes this sound—oink, oink Pig]. Variation: Make or buy tapes of sounds made by animals found on a farm. Children play them, finding the pictures of the animals making the sounds and putting them in the same order as on the tape.)

Alternate Activities

Simple Activities
- To show that they recognize which are farm animals, children will choose only farm animals to set up a farm scene when given a choice of an array of farm and zoo animals.
- Children will tell a short story about a farm animal of their choice to demonstrate their knowledge of this animal.
- To demonstrate knowledge of a farm animal, the child will choose a picture from several and tell the class its name and three facts about it. (Example: It comes in different colors; it's big, gives milk, and says "Moo" [cow].)

130

More Advanced Activities
• The children will demonstrate their knowledge of animals found on a farm by putting some pictures in boxes marked "farm animals," "zoo animals," and "other animals."
• The child will learn and recite finger plays—"Turtle in a Box," "Frisky Squirrel," "The Little Chicks," and "Funny Bunny"—to show knowledge of some of the animals found on a farm.

Design your own activities to meet the needs of individual children.

The child will learn ten farm animal sounds in terms of the animals that make them.

Objective 2

• While on a farm field trip, the child will reproduce appropriate sounds of animals as they are heard to show a knowledge of animal sounds.
• Given ample time to listen to the record "Sounds of the Farm," the children will make the correct sound as an animal is named, to demonstrate their knowledge of these sounds.
• When shown pictures of farm animals, the children will point to each picture and make the correct sound to show their knowledge of these sounds.
• To demonstrate an understanding of animal sounds, the child will make the correct sound of the animal mentioned as the *True Book of Farm Animals* is read

Activities

Simple Activities
• After discussion of three animal sounds, the child will role play animals singing in an animal drama to show a recognition of these sounds. Teacher sings, "Old MacDonald had a farm, ee-ii, ee-ii-oh. And on this farm he had some ducks, etc."
• To show their knowledge of animal sounds, the children, when given an animal name, will answer to milk call by using the animal's sound.

Alternate Activities

More advanced activities
• Each child will make the appropriate sound of a farm animal as models are handed to him/her, to demonstrate a knowledge of these sounds.
• To show their knowledge of animal sounds, the children will pretend to be animals on the farm with sound effects in an animal play they have prerecorded.

Design your own activities to meet the needs of individual children.

The children will learn to tell how some farm animals are protected and how some are beneficial to people.

Objective 3

• After a field trip to a farm, viewing pictures, and having a discussion, each child will tell that coloration is protection for certain animals, to demonstrate knowledge of ways these animals protect themselves.

Activities

131

• The children will tell which animals can protect themselves with their hoofs to demonstrate their knowledge of one means of protection, after seeing this on the farm, in a rodeo, on film, or in a story.

• After watching a movie on squirrels, deer, and rabbits, the children will demonstrate knowledge of one means of protection by naming animals protected by being able to run fast. (They may see this on the visits to the farm.)

• After the teacher shows cartoons that a child has drawn of hogs, cows, and chickens and the food we get from them, the child will relate knowledge of the benefit of one animal by saying that we get pork chops from hogs, milk and beef from cows, or eggs and meat from chickens.

Alternate Activities

Simple Activity
Given several pictures, a child will demonstrate knowledge of beneficial animals by pointing to one, such as the cow, and telling how it benefits man. (The child will need pictures of animals and the animal products to match.)

More Advanced Activities
• To demonstrate knowledge of beneficial animals, the child will select a picture of sheep or another animal fastened to a large envelope and will put the product—a piece of wool and a small picture of veal— inside the envelope.

• To demonstrate knowledge of the ways animals protect themselves, each child will draw or paint an animal that protects itself during the winter season by growing a heavier fur coat or changing its color. (Variation: They can robe themselves in one piece of cloth for summer and another for winter to dramatize what happens to certain animals that undergo color change.)

Design your own activities to meet the needs of individual children.

Postassessment

The postassessment is the same as the preassessment. After the postassessment, exit from the module or proceed to additional activities.

Additional Activities

• To demonstrate knowledge of farm animals, a child will sing with the teacher or tape familiar songs such as "Farmer in the Dell," "A Getting up Song," "Baa-Baa, Black Sheep," and "Old MacDonald's Farm."

• Children will draw, color and/or paint three animal homes to show their knowledge of animal habitats after a visit to animal homes in the vicinity.

• Classmates will demonstrate their recognition of animal sounds by correctly identifying the name of the animal sound another child is making.

Resources

Brown, Margaret W. *Wait 'til the Moon is Full.* Harper, 1948.
Bryan, John. *The True Book of Farm Animals.*
Childcraft.

Collins, Henry H., Jr. *Complete Field Guide to American Wildlife.*
   Harper and Brothers, 1959.
Compton's Encyclopedia.
Davis, Daphine. *The Baby Animal Book.*
Duvoisin, Roger. *Petunia.* Knopf, 1950.
Ets, Marie H. *Just Me.* Viking, 1965.
Fisher, Aileen. *Filling the Bill.* Bowman, 1973.
Flack, Marjorie. *The Story About Ping.* Viking, 1933.
Frasier, George. *We See.*
Gans, Roma. *It's Nesting Time.* Crowell, 1964.
George, J. C. *All Upon a Stone.* Crowell, 1971.
Hawkinson, John. *The Old Stump.* Whitman, 1965.
Hutchins, Pat. *Rosie Walk.* MacMillan, 1968.
Leaf, Munro. *The Story of Ferdinand.* Viking, 1936.
Leen, Nina. *And Then There Were None.* Rinehart and Winston, 1973.
Mari, Iela and Enzo. *The Children and the Egg.* Pantheon Books,
   1969.
McCloskey, Robert. *Make Way for Ducklings.*
Piatti, Celestino. *The Happy Owls.* Atheneum Press, 1964.
Podendorf, Lila. *True Book of Animal Homes.*
Potter, Beatrix. *The Tale of Peter Rabbit.*
Pringle, Lawrence. *Let's Get Turtles.* Harper, 1965.
Rockwell, Anne and Harlow. *Toad.* Doubleday, 1972.
Rojankovsky, Feodor. *Animals on the Farm.* Knopf, 1967.
Showers, Paul. *Find Out by Touching.* Crowell, 1964.
Tresselt, Alvin. *The Beaver Pond.* Lothrop, 1970.
Woodcock, Louise, and Parks, Gale. *This is the Way the Animals Walk.*

6.2 Zoo Animals

Rationale

Children who do not live on a farm or who have little opportunity to see animals in their environment need to have many chances to see, firsthand, animals from near and faraway places. Television helps, but lions are not two-dimensional animals most often found in black and white.

The nice thing about zoos is that they group and therefore classify animals, so that through many visits the child can draw some scientific conclusions about size, shape, smell, sound, behavior, and habitat. Many zoos no longer put tigers in cages, but simulate the terrain of their natural habitat so that visitors can see them more realistically. Some zoos even allow the children to visit baby animals, to feed and pet them. A few zoos send out people with animals to schools so that children can observe the animals up close and ask questions about them.

This module enables the young child with limited or no knowledge of zoo animals to extend his/her understanding.

Prerequisites

Gather various library books listed in the resources section or make substitutes as needed. Any filmstrips or pictures concerning zoo

6.2 Teacher admiring clay sculpture of zoo animal

animals will help. If some students have stuffed zoo animals or animal puppets, they could bring these. They would make the room more attractive, and their presence is educational. Children will also enjoy records and songs about zoo animals. Needed, too, would be a film projector and a record player. Various art supplies will also be needed.

Preassessment

• The children will show their recognition of zoo animals by naming twenty zoo animal pictures. (Show twenty-five to thirty pictures of zoo animals.)
• The children will demonstrate their knowledge of some characteristics and traits of ten zoo animals by telling three descriptive facts concerning each of them. (Example: elephant—what it eats, that it is bigger than any other animal on land, and what it uses its trunk for.) After the preassessment, exit from the module or proceed to the objectives.

Objective 1

The children will learn to recognize and name zoo animals.

Activities

• Following a field trip to a zoo, the children will demonstrate recognition of zoo animals and names by picking out from a series of

134

pictures all they can recognize, and by naming them.

● After hearing the books listed in the resources section and a discussion of each, the child will show knowledge of zoo animal names by role playing the way the animal walks and reciting a chant. The chant might go like this: "I am an elephant, a big, big, elephant. I swing my trunk up, I swing my trunk down, and when I walk, I shake the ground."

● Using paints or crayons of his choice, the child will demonstrate recognition of zoo animals by painting or coloring impressions of ten of them, one at a time, on different occasions, using pictures or photos as a reference. (Variation: sculpting the animals in clay.)

Simple Activity
To show they recognize zoo animals, children will set up a zoo using only zoo animals from the model animals box.

More Advanced Activity
After hearing an animal riddle, each child will answer correctly the animal name to show recognition of zoo animals and their names. (Example: I live in the zoo. I am tall as a house, have spots, and my neck is very long. Who am I? [Giraffe]

Design your own activities to meet the needs of individual children.

The children will learn some characteristics of zoo animals.

● Following another field trip to a zoo, a child will demonstrate knowledge of characteristics of zoo animals by correctly naming the animal picture pinned to his/her back by asking clue questions as, "Does it have four legs; does it have horns; does it go baa-baa?" (Other children can answer only "yes" or "no.")

● To demonstrate a more complete knowledge of zoo animals in their habitats, each child, after hearing a story about a number of zoo animals, will tell the class a short story about it or tape record its story for others to hear as they look at its picture.

Simple Activity
After the zoo representative brings animals to the school or after a film about certain animals is shown, each child will choose four animal pictures from ten and tell facts about each one to the teacher to demonstrate a knowledge of animal characteristics.

More Advanced Activity
After his listening to a tape prepared by the teacher in which the zoo animal says, "Hello, I am a hippopotamus who likes to spend his time in the water to keep cool," etc., each child will demonstrate knowledge of other characteristics of zoo animals by telling how five of these zoo animals protect themselves.

Design your own activities to meet the needs of individual children.

Alternate Activities

Objective 2

Activities

Alternate Activities

Postassessment The postassessment is the same as the preassessment. After the postassessment, exit from the module or proceed to the additional activities.

Additional Activities
- In a discussion with the teacher about his/her favorite zoo animal, each child will tell two facts concerning the zoo animal and will show the teacher that he/she can pick pictures of his/her favorite animal from an array of pictures.
- After discussing with the teacher those animals that run fast, those that bite and claw, and those that hide, each child will demonstrate knowledge of zoo animals by classifying pictures of zoo animals into these three categories.

Resources
Bridges, William. *The Golden Book of Zoo Animals.*
Brown, Margaret. *The Sleepy Little Lion.*
Childcraft.
Compton's Encyclopedia.
Count the Baby Animals. Wonder Books.
Geddes, Barbara. *I Like to Be Me.*
Green, Carla. *Zoo-Keeper.*
Greenberg, Sylvia, and Edith R. Roskin. *Homemade Zoo.* David McKay, 1952.
Hader, Berta. *Lost in the Zoo.*
Kranzer, Herman C. *Nature and Science Activities for Young Children.* Baker, 1969.
Kuskin, Karla. *Roar and More.*
Malter, Morton. *Our Largest Animals.*
Meeks, Ester. *Something New at the Zoo.*
Ranger Ricks. *Nature Magazine.* National Wildlife Federation.
Rojankovsky, Feodor. *The Great Big Wild Animal Book.*
Scarry, Richard. *Polite Elephant Book.*
Victor, Edward *Science for the Elementary School. MacMillan, 1970.*
Weil, Ann. *Animal Families.*
Wiltrout, Dorothea. *Let's Sing and Play.*
World Book Encyclopedia. (Find animal or regional name in index.)

6.3 Machines Work for Us

Rationale Children are constantly encountering machines that make work easier. At home, on their way to and from school, and at play, there are machines that are fun to look at and fun to try to analyze.

As preparation for living in our machine age and in the still more complex machine ages to come, it is highly desirable that children become familiar with some basic concepts underlying the operation of all machines.

The purpose of this unit is to give children an increased awareness of the useful machines about them so that they will become more observant and learn to appreciate man's ingenuity. They will also develop a simple nontechnical vocabulary to be able to talk about the labor-saving devices that we use in everyday work.

The teacher should collect some machines, such as scissors, saws, hammers, pulleys, and other small devices, and have pictures of these machines as well as those that could not be brought to the classroom.

Given a series of twenty pictures of simple machines, each child will tell the names of ten machines and the type of work they do to show knowledge of machine names and functions.
After the preassessment, either exit from the module or proceed to the objective.

Each child will learn the names of ten machines and the type of work they help us do.

• After a demonstration of how to replace a washer on a faucet, each child will demonstrate knowledge of the wrench by selecting it from a group of machines and telling how it works.
• After visiting a building under construction, each child will show knowledge of machines by naming five that he saw and telling what work they did.
• Given some nails, a board, a screwdriver, pliers, and a hammer, each child will pick the correct machine (hammer) to drive the nail to show understanding of the function of the hammer. (Variation: demonstrate how three other simple machines are used. Call for work to be done, and see if the child chooses the right machine.)
• Given a saw, a knife, a pair of scissors, and a miniature axe, each child will show knowledge of machine names and functions by telling correctly what to use in cutting a cake, threading a needle, cutting a tree, cutting a pie, and slicing a loaf of bread. (Variation: Set up similar simulations.)
• Continue preceding activity using the lever, the pulley, and the wheel.

Simple Activity
Given a series of ten pictures of machines, children working in pairs will pantomime the kind of work done by each machine to show their understanding of the functions of machines, while the others guess the machine and the work.

More Advanced Activity
After observing the flag pulley, stage curtain pulley, and window shade pulleys in your school, each child will show an understanding of the functions of the pulley by constructing Tinker Toy pulleys or by using dowels and spools.

Design your own activities to meet the needs of individual children.

The postassessment is the same as the preassessment. After the postassessment, exit from the module or proceed to additional activities.

Additional Activities

- Have a class discussion about machines that help us travel. Given a collection of six toys, each child will pick two toys that make traveling easier to show knowledge of the kinds of machines used for travel.
- After viewing the film *Machines That Help the Farmer,* each child will show knowledge of machines that help the farmer by drawing one machine that helps and telling a small group of children how it works. (Variation: The child can construct a model of the machine and then share his model with others.)
- After viewing the filmstrip *Simple Machines Help Us Work,* each child will pantomime the kind of work done by one machine to show understanding of the functions of machines.

**Resources
Books**

Hubner, Clark. *Working with Children in Science.* Houghton-Mifflin, 1957.

Kanzer, Herman C. *Nature and Science Activities for Young Children.* Baker, 1969.

Schneider, Herman and Nina. *Science for Work and Play.* 1961.

Films

How Machines and Tools Help Us. Coronet Instructional Films.
Machines That Help the Farmer. Film Associates of California.

6.4 Magnets Attract?

Rationale

In addition to the enjoyable experiences of handling and playing with magnets, the children are going to learn some simple but basic facts about magnets. Working with magnets on the kindergarten level calls for a great deal of individual manipulation. Children learn by watching others, but their learning should not be limited to what they hear others describe. When they do things themselves they learn through all the senses, including some that are rarely considered, such as kinesthesia.

Prerequisites

The teacher should collect a generous supply of small horseshoe magnets, paper clips, nails, brads, and drinking straws, and two boxes in which to place magnetic and nonmagnetic materials. Also, have available a "beauty parlor" doll, hairpins, sand, needle, cork, and styrofoam.

Preassessment

Given magnetic and nonmagnetic objects, each child will show understanding of magnets attracting iron objects by telling which of the objects the magnet will attract. Before asking the child to do this the teacher should tell what material each object is made of (iron, paper, aluminum, etc.).

After the preassessment, exit from the module or proceed to the objective.

138

The children will learn to recognize the materials or objects which are magnetic. **Objective**

• Each child will demonstrate an understanding that magnets attract iron objects by using a magnet to pull the hairpins out of a "beauty parlor" doll's hair. **Activities**
• The teacher will demonstrate that some magnets are stronger than others. Given a nail between two magnets, each child will show understanding of magnets by telling which magnet is stronger when pulling the magnets apart.
• When the children bring a collection of different toys to school, each child will put magnetic and nonmagnetic toys into two separate boxes to show knowledge that magnets attract iron objects.

Simple Activity **Alternate Activities**
Using a bowl of sand and paper clips, each child will demonstrate understanding of magnetic attraction by using a magnet to remove the clips.

More Advanced Activity
Given a bowl of water, a magnet, a needle, and a cork or piece of styrofoam, the children will show their understanding of magnets by making a compass. (Rub the needle with the magnet. Place needle on cork and float in water. Needle will point North and South.)

Design your own activities to meet the needs of individual children.

The postassessment is the same as the preassessment. After the postassessment, exit from the module or proceed to additional activities **Postassessment**

• Given ten drinking straws with the ends bent, each child will demonstrate knowledge of magnets by using a magnet to determine which straw has a nail in it. **Additional Activities**
• Using some safety pins in a transparent container of water, each child will show an understanding that magnets attract iron pole objects by using magnets fastened to a string or a pole (like a fishing pole) to take the pins out of the water.

Parker, Bertha. *Magnets.* Row, Peterson and Co., 1944. **Resources**
Piltz, Albert, et al. *Discovering Science, A Readiness Book.* Charles E. Merrill, 1968.
Schneider, Herman and Nina. *Science for Work and Play.* D. C. Heath and Co., 1961.
Thurber, Walter A. *Exploring Science.* Allyn and Bacon, Inc., 1957.

6.5 Day and Night

Rationale

This unit will give the young child a "first time around" introduction to his home planet. He/she will absorb and accept the ideas that we have daytime when the earth faces the sun, and nighttime when it faces away from the sun, and all this happens because the earth is turning.

Prerequisites

Arrange, if possible, a visit to a planetarium. Materials needed: flashlight, globe, old magazines and catalogs, flash cards of moon, sun, stars, and chenille sticks or pipe cleaners.

Preassessment

• Each child will show an understanding of day and night by telling scientifically why we have day and night and by stating some features of each.
• Given an array of ten geometric figures (ball, toilet roll, dowel [cylinder], a cube [block], a plastic egg, etc.), the child will show that he/she knows about the earth by pointing to the object that has the same shape as the earth and by picking it up and showing the teacher what the earth does (spin).
After the preassessment, exit from the module or proceed to the objectives.

Objective 1

The child will learn that we have night and day because of the rotation of the earth, and will learn some features of both night and day.

Activities

• After a demonstration by the teacher, each child will show an understanding of day and night by touching the dark part of the earth and then the light part as he operates a flashlight and spins the globe (or ball).
• Each child will demonstrate knowledge of night and day by cutting from old magazines and catalogs pictures of two things to do in the daytime and two at night.
• After the teacher reads *A Time for Sleep* (see the resources section), the child will indicate knowledge of how animals sleep by naming an animal and telling when it sleeps (day or night).
• Using a chart and flash cards of moon, star, sun, and other astronomical bodies, the child will show understanding of what he/she sees in the sky by placing each card under the appropriate heading of night or day.
• By using one child to represent the earth and one holding a light to represent the sun, the children will display their knowledge of the earth's rotation by telling which child should turn.

Alternate Activities

Simple Activity
After the teacher discusses night and day, each child will show an understanding of night and day by painting a picture of each, using tempera paints or watercolors.

6.5 A globe is round like other things.

More Advanced Activity
After visiting a planetarium, the children will show their ability to recognize the moon and dippers by finding them on flash cards. A discussion should follow about why we usually see these objects only at night.

Design your own activities to meet the needs of individual children.

The children will learn the shape of the earth.

Objective 2

• Given several objects, the teacher will discuss the shape of each, and the child will show ability to recognize the shape of each by picking out only the objects shaped like the earth.
• The child will take a chenille stick or pipe cleaner and demonstrate knowledge of a circle by shaping it to form a circle, like the shape of the earth.
• Given pictures of objects, each child will show knowledge of what is round by bringing to school round objects shaped like the earth.
• After looking at pictures of the earth and sky, each child will show knowledge of the shape of the earth by naming other things, such as sun and moon, that are shaped the same as the earth.

Activities

Simple Activity
Given some clay, the child will show a knowledge of the earth's shape by modeling the correct shape and putting in a toothpick to show his/her location as he/she thinks it should be.

Alternate Activities

More Advanced Activity
After looking at a globe from either side, the child will show

knowledge of the earth's shape by drawing a picture of the earth as if it were cut in halves.

Design your own activities to meet the needs of individual children.

Postassessment

The postassessment is the same as the preassessment. After the postassessment, exit from the module or proceed to additional activities.

Additional Activities

• Each child will demonstrate knowledge of the earth's shape by forming a circle and singing "Twinkle, Twinkle, Little Star" while looking up, holding his/her arms up, and walking in a circle.
• The children will show their knowledge of night and day by dramatizing the two different times of day. One child turns slowly around, wearing a sign saying "day" on his/her chest and "night" on his/her back. (Let as many as possible play the role of earth.)

Resources
Books

Craig, Gerald S., and Lembach, Margarite W. *Science Everywhere.* Ginn and Co., 1958.
Science for Work and Play. D. C. Heath & Co., 1961.
Selsam, Millicent. *A Time for Sleep.* William R. Scott, Inc., 1953..
Schneider, Herman and Nina. *Follow the Sunset.* Doubleday and Co., 1952.
Schneider, Herman and Nina. *How Big is Big?* William R. Scott, Inc., 1946.

Film

"What Makes Day and Night." Young American Films.

6.6 Weather

Rationale

Most youngsters peer through the window when they first get up in the morning. They know the importance of what kind of day it will be. Weather, even at this early age, affects their lives. Each weather condition means something special; what to wear, what to play, and where and how to go. The children are eager to explore this exciting and stimulating aspect of their environment. Young children, learning about the weather, are more concerned in organizing their observations and relating them to their own lives than in going deeply into causes of weather.

Prerequisites

Materials needed: articles of clothing appropriate for different days, weather symbols, model-airplane propeller, cotton, flash cards showing rainy, sunny, windy, and cloudy days, and a weather costume box.

Preassessment

After looking at five weather flashcards, the child will show knowledge of the different types of days by naming the days (e.g., sunny, windy),

choosing what should be worn on each day (from the weather
costume box), and telling how the sky will look.
After the preassessment, exit from the module or proceed to the
objective.

The child will learn about the different types of weather and will know
what is suitable to wear on those days.

Objective

- Given different articles of clothing, the child will demonstrate
knowledge of what to wear by dressing a flannel cut-out doll to suit
the weather outside.
- After discussing and observing the rain falling, the child will show an
understanding of this weather by telling how the sky looks before it
rains and how we should dress.
- The child will show that he/she understands the weather outside by
entering daily on a weather chart such symbols as a yellow smiling
sun, cotton clouds, an umbrella, and a face with puffed cheeks to
represent windy weather. (Variation: Expand these symbols as children
learn a set.)
- The teacher will fasten a model-airplane propeller to a stick outside
the window and the child will display knowledge that the wind is
blowing by observing the stick and telling if it is turning, not turning,
turning slowly, turning very fast, or turning now and then (gusts).
- After performing an experiment to show how plastic or rubber
clothing will keep us dry on rainy days, the child will indicate
knowledge of the importance of raincoats and boots by naming when
these should be worn and why. (Variations: Dress up as you recite and
pantomime A. A. Milne's "Happiness"; children pantomime "The
Engineer" as the teacher reads the poem by Milne.)

Activities

Simple Activity
Given an item of clothing, the child will show that he/she knows on
what type of day this should be worn by naming the weather for that
day.

More Advanced Activities
- Studying the propeller outside the window, the child will demonstrate
knowledge of clouds by tearing cotton and gluing it onto a piece of
paper to show the shape and closeness of the clouds in relation to the
propeller's action. The child can use pastel chalks to give cotton
clouds color where needed, if this is what he/she sees.
- Each child will show an understanding of weather by observing the
sky and drawing a weather prediction.

Alternate Activities

The postassessment is the same as the preassessment. After the
postassessment, exit from the module or proceed to additional activities.

Postassessment

- After showing and discussing flash cards of sunny, rainy, windy, and
cloudy days, the child will demonstrate how much he/he knows about

Additional Activities

143

different weather by naming each kind of card the teacher flashes. (Variation: child makes up a weekly weather story by putting the cards in any order and saying sunny, rainy, etc.)

• Keeping a weather diary. To show understanding of weather, each child will keep a weather diary for four weeks, each day drawing a picture of the weather. The teacher will add the date to each picture.

Resources
Books

Bendick, Jeanne. *All Around You.* McGraw- Hill Books, Inc., 1951.

Croft, Doreen J., and Hess, Robert D. *An Activities Handbook for Teachers of Young Children.* 2d ed. Houghton Mifflin Co., 1975.

Kranzer, H. C. *Nature and Science Activities for Young Children.* Baker, 1969.

Milne, A. A. *Now We Are Six.*

————. *When We Were Very Young.*

Schneider, Herman and Nina. *Let's Find Out.* William R. Scott, Inc., 1946.

Science for Work and Play. D. C. Heath & Co., 1961.

Thurber, Walter A. *Exploring Science.* Allyn and Bacon, Inc., 1957.

Weather. Grossett and Dunlap, 1960.

Zim, Herbert S. *The Sun.* William Morrow and Co., 1953.

Film

Ways to Find Out. Churchill-Wester Film Productions.

144

7
Creative
Arts

Every child is an artist, a music maker, an actor, and a dancer—sometimes openly, but always in his soul. The teacher is there to make him/her aware that he/she can express himself/herself through the creative arts. If the child learns of the potential of a paint brush, scraps of material in a box, the box itself, the musical beat of a tambourine, he/she will use this information in his/her own unique ways.

Call it self-expression or art. They are one and the same for the young child. The teacher is not a judge of artistic expression. The teacher is a patron of the arts. His/her role is to be a provider of materials, an adviser to the child concerning some of the potentials of the materials, and a patron who encourages the child to express himself/herself.

The modules in this component on creative arts were designed to help the teacher be a patron of student arts. The modules are the beginning of a creative arts curriculum for young children.

The modules, or units of learning, in the creative arts component are as follows:

7.1 Shapes
7.2 The Container with Six Sides
7.3 Print Making
7.4 Painting
7.5 Scraps
7.6 Paper Folding
7.7 Working with Clay
7.8 Keeping Time to the Music
7.9 Creative Movement to Music
7.10 Knowing the Instruments
7.11 Making Music

7.1 Shapes

Rationale

Learning the basic shapes is fundamental to readiness in math as well as art. Once the child learns to recognize and name shapes, his/her awareness of objects and the world about him/her is sharpened. The

145

child needs to realize that all objects are basically circles, squares, triangles, rectangles, and ovals, or combinations and variations of these and other basic shapes.

Prerequisites

For objective number one the teacher will need multicolored construction paper, cardboard, potatoes, tempera, large paper, stencils, a blindfold, basic shapes in felt, tagboard, a tape recorder, and tapes.

For objective number two the teacher will need colorful pages from magazines, newspapers, a reproduction of Pablo Picasso's *The Three Musicians,* stencils, construction paper, cans, and boxes with pictures from the supermarket.

Preassessment

• After placing various-sized felt squares, triangles, circles, rectangles, and ovals on flannel board, each child will demonstrate knowledge of the names of these basic shapes by naming them correctly.
• Given different sizes of the above-mentioned shapes combined to make five pictures of familiar objects, each child will demonstrate awareness of the basic shapes in all pictures by naming the familiar object and finding two basic shapes (e.g., a triangle and a circle) in each object. (Example: Combine to form a bird, a star, a man, etc.) After the preassessment exit from the module or proceed to the objectives.

Objective 1

The child will learn the names of the basic shapes (triangle, rectangle, circle, square, and oval), the shapes themselves, and be able to correctly identify each.

Activities

• As the teacher calls out the name of one of the basic shapes and holds up a representation of such, each child will show knowledge of the name of the shape by bringing the teacher an item in the room that is the same basic shape.
• Using different sizes and colors of each basic shape, each child will demonstrate knowledge of the proper names of shapes by correctly sorting by classification into boxes (all circles in the circle box) as called for on a teacher-prepared tape.
• Following a discussion on the differences in shapes, each child will show knowledge of shapes by feeling a cardboard shape in a "feely box" and correctly naming it. (Then the child may take out the shape to see if he/she was right.)

Alternate Activities

Simple Activity
Given paint, a large sheet of paper, and a potato with one basic shape carved out, each child will demonstrate knowledge of the one shape by identifying it while "printing" with it. Repeat, substituting a different shape until all shapes are available for the child to use.

More Advanced Activity
Given the ditto of the outlines of the basic shapes, each child will color the circles red, squares blue, ovals green, rectangles brown, and triangles orange as directed by the teacher.

Design your own activity to meet the needs of individual children.

The child will learn to see shapes in pictures and to realize that all works of art are basic shapes or variations of such.

Objective 2

• After discussing Pablo Picasso's *The Three Musicians* and emphasizing his use of cubic shapes, the child will demonstrate an ability to use shapes to form works of art by making a collage using circles, triangles, rectangles, squares, and ovals cut from magazines and other printed materials. Repeat, using the works of other artists from the cubist school.
• Each child will show that he/she can recognize the basic shapes in pictures by outlining a shape (such as a triangle) with a magic marker every time he/she finds one in magazine pictures.

Activities

Simple Activity
Given a reproduction of the stencil shown, the child will illustrate an understanding of all pictures as shapes by redrawing with a green pencil the triangles on a plastic overlay added to the stencil.

Alternate Activities

More Advanced Activity
Given crayons and paper, the child will demonstrate an ability to recognize shapes in art by drawing a picture using only rectangles and squares (or triangles and circles).

Design your own activity to meet the needs of individual children.

The postassessment is the same as the preassessment. After the postassessment exit from the module or proceed to additional activities.

Postassessment

• Given circles identical in color and size, the child will show knowledge of the names of shapes by calling aloud the correct name while separating the shapes into the box of the same shape. Also have boxes for the other basic shapes.
• To demonstrate an understanding that basic shapes are in pictures, each child will point out these shapes in pictures found on cans and boxes from the supermarket.

Additional Activities

Gradsky, Shirley. *Art Assemblies.* Arkansas State University, 1968.
Lewis, H., and Luca, M. *Understanding Children's Art for Better Teaching.* Charles E. Merrill, 1967.

Resources

147

7.2 The Container
with Six Sides

Rationale

Most young children are fascinated by boxes. It is a rare child who never discards a carefully selected gift, but clutches tightly its cardboard container. You can educate these children to recycle these six-sided boxes into unique objects or uses. The beauty of boxes is that the student has six sides on which to work, they can be painted and repainted many times and can be knocked down for easy transportation. Children enjoy variety, and through the medium of the box they begin to realize that there are many different uses for that empty, six-sided container.

Prerequisites

The children and the teacher should bring in as many big and small boxes as they can find. Paper, paint, glue, old sheets, buttons, aluminum foil, fasteners, marking pens, and other media will also be required.

Preassessment

Given six boxes, each child will demonstrate effective self-expression by telling eight ways to use these boxes. (Possibilities: for building something, for a costume, for changing to look like a truck or plane, for living or hiding in, for putting things in, for painting on, for pitching beanbags into as a game, for making a Jack-in-the-Box, as a mail box or bank, for sitting on.

Following the preassesssment, exit or proceed to the objective.

Objective

After learning some of the many things that can be done with a box, each child will learn effective self-expression using a box or boxes.

Activities

• After a discussion of sizes by the teacher and after being given two boxes of different sizes, each child will demonstrate knowledge that boxes can be stacked for building by using some to build an object for play such as a fireplace, a bridge, or a house.
• After discussing how boxes can be used for painting, each child will show understanding of this concept by painting a box to look like a turtle or other favorite animal.
• After hearing a story about strange animals (*Where the Wild Things Are*) and being given a small box, each child will show an understanding that boxes can be monsters by creating his own box creature using a box, paper scraps, crayons, buttons, aluminum foil, glue, and staples.
• After children have brought textured objects to the classroom and after being given a box with a lid, each child will demonstrate that a box can be a treasure chest by making a "feely box" to put these textured objects into and play with.
• After listening to "Cinderella" and being given as many boxes as needed, each child will show knowledge that boxes are for building by combining these boxes to represent Cinderella's castle. (Some may want to represent the carriage or the house where Cinderella lived with her stepmother.)
• The children will discuss a popular children's TV show. Then, given a

grocery box, each child will indicate an understanding that boxes can be costumes by making a costume of a character from that show out of the grocery box. (Directions: glue old sheets on box, cut holes in bottom and top of box, add straps so that the box can be held up by crossing over shoulders, and then paint or decorate. Pastel chalks for color on the boxes work well if sprayed with a fixative so that chalk doesn't smear.)

• The children will hear a talk by a railroad worker and take a field trip to the railroad station. Then, given a large box, each child will demonstrate knowledge that a box can be a train by making a railroad car from the large box. (The teacher lashes the boxes together in threes to form trains that the children can pull around the room.) (Variations: Boxes can be autos, boats, or airplanes.)

• After listening to a play, each child will demonstrate that boxes can be scenery by designing with paint on a box (height of tallest child) a part of the scenery to be used when acting out the play.

• Given a good sturdy box without a top, or a sturdy box lid, the children will be taken to a steep hill after a layer of snow has fallen and each will indicate that a box is a sled by using this box for sliding down the hill. (You can sit on it or belly flop with it. A coat or two of shellac will help your sled last for many slides.)

• The children will take a field trip to the community buildings around the school. Then, given an assortment of boxes, each child will create a model of a building in the community. By adding it to his/her classmates it will become the whole community around his/her school. (One-half-pint milk cartons are good for this activity.)

• After the teacher discusses houses, each child will show that he/she understands that you can build a playhouse with boxes by stacking or spreading as many large boxes as needed to become a miniature playhouse for the classroom. (This could be done as a group activity. Children can add paint, windows, door, or whatever they want to their house.)

• After a discussion of types of furniture, each child, given many boxes of different sizes, will show that boxes can be furniture by designing box furniture for the playhouse in the preceding activity. (Examples of furniture you can make: tables, television set, washer, dryer, sink, fireplace, bookcases, chairs, beds, and dressing tables.) (Children may want to cover the whole box with construction paper first and then draw or paint places for burners for stove; continue similarly with the rest of the furniture.)

• During a study of rock collecting, each child, given a cigar box or box of similar depth and size, will indicate that boxes can be used to display things by effectively making a shadow-box to display his rock collection.

• Same as preceding activity, but substitute butterfly collection or collections of baseball cards, old jewelry, and shells.

• After a discussion of the numbers needed, each child, given a large cardboard box, will demonstrate that boxes are for games by playing "Roll the Ball" and adding his total score at the end of the game. (Variations: Toss bean bags into boxes; put all smaller boxes into one box.)

Simple Activity
After a discussion in class by the teacher about saving money, each

Alternate Activities

child, given a small box, will show that boxes can be banks by making a bank for his/her money from the box.

More Advanced Activity
After hearing a story of "Red Riding Hood" and being given a large box, each child will show that the sides of the box can tell a story by making a scene on each side of the box to represent the story. (Examples: first scene, Little Red Riding Hood's house; second scene, the woods on the way to Grandmother's house; third scene, the wolf in Grandmother's house; and fourth scene, Little Red Riding Hood with the wolf in Grandmother's house.)

Design your own activity for certain children according to their needs and learning styles.

Postassessment

The postassessment is the same as the preassessment. After the postassessment, exit or proceed to additional activities.

Additional Activities

• After a discussion of the numbers needed, each child, given many small boxes, will show that boxes are for counting by lining up these boxes and counting the number of boxes he has lined up.
• Each child takes a box and gets in it, and given many boxes, will learn effective self-expression by creating a hideout from as many boxes as needed.
• After listening to the record of *The Jungle Book* and being given a box from cereal variety packages, each child will indicate that boxes make puppets by creating a puppet to represent a character from "The Jungle Book" and then role playing that character to the music. (Directions for puppet: Cut through the middle of the box on three sides, leaving the fourth side as the hinge for the mouth. Your fingers fit perfectly into each half of the box, so you can open and close the puppet's mouth. You can cover the box with patterned adhesive paper. Buttons glued to paper circles form eyes. Burlap ears can be stiffened with pipe cleaners and sewn on. Yarn forms the hair.)
• After each child receives a picture letter from his teacher and the class discusses the mailman, each child will show that boxes can be mailboxes by creating from a shoebox his/her own mailbox for delivering classroom papers to his/her mother. (Variation: valentine boxes.)

Resources

Alkema, Chester Jay. *Puppet Making*. Little Craft Book Series.
Childcraft. "Make and Do," vol. 9. Field Enterprises Educational Corp., 1968.
"More Creative Craft Activities." *Highlights for Children*. Highlights for Children, Inc., 1973.
Laliberte, Norman, and Kehl, Richey. *100 Ways to Have Fun with an Alligator and 100 Other Involving Art Projects.*. Art Education, Inc., 1973.
Little Red Riding Hood (book and record). Peter Pan Records.
Scott, Beatrice. *Instructor*. January, 1972.
Sendak, Maurice. *Where the Wild things Are*. 1963.
Walt Disney Productions. *The Jungle Book* (book and record). Western Printing and Lithographing Co., 1967.

7.3 Printmaking

Young children who know the basic techniques of printmaking are more aware of the world around them, since many familiar objects can be used to print with. Through printmaking, children become aware of letters and words and of books as the basis of a literate society. Printmaking can teach children to combine shapes and spaces and can expose the children to basic printing methods.

Rationale

Have on hand vegetables and fruit, tempera paints, table knives, sponges, ink pads, glue, heavy cardboard, brayers, cookie sheets, potato mashers, instant chocolate pudding, newspapers, small objects suitable for making a collage, finger-painting papers, *Watch My Tracks* by Bob Kaufman; a filmstrip, *Printmaking,* by John Lidstone; and a printmaking set of letters and ink pad.

Prerequisites

Given the needed materials suggested in the prerequisites, each child,when the teacher asks him/her to make certain designs with the materials before him/her, will show an understanding of the basic principles of printmaking by making vegetable and fruit prints, a potato block print, a sponge print, a fingerprint, and a potato masher print.

After the preassessment, exit from the module or proceed to the objective.

Preassessment

Each child will experience and learn the basic processes of printmaking.

Objective

• After the teacher reads the book *Watch My Tracks* (see the resources section), each child will show knowledge of the basic process of printmaking by discussing how animals leave their footprints on the ground and how different animals leave different kinds of print. (Variation: Children make a trail of their own hand- and footprints using tempera paints and large sheets of brown paper.)
• After viewing the filmstrip *Printmaking,* each child will demonstrate the different ways of making prints by trying out the different methods used in the filmstrip.
• Given different kinds of vegetables and fruits cut in half—cucumbers, mushrooms, green peppers, onions, oranges, and apples—each child will indicate an understanding of the process of vegetable printing by pressing the items into tempera paint and then pressing them onto paper.
• After a demonstration from the teacher on how to make a potato block, each child will show how to make a potato print by carving a design in the potato with a dinner knife and using the design to print with tempera paint on paper.
• Given sponges of assorted sizes and shapes, each child will show knowledge of printmaking by making his own designs using sponge prints with tempera paint on paper.
• Given an ink pad and paper, each child will show an awareness of a

Activities

7.3 Foot printing

type of printmaking by making designs on paper after pressing his/her fingers and parts of his/her hand on the ink pad. (Children may wish to draw with a felt-tip pen to finish their designs.) (Variation: printing with letters, ink pad, and paper.)

● Given the materials necessary to make glue prints, each child will demonstrate how to make his/her own designs and prints by following these steps: (1) squeeze glue onto heavy cardboard and let it dry thoroughly, (2) cover a brayer with paint, (3) roll brayer over glue design until all raised surfaces of glue are covered with paint, (4) lay a piece of paper on top of cardboard design, and (5) press evenly to make a print.

● Given at least two kinds of potato mashers, each child will demonstrate printmaking by dipping the end of the potato masher into the paint and pressing onto paper until he/she has covered a large piece of paper with designs.

Simple Activity
After placing one hand on a plate of tempera paint, each child will show how to make a hand print by pressing the hand onto a piece of paper. For the purpose of varying the design, the child should be encouraged to try one finger at a time, knuckles, and fingertips.

More Advanced Activity
After children have glued small objects onto cardboard (buttons, string, rice, paper clips, hairpins, and anything else the children can think of), each child will demonstrate how to make a collage print by rolling a brayer full of paint over the objects and printing the cardboard block onto paper.

Design your own activity for certain children according to their needs and learning styles.

Alternate Activities

The postassessment is the same as the preassessment. After the postassessment, exit or proceed to additional activities.

Postassessment

• Given instant chocolate pudding ready for eating, each child will learn another way to make a print by finger painting with pudding and then pressing a clean sheet of paper on top of pudding design. (Don't tell the children they are using chocolate pudding: see how long it takes them to realize it through smell and taste.) (Variations: other puddings; men's shaving cream to which several drops of cooking oil and food coloring have been added.)
• Given lots of newspapers placed on the floor, the children will experience foot printing by dipping the bottoms of their feet into small tubs of tempera paint and walking on the newspapers. (Encourage them to try tips of toes, balls of heels, and knees.)

Additional Activities

Katz, Marjorie P. *Finger Print Owls and Other Fantasies.* M. Evans and Company, Inc., 1972.
Laliberte, Norman, and Kehl, Richey. *100 Ways to Have Fun with an Alligator and 100 Other Involving Art Projects.* Art Education, Inc., 1973.
MacStravic, Suellen. *Printmaking.* Lerner Publications, 1973.
Pitcher, Evelyn G. *Helping Young Children Learn.* 2d ed. Charles E. Merrill Publications Co., 1974.
Rockwell, Harlow. *Printmaking.* Doubleday & Co., 1973.
Wiseman, Ann. *Making Things.* Little, Brown and Co., 1973.

Resources

7.4 Painting

Art is an essential school experience for all children because it helps develop the whole child, not merely his mental and verbal capacities. In creative art activities the child uses and integrates his motor,

Rationale

emotional, and mental capacities. Art experiences help develop personal sensitivity and reliance on one's own taste and judgment. Inner resources are tapped; a sense of personal satisfaction and confidence is achieved; lifelong interest in looking at or creating art develops. But an awareness of many art materials and of many means of expression is necessary if the young artist is to find his/her medium and to appreciate the medium another uses.

Prerequisites

Have on hand tempera paint, primary colors, Gerber baby food jars and lids (large) or tin cans, a few cloves or drops of wintergreen to prevent odor in each jar, long-handled brushes ¾" to 1" wide (round bristles, flat bristles or soft camel hair No. 12), 18"-by-24" newsprint or manila paper on easels or improvised painting surface, 22"-by-28" cardboard taped to blackboard or set in chalk tray, masonite boards or primary tables covered with newsprint or oilcloth, string, cord, yarn, used wooden match sticks (cut in half), a place to put papers to dry, fingerpaint (thinner type), 1 pint liquid starch, 1 cup Ivory Snow, powdered tempera (thicker type) to color, 1 pt. prepared starch, ½ cup talcum powder, ½ teaspoon oil of cloves, smocks or father's old shirt *with sleeves cut out* (or apron made from a half fold of newspaper with string through fold for tying around child's chest), slick finished paper or fingerpaint paper, instant chocolate pudding already mixed, catsup, water, sponges, and records with different tempos.

Preassessment

• When provided with a paint brush and tempera paint, the child will show he is able to make designs on a sheet of paper. The designs should include circles when asked to show a tricycle, vertical lines when asked to show a house, diagonal lines when asked to show a sliding board, and horizontal lines when asked to show a sidewalk.
• When the teacher asks, "Which of these can you use to make designs?" each child will demonstrate an awareness of painting as a medium of expression by choosing at least three different tools and three materials from an array of six fingerpaint materials and paper. After the preassessment, exit from the module or proceed to the objectives.

Objective 1

Using a brush, the child will learn how to make designs, including circles, diagonal lines, horizontal lines, vertical lines, colors on top of colors, and colors beside colors.

Activities

• After the teacher's demonstration and given one color and brush, the child will tap, twist, press, drag, and roll the brush like a rolling pin across the paper to show that he can manipulate his brush in several ways.
• Using one color with the paint brush, the child will let it dry in one area of the paper then apply a second color on top to show his ability to use different colors on top of one another in designs.
• To become aware of the different combinations of paint designs the child will show his awareness of design by dropping different puddles of paint on the paper then using another color before the first dries to see the interesting effects.

154

• After riding a tricycle, running inside circles painted on the playground, or playing on the merry-go-round, the child will show his awareness of this spatial design by drawing it on paper using circular strokes.

• After sliding down a slide, walking up and down an inclined plane made of blocks, using a wedge to split wood, and walking in rain slanted by the wind, the child will show his awareness of the design slanted strokes by painting it voluntarily.

• After walking or playing on a balance beam, a low concrete fence, a sidewalk, a level bridge of blocks and a low table, the child will show his awareness of horizontal lines by painting them voluntarily at free play or painting time.

• After a walk through tall trees, a class discussion on a picture showing a line of telephone poles, and watching the rain come straight down, each child will indicate an awareness of vertical lines by using these voluntarily in his painting when he chooses to paint as an activity.

• The child will show an awareness of design by wedging one half of a match stick in the middle of the bristles of a brush and moving the brush across the paper, using different colors to make a design.

Simple Activities
• While a child and the teacher are mixing tempera using a brush, the child will demonstrate an awareness of the four kinds of strokes by using them when painting on paper. (The teacher moves the child's hand on the paint brush in the jar to make the four kinds of strokes).

• To show an awareness of color's relationship to design, the child will move a brush across paper, exploring the area, adding one color at a time to make a design.

More Advanced Activity
Using many different colors, the child will paint a picture with the four kinds of brush strokes, later naming the objects in the picture and telling about them to show an awareness of objects or space to what he/she has painted.

Design your own activities to meet the needs of individual children.

The child will learn to use his/her hands and other instruments to make creative fingerpaint designs on paper.

Objective 2

• After the teacher's demonstration, the child will demonstrate an awareness of materials and designs by covering a paper with finger paint, and then using palm, finger, fingers, fist, knuckles, and side of hand to make a design.

• Using fingers and sponges, the child will make a picture to show he/she is aware of design-making in this medium.

• To show an awareness of the relationship of materials to design, the child will fingerpaint with two colors, first with separate hands for separate colors on the paper then by mixing the colors together to see the two effects as well as feel them.

Activities

• Using media with different textures (e.g., mustard, catsup, and pudding with raisins), the children will create pictures on tabletops to show their awareness of materials and designs.

Alternate Activities

Simple Activity
The teacher will show the child how to place one palm in the fingerpaint on the paper and how to move it from side to side to get the feel of the paint and movement in order to make a design. After this demonstration each child will experiment in the same way, showing an awareness of the tool and the design.

More Advanced Activity
To show an awareness that parts of the body can be used as painting tools, the child will experiment with at least four parts of the body while finger painting. (Examples: nose, lips, elbows, feet, hands.)

Design your own activity to meet the needs of individual children.

Postassessment

The postassessment is the same as the preassessment. After the postassessment, exit from the module or proceed to additional activities.

Additional Activities

• The child will use brushes of various sizes as well as different textured paints, such as water paint, to show that he/she can make varied designs with any materials provided.
• The child will use squeeze bottles, rollers, corrugated paper, shoe polish applicators and other unusual objects to show that he/she can manipulate the fingerpaint in unusual ways.

Resources

Art in the Elementary School. New York Board of Education, 1969.
Brantlinger, F. *What to Do for Kindergarden and Primary Art.* Hayes Publishing Company.
Hoover, F. Louis. *Art Activities for the Very Young.*
Whitman Creative Art Book, A. Whitman Co., 1966.

7.5 Scraps

Rationale

Children learn best when they feel free to explore materials and ideas. Art is one of the ways young children can feel free to communicate their feelings. To develop art communication, the child must have many opportunities to try out materials and ideas. He/she must become aware that there is more to "art" than painting and crayons. The purpose of this module is to help the child understand that almost anything available can be united with other elements for full self-expression.

7.5 Making a sock puppet

The teacher will need the following materials: glue, small stones, cereal, beans or buttons, cardboard squares for each child (8"-by-10"), wood scraps, paint, egg shells, straws, pipe cleaners, socks, construction paper (or buttons for eye), material scraps, tin cans, 3"-4" round flat stones, and ½ pint boxes.

Prerequisites

Given glue, small stones, cereal, beans or buttons, paint and paper, the child will show an ability to create forms from scraps by interpreting a chosen object using the scrap materials rather than just painting a picture.

After the preassessment, exit from the module or proceed to the objectives.

Preassessment

The child will learn to create personal art from common materials or scraps.

Objective

• Using small scraps of wood, glue, paint, colored paper, and cloths, the child will demonstrate creativity with scraps by arranging the wood to form a sculpture and decorating it with paint and paper in a pleasing way.
• Following a discussion on animal structure and decoration of the room with many animal pictures, each child, when given clean, hollow eggs, pipe cleaners, and drinking straws, will combine the scraps to create an animal representation.

Activities

157

• Using a sock, glue, and construction paper, a child will show knowledge of combining scraps to form art by creating a hand puppet successfully.

Alternate Activities

More Advanced Activity
Given various textures and colors of materials, buttons, glue, and cardboard, the child will show awareness of art with scraps by constructing a collage of the materials on the cardboard to form a self-satisfying picture.

Simple Activity
Given a clean tin can with glue and paper and scraps of various colors, the child will demonstrate an ability to create beauty from scraps by successfully decorating the tin can.

Design your own activity to meet the needs of individual children.

Postassessment

The postassessment is the same as the preassessment. After the postassessment, exit from the module or proceed to additional activities.

Additional Activities

• After a stone painting demonstration by the teacher, the child, given paint and a stone about the size of a hand, will show a knowledge of how to transform scrap material into art by decorating the stone to his/her satisfaction. (In the demonstration the teacher should paint the sides of a rock different colors, paint a picture on one side, paint a rock one color all over, and paint a design such as polka dots.)
• Using a small box (e.g., a ½ pint milk carton), paint, paper, and glue, the child will illustrate a knowledge that scraps can be turned into art by creating an animal, a house, or another familiar object from the box.

Resources

Laliberte, Norman, and Kehl, Richey. *100 Ways to Have Fun with an Alligator and 100 Other Involving Art Projects.* Art Education, Inc., 1973.
Meilach. *Creating Art from Anything.* Reilly and Lee.
Paine, Irma Littler. *Art Aides for Elementary Teaching—A Handbook.*
Reed, Carl, and Orze, Joseph. *Art From Scrap.* Davis Publications, Inc., 1960.
Stribling. *Art from Found Materials.* Crown.
Surderlin, Sylvia, ed. *Creating with Materials for Work and Play.* Association for Childhood Education International, 1969.
Wiseman, Ann. *Making Things: The Handbook of Creative Discovery.* Little, Brown and Co., 1973.
Wurman, R. S. *Yellow Pages of Learning Resources.* Group for Environmental Education, Inc., 1972.

7.6 Paper Folding

The progress or success of a paper-folding activity depends primarily upon the teacher. Paper is readily available, but it is also weak, frustrating to the child because it is easily destroyed or torn apart. Care must be observed if the finished products are to be taken home and admired for future pleasure.

Paper folding may offer a new and wonderful challenge to the child. For some children it may give an opportunity to share already stored knowledge. Whtever the experience of the child, guidance on the teacher's part must be carefully exercised and followed if the activity is to be a successful experience in art for young children.

The most generally used paper is 8½"-by-11" or 9"-by-12". Much smaller paper or larger paper generally becomes unmanageable for the child and thus causes frustration. The following activities call for a square sheet of paper.

When given the following commands by the teacher, the child will show knowledge of paper folding by responding to five of the commands correctly.
- Fold the paper in half.
- Fold the paper in fourths—four equal parts.
- Make a glider like this. (Show the finished product.)
- Make a fan like this. (Show the finished product.)
- Make four squares like these. (Show four squares made from folding a square into fourths and cutting it into four equal pieces.)
- Make a soldier's hat like this. (Show the finished product.)

After the preassessment, exit from the module or proceed to the objective.

Each child will know and understand the fundamentals of folding paper to make a variety of paper designs and products.

- After first showing and discussing what a square is, the children will pick out a square piece of paper from a variety of different shapes to show that they understand how paper may be used for folding.
- Using the square sheet of paper, the teacher will demonstrate how to fold a square sheet of paper from top to bottom and then once more from side to side into a four-square piece of paper. After this demonstration, each child will show an understanding by imitating the teacher as the demonstration is done three more times.
- After seeing this demonstration, each child will fold his/her own square sheet as shown by the teacher.
- When given a newspaper measuring 18"-by-18", the child will show an understanding of the process of paper folding by producing a four-square fold and then taking a single fold of one side to the opposite side, producing a soldier's hat.

Alternate Activities

Simple Activity
Taking a square sheet of paper, the child will fold or crease the paper in half and then proceed to illustrate half the paper with a favorite animal to show understanding of one simple fold. (Variation: folding in fourths.)

More Advanced Activity
After seeing the steps and the finished design of a paper glider, the child will (1) fold a 9"-by-12" paper sheet lengthwise down the middle and then lay it flat (not folded), (2) fold the top corners down to the center fold so that each new panel forms a triangle one leg of which coincides with the center fold, (3) fold both newly formed corners (one on each side) toward the center slightly below the midpoint, forming a triangle one leg of which coincides with the center fold, (4) repeat step 3, (5) turn the paper over, and (6) refold it along the original center line so that the panels are on the outside.

Design your own activity to meet the needs of individual children.

Postassessment

The postassessment is the same as the preassessment. After the postassessment, exit from the module or proceed to additional activities.

Additional Activities

• Given a piece of paper, each child will show knowledge of paper folding by making one-half-inch folds across the paper, keeping the folds together while folding—thus making a paper fan.
• After reviewing the procedure for making a four-square fold, the child will cut apart the individual squares on the fold lines and then make a four-series coloring book to indicate an understanding of paper folding.
• When given a large sheet or square of construction paper, the child will fold it in half and then proceed to make colorful designs on one side for a stand up "show-and-tell" book to demonstrate a knowledge of paper folding.

Resources

Campbell, M. W. *Paper Toy Making.* Dover Publications, Inc., 1937.
Nelson, L. *Instructional Aids.* 1958.
Murray, W. D., and Rigney, F. J. *Paper Folding for Beginners.* Dover Publications, Inc., 1975.
Osborn, D. *Creative Activities,* 1964.
Phillips, Jo. *Right Angles: Paper-Folding Geometry.* Crowell, 1972.

7.7 Working with Clay

Rationale

The child who works with clay lays a good, structural foundation for building muscles needed for many school activities. Clay modeling

7.7 Making bowls from clay ropes

enables a child to use various muscles while gaining understanding of the environment. Using clay is fun, too. Children can pound, roll, sculpt, and redo to their hearts' content. Sometimes the child role plays while interacting with the material. Sometimes the child is reflective. All he/she needs is the awareness of how to use the material effectively.

Before using clay—any type of clay—have a moist table or cloth to lay the clay on while in use. It is best, too, to have a bowl of water handy to keep your fingers wet while working with the clay. Other materials may include fingernail files for cutting, toothpicks, and possibly tempera paint to paint the finished products.

Prerequisites

The child will take a lump of clay and be able to construct a chosen clay man or animal, demonstrating an awareness of how to use clay by doing five of the following: wetting fingers to work, pounding, rolling into a ball or a rope, putting pieces together and smoothing seams, indenting with tooth picks, cutting with a file, or pressing clay flat.

   After the preassessment, exit from the module or proceed to the objective.

Preassessment

Each child will learn some simple techniques of working with clay.

Objective

161

Activities
- Using a lump of clay, the teacher will first discuss the fundamentals of playing with clay and demonstrating the procedures for (1) rolling the clay into a ball, (2) rolling the clay into ropes, (3) pressing clay flat with the palms, and (4) wetting fingers to keep clay moist and easy to work with.

  Each child will show an understanding of the four principles by demonstrating each while working with clay.
- When provided with individual clay, each child will show knowledge of how to make a ball, a rope, and a flat piece of clay by making each as the teacher tells a made-up story about a clay ball that changes shape as it gets into some tight places.
- After looking at and discussing pictures of animals and people, each child will take a piece of clay and mold it into either an animal or a man, using the four principles in the first activity where appropriate, to show an understanding of how to work with clay.
- Using three different sizes of clay balls, each child will make a clay man by placing the largest ball on bottom, the middle-sized in the middle and the smallest on the top, and will then proceed to paint the finished product to show knowledge of the principle that clay can be rolled into balls.
- Using a lump of clay, the teacher will first discuss the fundamentals of playing with clay and demonstrating the procedures for (1) pasting pieces together and smoothing seams with fingers and water, (2) indenting with toothpicks to make such things as eyes, nose, hair, and mouth, (3) cutting pieces of clay with a nail file, (4) making indentations with the side of the file, and (5) coring with the file to make a hole.

  Each child will show knowledge of the five principles above by demonstrating them while working with clay.
- After a demonstration by the teacher, each child will show, by making several bowls, an understanding that a bowl is made by building up the clay in a circular fashion using a clay rope.

Alternate Activities

Simple Activity
After rolling a piece of clay flat on a table top, the child will etch out with a fingernail a drawing of an animal or a face to show an understanding of how the fingernail can be used in working with clay.

More Advanced Activity
Given a series of picture designs and a demonstration by the teacher, the child will trace a design on the flattened clay with a nail or other pointed object and then cut away the excess clay with the nail file, showing a knowledge of how to work with clay.

Design your own activity to meet the needs of individual children.

Postassessment

The postassessment is the same as the preassessment. After the postassessment, exit from the module or proceed to additional activities.

Additional Activities

- Given a combination of five clay balls, the child will flatten each clay ball and then roll it into balls again to show knowledge of how to make balls and pancakes with clay.

• Using at least a pound of clay, the child will roll the clay into snakes or ropes until it is as tall as he/she is and then tell an impromptu story about long snakes, indicating an understanding of how to roll clay into a rope.

• When looking at a model of a clay man made from round balls, the child should be able to point to the three different sizes involved in making the man and tell why one ball is larger than another, showing an understanding of this principle in clay building.

Nelson, L. *Instructional Aids.* 1958.
Osborn, D. *Creative Activities.* 1964.
Sunderlin, Sylvia, ed. *Creating With Materials for Work and Play.*
  Association for Childhood Education International, 1970.
Wankelman, W. *A Handbook of Arts and Crafts.* 1961.

Resources

7.8 Keeping Time
to the Music

A rhythmic response to music serves as body exercise, affords opportunities for the child to develop a feeling for and a sense of rhythm, and develops motor coordination and grace. Bodily activity is a natural response to music; it will develop the awareness necessary for a better appreciation of music.

Rhythm exists not only in music, but in poetry, art, and nature. Sequels to this module might be units on keeping time to poetry, the rhythm in painting, sculpting, or other art activities, and the rhythm in nature.

Rationale

Have on hand wood blocks, coconut shells, bells and bracelets, Millie Burnett's *Melody Movement and Language: a Teacher's Guide of Music in Same Forms for the Pre-School and Primary Grades.* San Francisco: R & E Research Associates, 1973.

Prerequisites

• Each child will show a knowledge of rhythm by synchronization of hand clapping with the rhythm of music after a demonstration by the teacher, using "One-Two, Buckle My Shoe," "Three Potatoes," "Sing a Song of Sunshine," and "Another Rain Song," from Burnett's *Melody* (see prerequisites).

• Given blocks, bells, and bracelets, the child will demonstrate a knowledge of rhythm by keeping time with the music, using each instrument separately to 4/4 and 3/4 time.

After doing the preassessment, exit from module or proceed to the objectives.

Preassessment

The child will learn rhythm by clapping hands or moving other body parts to music.

Objective 1

7.8   Keeping time to music

Activities

• While hearing the song, "Greetings," the children will show their understanding of the rhythm by clapping their hands to the melody and moving about pretending to greet others. (Variations: snap fingers, snap and clap, stamp foot.)

• The children will show their understanding of rhythm by knee slapping to the song "This Train."

• While playing the song, "Yankee Doodle," the children will demonstrate their knowledge of rhythm by marching and clapping in time with the music.

• Hopping to "Hop Up, My Children" in time with the music.

Alternate Activities

Simple Activity
The children will demonstrate their knowledge of rhythm by clapping to the chant "One, Two, Buckle My Shoe," instead of music.

More Advanced Activity
The children will show their ability to perform with the rhythm of the music by skipping and clapping simultaneously to a record of "Skip to My Lou," a folk song.

Design your own activity to meet the needs of individual children.

164

The child will learn to keep time to music with musical instruments.

Objective 2

Activities

• Given bells, blocks, and coconut shells, the children will show their skill in rhythm by imitating trotting horses and sleigh bells to the song "Jingle Bells."
• Given blocks and bells, the children will show their knowledge of rhythm by keeping time to the song "Bingo."

Alternate Activities

Simple Activity
Given bells and bracelets, the children will demonstrate their skill in rhythm by keeping time to the music of "Row, Row, Row Your Boat" while others keep time by rowing a pretend boat on cue.

More Advanced Activity
The children will show their rhythmic skill by playing in time to the music of the song "Hallowe'en" while being a witch (drum), a cat (triangle), or a tiger (sand block).

Design your own activity to meet the needs of individual children.

The postassessment is the same as the preassessment. After the postassessment, exit or proceed to additional activities.

Postassessment

• The children will show their skill in rhythm by marching and clapping to the song, "I've Been Working on the Railroad."
• By skipping or striking rhythm sticks together to the chant, "A Treasure Hunt," the children will show their knowledge of rhythm.

Additional Activities

Foster and Headley. *Education in the Kindergarten.* American Book Co., 1966.
Nye, Robert E., and Bjornar, Bergethon. *Basic Music.* Prentice-Hall, 1968.
Pitcher, Evelyn G., et al. *Helping Young Children Learn.* 2d ed. Charles E. Merrill Publishing Co., 1974.

Resources

7.9 Creative Movement to Music

Body movement helps develop muscular coordination, poise, and self-control, and it quickens awareness of how to express one's feelings and ideas to music. Children who have not learned how to hop, skip, jump, walk, run, or gallop have been deprived of some fundamentals of self-expression. Once the child has mastered these, expression of self to music is easy.

Rationale

Prerequisites

Have on hand the book *Singing Fun*, the record *Mary Poppins*, and a tape recorder and blank tapes. The teacher should record sections needed for a specific activity.

Preassessment

The children will demonstrate that they can express themselves to music through body movement by matching high and low notes in a song with high and low body movement, and by moving to music like a hippopotamus, a floating leaf, a spinning top (on one foot), a cowboy riding a horse (using whip, reins, and trot or gallop), and a bouncing ball (by skipping as well as jumping).

After the preassessment, exit from the module or proceed to the objective.

Objective

The children will demonstrate that they can express themselves to music through the fundamental body movements.

Activities

• To indicate a knowledge of body movement, the child, while listening to the song "Pussy Willow," will demonstrate ability to express self to music through body movement by moving from a crouched position to tiptoes, then back to a crouch, and then jumping on the word *scat*.

• While listening to the song "Let's Go Fly a Kite," from *Mary Poppins*, the children will show their understanding of basic movements by pretending with body movement that they are flying kites while skipping in circles. (Variation: walking up and down with kites, running with kites.)

• While singing the song "Ten Little Indians," the children will show their understanding of body movement by trotting in a circle around the room pretending they are Indians riding ponies. (Variation: repeat, using the gallop.)

• To demonstrate their knowledge of light and heavy movements, the children will move on tiptoe (light), stamp their feet (heavy), and stamp while in a crouched position as the teacher plays and sings "The Animals in the Zoo." (Burnett's *Melody*, in resources section.)

• To show that they understand how to jump and hop, the children will jump on "the farmer hoes the corn," and hop on "Heigh, ho, the dairy oh," singing "The Farmer in the Dell" (see Burnett's *Melody*, in resources section).

Alternate Activities

More Advanced Activity
While listening to a song like "Susie Snowflake," the children will demonstrate their ability to coordinate body movement to music by pretending they are snowflakes.

Simple Activity
The children will demonstrate their ability to coordinate their body movement to music by rocking back and forth as they sing the lullaby "Rock-a-Bye-Baby."

Design your own activity to meet the needs of individual children.

166

The po̲assessment is the same as the preassessment. After the postassessment, exit from the module or proceed to additional activities.

* The children will show how body movement relates to music by stamping to the song "She'll Be Comin' 'Round the Mountain." (Variation: gallop as a horse to the music.)
* The children will show how body movement relates to music by making hand motions to the song "Mulberry Bush."

Andrews, C. *Creative Rhythmic Movement for Children.* Prentice-Hall, 1954.

Burnett, Millie. *Melody, Movement and Language.* R & E Research Associates, 1973.

Driver, Ann. *Music and Movement.* Oxford University Press, 1952.

Findlay, Elsa. *Rhythm and Movement.* Summy-Birchard Co., 1971.

Foster and Headley, *Education in the Kindergarten.* American Book Co., 1966.

Hayes, E. "Expanding the Child's World Through Drama and Movement," *Childhood Education.* April 1971.

Jones, Bessie, and Hawes, Bess. *Step It Down.* Harper and Row, 1972.

Jones, E. *What Is Music for Young Children?* National Association for the Education of Young Children, 1969.

Porter, L. *Movement Education for Children.* Association of Elementary, Kindergarten, and Nursery Educators, 1969.

Saffron, Rosanna. *First Book of Creative Rhythm.* Holt, Rinehart, & Winston, 1963.

Stecher, M. B. "Concept Learning Through Movement Improvisation: The Teacher's Role as Catalyst." *Young Children.* January 1970.

7.10 Knowing the Instruments

Music! Almost *every* child's world is filled with it from television, radio, record players, and even family members who play musical instruments. All this contributes to the development of a child's interest in music and how to make it.

Have on hand: record player, tape recorder, drum, sandblocks, small xylophone, rhythm sticks, melody bells, triangle, tambourine, crayons, paper, picture books of rhythm instruments (made by the teacher). Tapes of rhythm instruments playing two pieces (prepared by teacher) for preassessment below.

Given the nine rhythm instruments in the prerequisites, the child will demonstrate a knowledge of five of the instruments by saying the names of each, by showing how to handle them to produce the best tone, and by identifying the sounds of two or three instruments being played in a tape recording.

After the preassessment, exit from the module or proceed to the objective.

Objective   Each child will learn to recognize three out of five instruments, their names, how they sound, and how to produce the sound.

Activities   • After seeing all the instruments, each child will choose one instrument and demonstrate knowledge of it by repeating its name, listening to the teacher play it, and by playing the instrument as directed.
• Same as first activity, except that if the child does not demonstrate a knowledge of the names, the teacher will provide the child with a book on rhythm instruments and a tape that the child can listen to while following in the book. After listening, the child will demonstrate his/her knowledge by naming the three that were chosen.
• Given paper and crayons, each child will indicate recognition of the three instruments he/she chooses by drawing a picture of each and sharing it with teacher by naming each instrument drawn. (Teacher can write name of each instrument under the picture, and child can make into booklet.)
• After inspecting instrument by handling and producing a sound which gives the best tone, the child will demonstrate knowledge by showing the teacher.
• Same as preceding activity, but with another instrument. After the teacher demonstrates the correct way to produce a sound, the child will show understanding by handling the instrument correctly. (Give the child this same opportunity with all of the instruments.)
• After listening to tape recordings in which each of the rhythm instruments is used in simple songs, the child will indicate knowledge of the three instruments by pointing out what they are.
• Given a record to listen to, the child will show recognition of how to play the three instruments by playing them freely to the music to see how they sound.

Alternate Activity   Given a large piece of cardboard with notes colored to match the different colors of the melody bells or the xylophone keys, the child will demonstrate an ability to play a simple melody by looking at the colors and picking up the matching bell or hitting the matching key.

Design your own activity to meet the needs of individual children.

Postassessment   The postassessment is the same as the preassessment. After the postassessment, exit from the module or proceed to additional activity.

Additional Activity   After picking out a rhythm instrument, each child will demonstrate knowledge of that instrument by playing it to the beat of the music while other children are playing their rhythm instruments.

168

Aronoff, Frances Webber. *Music and Young Children.* Holt, Rinehart and Winston, Inc., 1969.
Myerson, E. "Listen to What I Made! From Musical Theory to Usable Instrument." *Young Children.* December 1970.

7.11 Making Music

In a good kindergarten, music becomes part of the child's life, part of the child's day, and a support to other areas of learning. A music program should stimulate love and appreciation of music through exploratory activities. Because children are natural explorers, they will find pleasure in trying out different kinds of percussive and melody instruments, manipulating them in a variety of ways and listening to the sounds they can make with them. These initial discoveries are important in opening the way to later musical understanding. Making music does not have to be a noisy or chaotic experience for the teacher. Music is an art form that requires self-discipline. Exploration does not mean turning the children loose to bang with rhythm instruments. That is noise, not music.

Rationale

Do Module 7.10 before this module.
Have on hand rhythm sticks (eight sets), cymbals, drums, tambourines, triangles, bells, wood and sand blocks, records, and, for teacher, music book and record player.

Prerequisites

Given an instrument, the child will show ability to play with the beat and up to tempo by accompanying several other children while the teacher is playing either the piano or a record. (Test only three or four children at a time. Use taped or recorded music so that you are free to watch and listen.)
   After this preassessment, exit from the module or proceed to the objective.

Preassessment

The children will learn to accompany each other and the music with three different instruments.

Objective

• Given an array of instruments at a learning center and teacher-prepared tapes of someone playing a rhythm instrument with recorded music, each child will show skill in accompaniment by playing, with the tape, the same instrument as is playing on the tape.
• Listening to a record or a piano playing "Marching Down the Street" (*Growing With Music Series*) or any other good march, half the children will use rhythm sticks to accompany first the music, and then other children marching, showing that they understand simple principles of musical accompaniment.

Activities

• The teacher, using different songs to introduce the playing of different instruments, will play these at different times to give children a chance to learn how it sounds to accompany. (Variation: Teacher records one child [then two, then three] accompanying the music.)

Alternate Activities

Simple Activities
• Using a record with an obvious beat or rhythm, the child will sway from side to side, later clapping, to show an ability to keep time with music as a way of indicating an ability to accompany up to tempo.
• The children will use one rhythm stick on the uncarpeted floor to show they can beat along with the clock sound while the teacher plays "Hickory Dickory Dock," thereby demonstrating an awareness of how to accompany to the beat of the music.

More Advanced Activities
• The teacher will play "Our Instruments" (Prentice-Hall). The child, with the proper instrument, will come in when it is his/her turn, showing an ability to play on the beat (tambourines, bells, triangles, blocks).
• To demonstrate an awareness of what "up to tempo" means, the child will increase and decrease the speed at which he/she plays the instrument (without losing the beat) as the teacher plays a tape (teacher-made) of a piece played slower than written and up to tempo.

Design your own activity to meet the needs of individual children.

Postassessment

The postassessment is the same as the preassessment. After the postassessment, exit from the module or proceed to additional activities.

Additional Activities

• The children will form a circle and, using four different instruments, will play their instruments when the words "oats, peas, beans and barley" are chanted, showing they can come in at the proper time.
• As the children say a nursery rhyme such as "Mary Had a Little Lamb," each child picks out the word to play his/her instrument on, showing ability to coordinate hearing with playing. (For example: "Mary" is two beats on the drum, "little" is two hits on the tambourine, and "lamb" is one beat on the triangle.)

Resources
Books

Board of Education of the City of N.Y. *Teaching Music in the Elementary Grades.*
Growing With Music-K. Prentice-Hall, 1966.
Jones, Elizabeth. *What is Music for Young Children?* National Association of Educators of Young Children, 1969.
This is Music for Kindergarten and Nursery School. Allyn and Bacon, 1965.

Records

"Indian Dance," "My Rhythm Sticks," "My Tambourine" (record), "The Cuckoo Clock" (record), "My Triangle" (record). *American Singer,* book I. American Singer Series.

The Kindergarten Book, Albums 1 and 2. Bomar Educational Records.
"The Wood Sticks" (record), "The Triangles" (record), "The Drum"
(record), "The Cymbals" (record), "Making Music" (record),
"Marching to My Drum." *The Kindergarten Book.* Our Singing
World Series.
"Tick Tock," "Jack and Jill" (record), "Drum Song" (record), "The
Little Bells" (record). *Music Round the Clock.* Together We Sing
Series.

8
Nutrition and Health

Good health requires knowledge and practice. The young child hears about good health, but seldom sees its application to self. Children brush their teeth, for example, because their mothers insist. But learning good health habits early is much easier than breaking bad habits later. The teacher can help the children develop good health habits by making the process a daily adventure—by making it fun.

The modules (units of learning) in the nutrition and health component are as follows:

8.1 The Clothing Story
8.2 Appropriate Clothing
8.3 Seeing, Smelling, and Other Senses
8.4 Care of the Five Senses
8.5 Brushing the Teeth
8.6 Feeding the Teeth
8.7 Skin
8.8 Hair Care
8.9 The Food Machines
8.10 A Better Breakfast.

This component is not a complete curriculum in nutrition and health. The teacher will need to add modules to make it more comprehensive such as: The Art of Snacking (more activities on nutritional snacks); Posture Perfect (the need for certain healthful postures when sitting, standing, walking, lifting and so on); What To Do When (what to do in case of fire, burglars, strangers, injury); and Funny Feelings (what to do when you feel angry, afraid, sad, and lonely).

8.1 The Clothing Story

Since clothing is an important part of healthy lives, it is important to know where we get this clothing. Learning where cotton, leather, and

8.5 Brushing giant teeth

Rationale

173

wool come from enables the child to better understand the importance of clothing.

Prerequisites   Bring materials of cotton, wool, and leather; some cotton seed; a cotton plant; carpet, yarn, thread, and other wool products; pictures telling the cotton and wool stories; lots of magazines; a tape recorder and teacher-prepared tapes of an imaginary visit to a cattle ranch; felt story figures and a flannel board.

Preassessment   Given several pieces of material each made from cotton, wool, and leather, each child will match these with pictures of cattle, sheep, and cotton plants, classifying according to the source of each material. To exit from the module, the child will respond correctly 100 percent of the time.

   After the preassessment, exit from the module or proceed to objectives.

Objective 1   The child will learn that some clothing is made from cotton and that cotton comes from cotton plants.

Activities   • After a discussion, the children will show their knowledge of picking and processing cotton by role playing the cotton story.
   • After seeing the cotton plant and pictures that tell the story of cotton, each child will show knowledge of cotton as a clothing source by acting out planting the cotton seeds, hoeing the cotton, picking the cotton, and tramping the cotton in the wagon.
   • After learning the song with the teacher, the children will sing and act out songs about cotton such as "This Is the Way We Pick the Cotton" to the tune of "This Is the Way We Wash Our Clothes," showing their knowledge of processing cotton. (Variation: "Pawpaw Patch," folksong taught as "Cotton Patch.")
   • Have a cotton day. Each child wearing cotton this day will model for the rest of the class to demonstrate his knowledge of clothes made from cotton. (Variations: Leather Day and Wool Day.)

Alternate Activities   *Simple Activity*
   To show they know the feel of cotton, the children will make a picture by gluing cotton and pieces of cotton cloth to construction paper. They will then share the result with the others.

   Advanced Activity
   Each child will make a loom and show how cotton threads are woven by using cotton loops, demonstrating a knowledge of cotton production. (Variation: Given a six-inch square of cotton cloth, the child unravels it to discover how it was woven together.

   Design your own activity to meet the needs of individual children.

Objective 2   The children will learn that we can make clothing from wool and that wool comes from sheep.

174

• Each child will look through a microscope at wool fibers to see how closely these fibers are clinging together, then discuss what he/she sees, thus demonstrating knowledge of how these fibers keep the sheep warm by not letting in the cold. (Variation: Compare cotton and wool under microscope and ask how tightly each is woven and which is warmer.)
• After making a display table of wool objects, the children will show their knowledge of wool objects by examining and discussing these objects. Objects may include yarn, carpet, thread, sweaters, scarves.
• The children will sing "Baa, Baa, Black Sheep," indicating their knowledge of where wool comes from.

Alternate Activities

Simple Activity
After a review of what wool is like, each child will demonstrate knowledge of wool materials by bringing from home material made of wool for the class to examine.

Advanced Activity
After seeing pictures of sheep shearing and fleece processing, each child will demonstrate knowledge of the shearing process by acting out shearing the sheep and taking the wool to the mill.

Design your own activity to meet the needs of individual children.

Objective 3

The children will learn where leather comes from and understand that some clothing is made from leather.

Activities

• To show knowledge of what leather is, the children will examine and discuss leather and leather products on a display table. (Variation: Children will bring leather products to put on the display table.)
• On a teacher-prepared tape, each child will hear of an imaginary trip to a cattle ranch. To show a knowledge of where leather comes from, each child will place on a flannel board felt figures about the story as the figures are introduced on the tape.
• Using old magazines, the children will cut out pictures of products made of leather, showing their knowledge of clothing made of leather. (Variation: Cut out pictures of cotton and wool products to put in the cotton and wool scrapbooks.)

Alternate Activities

Simple Activity
To demonstrate a knowledge that clothes are made of leather, each child will wear to school some clothing made from leather.

Advanced Activity
After the teacher has told the story of "The Shoemaker and the Elves," the children will act out the story, demonstrating their understanding of how some shoes are made from leather.

Design your own activity to meet the needs of individual children.

Postassessment

The postassessment is the same as the preassessment. After the postassessment, exit from the module or proceed to additional activities.

Additional Activities

• After a trip to a cotton gin, the children will show their knowledge of how seeds are separated from cotton by picking seeds from parts of the cotton plant and telling how difficult it is to separate them by hand.
• By weaving paper, the children will show their knowledge of how cloth is woven from cotton and woolen threads.
• Each child will examine and make things from scraps of shoe leather (from a shoe repair store) to demonstrate knowledge that shoes are made from leather. (The teacher should have several pairs of shoes on the leather scraps table to remind the child of the whole.)

Resources

Nighbert, Esther. *The True Book of Cloth.* Childrens Press, 1955.
World Book Encyclopedia. (See wool, cotton, and leather.)
Wurman, R. S. *Yellow Pages of Learning Resources.* Group for Environmental Education, Inc., 1972.

8.2 Appropriate Clothing

Rationale

To feel comfortable we need to know what clothing is suitable for certain weather conditions. The following module deals with clothes that should be worn in the winter and in the summer. Cotton clothing is worn in the summer and wool in the winter because of properties that keep the body either cool or warm. Good health and wearing appropriate clothing are related. Children often wear just what Mother tells them to, but they need to become aware of appropriate clothing so that they can dress themselves more intelligently.

Prerequisites

Have several sets of paper dolls, pieces of heavy material, pieces of light, cool material, and catalogs. (Include cotton and wool materials.) Do Module 8.1 before doing this module.

Preassessment

Given a set of paper dolls and clothing made of cotton and wool as well as appropriate styles for summer and winter, each child will dress the dolls for summer play and then dress the dolls in suitable winter clothes. The child will be able to do this with 100 percent accuracy. After this preassessment, exit from the module or proceed to the objectives.

Objective 1

The children will learn the kind of clothing suitable for summer wear.

Activities

• Given scissors and catalogs, the children will show their knowledge of what clothes should be worn in the summer by cutting out a summer wardrobe for role playing summer activities.
• After the teacher discusses with the children the cool clothes, such

as cotton, that should be worn in the summer, each child will demonstrate his knowledge of suitable summer clothes by dressing paper dolls for warm summer weather.

• While on a trip to the department store, the children will point out a playsuit, shorts, swim suits, or the like for summer, demonstrating their ability to recognize appropriate clothing.

Simple Activity
Each child will show knowledge of which clothing is appropriate for summer by using crayons to draw clothes on a picture (supplied by the teacher) of a child playing outside in warm weather.

More Advanced Activity
To demonstrate knowledge that cool, light clothes are to be worn in the summer, each child will find in the scrap box some scraps of cool, light material for summer and then examine these scraps with the teacher, comparing these with heavier scraps.

Design your own activity to meet the needs of individual children.

The children will learn that clothes worn in winter differ from those worn in summer.

Objective 2

• Following a class discussion started by the teacher, the child will dress a paper doll in paper clothes to demonstrate a knowledge of clothes worn in winter.
• Given a situation of a cold day, a snowy day, and a rainy day, the children will dress each other for going outside to play, thus showing their knowledge of clothing suitable for winter. (Keep a box of children's summer and winter clothing so that the children can dress up.)
• With assistance from the teacher, each child will select and cut out a winter wardrobe from a catalog, thereby showing knowledge of clothing appropriate for winter.

Activities

Simple Activity
To demonstrate their knowledge of cloth used in making some winter clothing, the children will bring scraps of heavy, warm material and make a winter clothing mural with the teacher's help.

Alternate activities

More Advanced Activities
• Each child will bring different textures of material and examine them for a class discussion, thus demonstrating knowledge that warm clothes are heavier and more tightly woven than cool clothes.
• Each child will show that he knows about seasonal clothing by putting on a style show called "Summer and Winter."

Design your own activity to meet the needs of individual children.

The postassessment is the same as the preassessment. After the postassessment, exit from the module or proceed to additional activities.

Postassessment

Additional Activities

- To demonstrate their knowledge of summer and winter clothing, the children will have a dress review. The children will dress in different cothing, some for summer and some for winter. As they model, they will tell whether they are dressed appropriately for summer or winter.
- The children will make a chart of summer and winter clothing. Each child will cut out clothing from a catalog and place it on the right chart, thus showing a knowledge of appropriate clothing.

Resources

Chamber, Helen G. *Clothing Selection*. Lippincott, 1961.

8.3 Seeing, Smelling, and Other Senses

Rationale

The five senses are a very important part of every human being, since without the five senses a person could not function. Each sense is unique in itself. Each child needs to be made aware of the important part that each sense plays in his or her life. Too often the senses are just listed as parts of the body, not studied in detail as they should be. The children should appreciate and respect their senses, for it is through their senses that they learn as well as enjoy life.

Prerequisites

Read *Our Senses and How They Work* by Herbert S. Zim. Gather magazines that will have pictures of all five senses. Make a feely box and gather different types of food. Borrow a model of the tongue. Collect an eye patch, a pair of sunglasses, eye makeup, a radio, and a tape player. Bring objects with a variety of odors, tin mirrors, paint and brushes, magazines for cutting out pictures, taped animal sounds, soft drinks of different flavors, two identical hot water bottles, feely boxes, lemons, sugar, pickles, sweet and sour apples, bitter chocolate, bitter lemon, an onion in a covered can, room deodorizers, flowers, and objects for the tresure hunt.

Preassessment

After showing a picture of a man, each child will tell what part of the body is used for seeing, for hearing, for feeling, for touching, or for smelling, demonstrating a knowledge of the five senses.

After this preassessment, exit from the module or proceed to the objectives.

Objective 1

Each child will understand what part of the body is used for seeing.

Activities

- Given a patch, a pair of sunglasses, a pair of glasses, binoculars, goggles, eye makeup, and pictures of people who wear them, all located in the housekeeping center of the classroom, the children will discover the uses of the objects by experimentation to demonstrate their awareness of the five senses.

8.3 Using the eyes

• Each child will show a knowledge of the eyes by drawing a picture of his/her eyes (aided by a mirror) and all the things those eyes like to see.

• Using paint colors of their choice, paint brushes, and easel paper, the children will paint their impressions of what they see when they look around the classroom, showing awareness of seeing as a sense.

Simple Activity
Each child will demonstrate knowledge of where the eyes are located by putting his/her hands over another child's eyes. While the teacher asks, "Who is covering your eyes?" the other child listens to the first child or feels his/her face to determine identity.

Advanced Activity
Given a series of pictures with eyes in them, each child will show ability to identify what sense organ is used for seeing by picking the eyes out of the pictures when asked, "Where are the weepers?" "Where are the blinkers?" "What sparkles and tells people you are laughing inside?" "What do you use to watch TV with?"

Alternate Activities

179

Design your own activity to meet the needs of individual children.

Objective 2   Each child will understand what part of the body is used for hearing.

Activities
- Each child will explain where the ears are located by pointing to his/her own ears when the teacher says, "Bunnies have big, long ones to hear sounds in the forest. Where are yours?" "What are they called?" "What do you do with them?"
- After hearing a series of taped animal sounds, each child will demonstrate what was heard by imitating the sound.
- Given a radio, tape player, record player, and telephone located in the music center of the classroom, each child will find out about hearing by listening to each with and without ear muffs.

Alternate Activities

Simple Activity
Each child will demonstrate the sense of hearing by listening to a tape of the nursery rhyme "Old Woman in the Shoe" and then repeating it. (Tape should ask at the end if the children listened with their eyes, tongue, skin, or nose and so on.)

Advanced Activity
After listening to a series of soft and loud sounds, each child will demonstrate an ability to use his/her ears with comprehension by repeating the series of soft and loud sounds with eyes open and eyes closed.

Design your own activity to meet the needs of individual children.

Objective 3   Each child will understand what part of the body is used for testing.

Activities
- The children will demonstrate what sense organ is used for taste by drinking a bottle of their favorite soft drink with a straw, testing the liquid on the hand, holding the bottle near the ear, putting a drop on end of the tongue, the middle, and the back to see where taste occurs.
- After a food-tasting party, each child will explain what sense organ he used by moving the food around the mouth until it touches the taste buds the teacher has shown the class on a model of the tongue.
- The children will show what sense they use for identifying small discs of candy in different flavors.

Alternate Activities

Simple Activity
After cooking and eating popcorn, each child will show what sense organ is used in tasting by coloring a picture of the tongue with popcorn on it.

More Advanced Activity
After a discussion with the teacher, each child will demonstrate knowledge of the different kinds of taste (sweet, bitter, sour, and salty) by tasting and naming these different tastes when experiencing lemons,

180

lemonade before and after sugar has been added, sour pickle, sour apple, sweet apple, and bitter chocolate or bitter lemon (mixer for highballs).

Design your own activity to meet the needs of individual children.

Each child will understand what parts of the body are used for feeling.

Objective 4

• While blindfolded, the children will demonstrate the sense of feeling by putting a finger, an elbow, a toe, and their backs on a hot water bottle filled with hot water and an identical one filled with cold water.
• Given a covered box with several different types and kinds of objects, each child will show what feeling is by putting a hand into the box, describing the object handled, and telling what sense is used.
• Each child will demonstrate one use of feeling by touching five things in the room and telling the teacher how they feel (soft, smooth, rough, and so on).

Activities

Simple Activity
After a discussion on what feeling is, each child will show understanding of feeling by naming things that are hot and cold. (Variation: naming things that are sharp or dull, rough or smooth.)

Alternate Activities

Advanced Activity
Each child will demonstrate what feeling is by listening to a story and discussing the touching words in the story. (Choose a story for its touching words.)

Design your own activity to meet the needs of individual children.

Each child will understand what part of the body is used in smelling.

Objective 5

• Given a series of things to smell, each child will show what smell is by listening to an onion hidden in a smell can and then smelling it. The child will tell what sense was used to reveal what the onion was. (Variation: smelly objects besides onions.)
• The children will discover that things have different odors by smelling a variety of objects that have different odors and by smelling different objects that have been placed in the classroom for smelling, such as scented room deodorizers placed in three different parts of the room.
• After a discussion on what sense organ is used in smelling, each child will indicate what sense organ is used by making a nose of clay and putting something under it that is good to smell.

Activities

Simple Activity
After the teacher has shared three scented flowers with the class, such as a rose, a carnation, and sweet peas, each child will show what smell is by naming and describing something enjoyable to smell.

Alternate Activities

More Advanced Activity
After being blindfolded and while being led about by the teacher, each child will name as many classroom objects as possible that have a smell.

Design your own activity to meet the needs of individual children.

Postassessment

The postassessment is the same as the preassessment. After the postassessment, exit from the module or proceed to additional activities.

Additional Activities

• Given a picture of a man with the five senses removed, each child will show where the senses are by pasting the five senses in the proper places.
• The children will demonstrate their knowledge of the five senses by going on a treasure hunt using each of the other senses.)

Resources

Brenner, Barbara. *Faces.* E. P. Dutton, 1970.
Elgin, Kathleen. *Read About the Ear.* Franklin Watts, Inc., 1967.
_____. *Read About the Eyes.* Franklin Watts, Inc., 1967.
Froman, Robert. *The Many Human Senses.* Little, Brown, 1966.
Liberty, Gene. *The First Book of the Human Senses.* Franklin Watts, Inc., 1967.

8.4 Care of the Five Senses

Rationale

Taking care of the five senses is a very important part of health care. If the care of the five senses is neglected, a person's general health suffers, so important a role does each sense play in every human life. The role of the teacher is to help each child be more aware of the senses and how to keep them functioning effectively.

Prerequisites

Do Module 8.3 before doing this module.
Obtain a filmstrip on the care of the five senses. Bring to class a washcloth and soap. Have a model of each of the senses, puppets, a collection of objects, tapes and accompanying pictures as described, sunglasses, goggles, taped music, tissues, and stuffed toys such as teddy bears.

Preassessment

• Each child will demonstrate knowledge of how to care for the eyes and ears by answering the following questions: (a) Do we stick objects into our eyes and ears? (b) Why not? (c) Why should we wash our eyes and ears every day? (d) Why should we not hit anyone in the eyes or ears?
• Each child will explain his knowledge of how to care for the five senses by answering the following questions: (1) How do we take care of our sense of smell? (2) How do we take care of our sense of taste? and (3) How do we take care of our sense of touch?
After this preassessment, exit from the module or proceed to the objectives.

Each child will understand how to care for eyes and ears.

• After a discussion and demonstration on how to care for the eyes and ears, each child will show understanding by cleaning the eyes and ears. (Include instruction on not looking directly at the sun and not listening to music that is too loud.)
• To show understanding of proper care of eyes and ears, each child will, with puppets, explain why we should keep our eyes and ears clean, explaining what could happen to the eyes and ears if we did not keep them clean.
• After a discussion of what we don't put in the eyes and ears and why, each child will indicate an awareness by selecting from a collection of objects what can be used. (Example: washrag and water.)

Simple Activity
After the teacher demonstrates with a puppet why we do not hit a person in the eyes and ears, each child will show understanding by reenacting the drama with the puppets.

More Advanced Activity
After a filmstrip or film on the proper care of the eyes and ears, each child will explain how to care for these senses by drawing two ways to take care of each.

Design your own activity to meet the needs of individual children.

Each child will understand how to care for his/her senses of taste, smell, and touch.

• After hearing a story adapted from information in the resources of the module, each child will explain why the skin should be cared for, telling what could happen if it were not.
• After hearing a teacher-prepared tape on care of the nose, each child will show understanding by putting accompanying story pictures in order. (Pictures should include scenes of going to the doctor and of the pain caused by having an object removed.) (Variation: a tape and pictures on what we don't drink or eat and why.)
• After a discussion and a demonstration on how to clean skin, mouth, and nose, each child will demonstrate understanding by cleaning his/her own skin, mouth, and nose.

Simple Activity
After a review with the teacher, each child will show the proper way to care for skin, mouth, and nose by selecting from an assortment of pictures on the subject those scenes that show how to correctly care for skin, mouth, and nose.

More Advanced Activity
After watching a filmstrip on the care of the nose, skin, and mouth, each child will explain the correct way to care for these areas of the

body by role playing a teacher-written story such as "The Nose without a Tissue," "The Skin That Crawled," or "The Mouth That Wouldn't Listen" (and so burned itself).

Design your own activity to meet the needs of individual chidren.

Postassessment

The postassessment is the same as the preassessment. After the postassessment, exit from the module or proceed to additional activities.

Additional Activities

• Given plastic models of the eyes, ears, nose, skin, and mouth, each child will show how to care for each by washing them and by putting sunglasses or goggles on the eyes, playing soft music near the ears, and wiping the nose correctly with throw-away tissues.
• Each child will demonstrate skill in sense care by caring for a toy bear's senses.

Resources

Froman, Robert. *The Many Human Senses.* Little, Brown, 1966.
Puron, Heni. *The Sensations, Their Functions, Processes and Mechanisms.* Yale University Press, 1952.
Wilenty, Joan Steen. *The Senses of Man.* Crowell, 1968.
Zim, Herbert Spencer. *Our Senses and How They Work.* W. Morrow, 1956.

8.5 Brushing the Teeth

Rationale

People rarely do anything just because they are frightened into it; for example, few quit smoking for fear of lung cancer, or wear seat belts because they fear traffic fatalities. Instead, people do things because they are educated to do them, or because it simply seems to be the thing to do. Young children don't learn to take good care of their teeth only because it is good for them or because they develop painful, smelly, and ugly cavities if they don't. Children learn to care for their teeth because the teacher, a respected adult, stresses the importance of good dental care, including proper brushing and dental checkups.

Prerequisites

Obtain from a toothpaste company a free classroom supply of toothbrushes and toothpaste, or ask each child to bring a toothbrush and you as teacher supply the toothpaste. Also, invite a dental hygienist and have available a supply of dental floss, paper cups, and tin mirrors.

Preassessment

• Each child will demonstrate knowledge of the proper way to brush teeth. The child will then use dental floss.
• To demonstrate knowledge of brushing and having checkups, each

184

child will tell the teacher when a person should brush teeth (after meals) and have checkups (twice a year).
After doing the preassessment, exit from the module or proceed to the objectives.

Each child will learn the proper way to brush his teeth.

• Each child will demonstrate awareness of healthy teeth by drawing on plain paper a smile showing clean teeth.
• Each child will demonstrate knowledge of the parts of the toothbrush by drawing and cutting out a paper toothbrush.
• The children will use their paper smiles and toothbrushes to pantomime the teacher as she demonstrates the proper technique of brushing.
• Each child will demonstrate knowledge of proper brushing by doing so with a dry brush in front of mirror and the teacher.

Activities

Simple Activity
The children will play a guessing game as each child uses his/her finger as a brush to show either the correct or the incorrect way to brush a doll's teeth or a set of model teeth.

Alternate Activities

More Advanced Activity
The children will draw a picture of a girl or boy who brushes properly and a picture of a boy or girl who never brushes, showing and telling how the teeth of the children in their pictures are different from their own.

Design your own activities to meet the needs of individual children.

The children will learn the proper times to brush their teeth and to have dental checkups.

Objective 2

• After inviting a dental hygienist to their classroom to discuss proper ways and times to brush and to visit the dentist, each child will be able to tell the teacher when to brush and when to go to the dentist.
• After seeing and listening to the films about Dottie, the hand puppet (see resources), each child will answer correctly the question, "When should you brush your teeth?"

Activities

Simple Activity
The children will demonstrate their knowledge of the importance of brushing their teeth after they eat by including such a statement in an oral story of "The Things I Do Before I Come to School," dictated to the teacher or put on tape by the child.

Alternate Activities

More Advanced Activity
The children will demonstrate their knowledge of the importance of dental checkups by dramatizing a visit to a dentist office.

Design your own activities to meet the needs of individual children.

Postassessment

The postassessment is the same as the preassessment. After the postassessment, exit from the module or proceed to additional activities.

Additional Activities

• Using a clean toothbrush (no toothpaste), the children will act out the words as the teacher sing-songs the following chant:

Brush your teeth the way they grow, down from the top and up from below. This is what you need to know, brush your teeth the way they grow. Inside and out and on the top, brush them clean before you stop.

• The children will sing and act out "The Brushing Song," sung to the tune of "The Mulberry Bush:"

This is the way we brush our teeth, brush our teeth, brush our teeth. This is the way we brush our teeth, right after we eat.

After completing this module, study the children's needs and design activities for the individual students who are still having difficulties.

Resources
Books

Berland, Theodore and Seytor, Alfred. *Your Children's Teeth.* Meredith Press, 1968.
Jubelier, Ruth. *About Jack's Dental Check-Up.* 1961.

Films

Dottie and Her Dad and *Dottie and Dentist.* American Dental Association. (*Note:* these 4½ minute, 16mm films may be borrowed free of charge from the American Dental Association, Bureau of Audiovisual Service, 211 East Chicago Avenue, Chicago, Illinois, 60611.)

8.6 Feeding the Teeth

Rationale

Proper food is necessary for good health and a pleasing appearance. Kindergarten seems to be a good time to introduce children to the proper foods for their teeth, because early eating habits, when the teeth are forming, can affect dental health.

Prerequisites

Obtain from a dentist X-rays of good and bad teeth. (Borrower pays return postage via insured parcel post. Send request on school stationery about seven months in advance.) Have on hand pictures, combs, tin mirror, model of human teeth, pan and hotplate, apples, candy bars, block, soft drink, milk, sandwiches, sugar, water, potatoes, Dixie cups, toothbrushes, and dental disclosing tablets.

8.6 Feeding the teeth

Preassessment

● Given four pictures each of candy, fruits, and vegetables, each child will choose the four pictures of the candy when asked to pick out the foods that cause the most cavities.
● Given pictures of different liquids, each child will demonstrate knowledge of the importance of milk in developing good healthy teeth by correctly choosing the pictures of milk when asked to pick those liquids that are best for the teeth.
After this preassessment, exit from the module or proceed to the objectives.

Objective 1

Each child will learn that sticky foods (foods containing quantities of sugar) cause more cavities than do fruits or vegetables.

Activities

Each child will demonstrate the difficulty of cleaning teeth coated with sugar substances by using a toothbrush to clean the teeth of a comb that has been spread with syrup. This syrup should be made in the classroom from sugar and water cooked in a pan on a hotplate. Each child will compare the difficulty of cleaning the coated comb with that of cleaning the uncoated comb.
● Using mashed potatoes prepared in the classroom, each child will demonstrate the relative ease of cleaning teeth covered with this vegetable by using a toothbrush to clean the teeth of a comb spread with mashed potatoes.
● To show the relative ease of cleaning teeth coated with a fruit, each child will rub the teeth of a comb with a slice of an apple and then brush the comb clean with a toothbrush.

Alternate Activities

Simple Activity
To demonstrate that sticky foods (foods containing sugar) are more difficult to clean from teeth than fruits, each child will eat a candy bar,

187

brush his/her teeth, chew a dental disclosing tablet, rinse, look in a mirror and then repeat this procedure after eating an apple. Each child will then be able to tell why more red spots appeared after the candy.

More Advanced Activity
Each child will make a picture book of good choices of foods for snacks to show an understanding that fruits are less harmful to teeth than sweets (sticky foods).

Design your own activities to meet the needs of individual children.

Objective 2

Each child will learn that high protein foods are important in developing healthy teeth.

Activities

- After a discussion by the teacher on protein (its importance to good health and the foods that contain it), each child will demonstrate an understanding that milk contains the ingredients needed for healthy teeth by drawing a picture of milk when asked to draw a picture of the liquid that is best for teeth.
- Given pictures of a sandwich, a candy bar, milk, and soda pop, each child will show knowledge of the protein foods by picking the correct pictures when asked to choose the foods that would help make teeth stronger.
- Given blocks covered with pictures of protein foods, the children will use these to build with, showing their understanding that protein foods are the building blocks of healthy teeth.

Alternate Activities

Simple Activity
Each child will demonstrate knowledge of the importance of milk by correctly choosing, from small paper cups of milk, water, and soft drink, the one that is best for teeth and then drinking it.

More Advanced Activity
After seeing and discussing X-rays of healthy and unhealthy teeth, each child will demonstrate knowledge of what makes teeth healthy or unhealthy by making a paper hand puppet of a "good" tooth and a "bad" one and dramatizing a story of how each tooth got to be "good" and "bad" (i.e., what foods made it that way).

Design your own activities to meet the needs of individual children.

Postassessment

The postassessment is the same as the preassessment. After the postassessment, exit from the module or proceed to additional activities.

Additional Activities

- Each child will demonstrate awareness of the possible effects of frequently eating sweets by correctly matching pictures of fruits and vegetables with pictures of healthy teeth and pictures of candy with pictures of decayed teeth. (Pictures of decayed teeth can be made by cutting pictures of healthy teeth from a magazine and shading in spots to resemble cavities.)

• Given a small sandwich, candy bar, glass of milk, and soft drink, each child will show knowledge by picking the best foods when asked to choose the foods that will help make teeth stronger.
After completing this module, study the children's need and design activities for individual students.

Jameson, Dee Dee. "What Do They Know from Bacon and Eggs?" *Childhood Education,* January 1975, pp. 145-49.

Resources

8.7 Skin

It is very important that the young child learn some basics about the care of the skin if he/she is to develop into a healthy adult. Cleanliness will help control germs which can be transferred from the hands to foods the child puts in the mouth. A child who learns about the skin has learned something about the sense of touch as well as a few basic concepts to build on in later school units.

Rationale

Obtain a microscope, vitamin A and basic food group pictures, manicure sets, white towels, and skin care kits, including soap and washcloths.

Prerequisites

• Each child will show knowledge of skin care by telling four ways to care for the skin.
• Each child will show understanding of the skin's functions by stating three skin functions. (The skin is used for feeling temperature changes, and the texture of objects, as eyelids to keep dirt out of the eyes, and to detect shapes of objects.)
After this preassessment, exit from module or proceed to the objectives.

Preassessment

The children will learn some ways of caring for their skin.

Objective 1

• After the teacher demonstrates how to wash hands correctly, using soap, water, and a towel, the child will indicate knowledge of how to wash hands by washing his/her hands properly. (Child should clean fingernails, both sides of hands, and between fingers.)
• Given a manicure set, each child will show understanding of nail care by manicuring his/her fingernails after a demonstration by the teacher. (Nails protect the skin on the fingers and toes.)
• Following a class discussion of good and bad foods for the skin, the child will demonstrate skill in choosing foods that help produce a healthy skin by pointing to the best foods from a group of bulletin board pictures showing foods good and bad for the skin. (See books in resource section for best foods.)

Activities

• Interested students, through self-initiated activity, will demonstrate their understanding of skin care by using skin care kits correctly, after several class discussions on the importance of skin care.
• After hearing a talk on cleanliness from the school nurse, each child will show understanding of skin cleanliness by telling what times during the day hands should be washed.
• Immediately following a short talk from a dermatologist about skin care and the effects of the sun, each child will indicate a knowledge of skin care by telling several ways to protect or care for skin in severe weather.

Alternate Activities

Simple Activity
Given a simple picture to look at while the teacher makes comments about skin care, the child will show knowledge of skin care by telling what skin care activity the person in the picture is doing.

More Advanced Activity
After seeing a film on skin care (see resources), the child will demonstrate an understanding of skin care by pantomiming all of the ways skin should be cared for as shown on the film. The other children should guess the actions.

Design your own activity to meet the needs of individual children.

Objective 2

Each child will understand some of the functions of the skin.

Activities

• During a game where one child at a time is blindfolded and touched by some object, the blindfolded child will demonstrate an understanding that skin has feeling by saying, "I felt something," each time he/she feels an object.
• The students will observe the ridges on the fingertips by looking at their fingers under a microscope. After the teacher explains that the ridges can feel rough or smooth, the child will indicate an understanding of the function of the fingertip ridges by trying them out (while blindfolded) with sandpaper, corduroy, brick, smooth tile, a plastic bag, a piece of concrete, and a smooth pebble.
• Given an array of objects that differ in smoothness and roughness, each child will demonstrate skill in choosing rough objects and smooth objects by putting the smooth objects in one container and the rough objects in another container. (Variation: Try to sort objects using the toes, the back of the hand, the heel of the foot.)
• Following a discussion of fingernails and toenails as protectors for our fingers and toes, the child will show an understanding of the function of the fingernails and toenails by stating why we need them.
• After the teacher explains how eyelids keep dirt out of our eyes, the children will indicate that they know the function of our eyelids by telling of experiences when they got something in their eyes.

Alternate Activities

Simple Activity
After the child has been touched on the body with an object, each child will indicate an awareness that skin has feeling by telling where he/she was touched while blindfolded.

More Advanced Activity
While looking at a covered bowl, the child will demonstrate knowledge of the function of eyelids by telling how the cover over a bowl is like an eyelid over the eye. (The cover protects or keeps dirt out.)

Design your own activity to meet the needs of individual children.

The postassessment is the same as the preassessment. After the postassessment, exit from the module or proceed to additional activities.

Postassessment

• After the child is given assistance in skin care, he/she will indicate an understanding of skin care by telling one way to care for the skin.
• After listening to stories adapted from books on functions of the skin and while looking at pictures in the books, the child will show a knowledge of skin functions by telling three functions of the skin.

Additional Activities

Adelborg, Ottilia. *Clean Peter and the Children of Grubbylea.*
Elgin, Kathleen. *The Eye.* 1967.
McCullers, Carson. *Sweet As a Pickle and Clean As a Pig.* 1964.
McGovern, Ann. *The Question and Answer Book about the Human Body.* 1965.
O'Neill, Mary. *Fingers Are Always Bringing Me News.* 1969.
Showers, Paul. *Your Skin and Mine.* 1965.
Steinsiek, Ruth. *Some Days Are Magic Days.*
Weart, Edith Lucie. *The Story of Your Skin.* 1970.
Wilcox, Charlotte, and Bolton, William. *Healthy Days.* 1961.
Zim, Herbert S. *Our Senses and How They Work.* 1956.

Resources
Books

Soapy, the Germ Fighter. MacMullan Films, Inc. 1974.

Film

8.8 Hair Care

Because well-groomed hair does contribute greatly to the health and appearance of an individual, teachers need to impress upon the young child the importance of caring for his/her hair. Hair is also a protecion to the head against cold, heat, and injury. It deserves the very best treatment.

Rationale

Have on hand shampoo and several mirrors. Have each child bring a comb, brush, and towel.

Prerequisites

The children will show their understanding of hair grooming by telling of four ways to care for the hair. (Trimming makes it neater and easier to brush or comb; keeping the scalp clean leads to a healthy

Preassessment

scalp without lice; brushing and combing correctly using one's own comb and brush prevents the spread of germs; washing the comb and brush frequently keeps the hair clean.)

After the preassessment, exit from the module or proceed to the objective.

Objective   Each child will learn some ways to keep the hair healthy and well groomed.

Activities

• The children will take a trip to the barber shop, where the barber will discuss how trimming the hair makes it neater and easier to brush and comb, and then the barber will give a demonstration by trimming someone's hair. Later, as the children trim doll hair in their barber shop at school, they will indicate their understanding of the purpose of trimming the hair.

• Shortly after a trip to the beauty shop to see the beauty operator wash hair as she explains the importance of keeping the hair and scalp clean, the children will show, by stating the reason, that they know the purpose for washing hair regularly.

• The children will show an understanding of how to comb and brush the hair by combing and brushing their hair properly after the teacher demonstrates and discusses the importance of each. The children will sing, "This Is the Way We Comb (or Brush) Our Hair" to the tune of "This Is the Way We Wash Our Clothes."

• Supplied with shampoo, water, and towel, each child will indicate knowledge of how to wash the hair by washing a doll's hair under the supervision of the teacher.

• After class discussion and hearing books read on the subject, each child will indicate an awareness of the importance of using one's own comb, brush, and towel by stating the reasons.

Alternate Activities

Simple Activity
While looking at several objects that do and do not pertain to caring for the hair, the child will show an understanding of hair grooming by pointing to and saying the names of all those things used in taking care of the hair.

More Advanced Activity
After he has had opportunity to learn about proper hair care, the child will indicate an awareness of good hair grooming habits by deciding upon and drawing five things needed to care for the hair.

Design your own activity to meet the needs of individual children.

Postassessment   The postassessment is the same as the preassessment. After the postassessment, exit from the module or proceed to additional activities.

Additional Activities

• After the teacher discusses several things that contribute to good hair care, the child will show knowledge of hair grooming by telling

192

about one thing used in hair care.

● Given several hair grooming pictures to look at, the child will demonstrate skill at hair care by performing each of the actions suggested, playing in the Barber Shop/Beauty Parlor Learning Center in the classroom.

Keen, Martin. *The How and Why Wonder Book of the Human Body.* 1961.

Leaf, Munro. *Health Can Be Fun.* 1943.

Schneider, Robert. *Health and Growth.* 1967.

Resources

8.9 The Food Machines

Rationale

Most textbooks omit nutrition or good nutritive habits in young children as a part of the curriculum. Does this mean that the parents are the sole teachers of this part of the curriculum? The elementary school curriculum usually covers the basic food groups, but eating habits start much earlier than that.

A health hazard to young children, older children, and adults is lack of knowledge of what to eat or not eat from the many food-dispensing machines. The machines seem to be everywhere. They contain gum, candy, soft drinks, milk, other beverages, pies, crackers and cheese, crackers and peanut butter, sandwiches, and many other foods. The problem is to learn to select what the body needs. It is a matter of good nutrition and nutritive habits.

It would be unrealistic for the teacher to say that children should never eat from the food machines, because they are going to anyhow. It is more realistic to say that milk is better than coffee, tea, or soft drinks. With the milk the child could eat a pie for dessert after a balanced meal, or cheese and crackers for a snack.

To prepare for teaching from this module, the teacher should observe what the students buy from food machines and what kinds of food machines are in the community—to see what is sold that might make a nutritious snack, dessert, or lunch. The student's present habits and the foods available in machines become the teacher's starting point for improving nutritive habits in the children. Part of the module might deal with sharing the information with parents so that they can better supervise what the children buy.

Prerequisites

Have on hand many examples of food from food machines (you can save money by using an empty milk carton, an empty candy wrapper, cap labels and similar items); a simulated food machine with a money slot, play money, and pictures of what can be bought (changed according to the lesson) with a child behind it to catch money and operate the machine with simulated products; flannel board, and felt cutouts of foods.

Preassessment

● To demonstrate that they know how to choose a healthful snack from food machines, the children will choose from an assortment of

food machine items (on a table) the best snack items. Examples: milk with cheese and crackers, an orange, or an apple.
• To demonstrate knowledge of what is best to buy for a good lunch, each child will choose from a combination of items on a display table of food-machine items those that make the most nutritive lunch (e.g., milk with cheese or meat sandwich and an orange; soup, milk, a sandwich, and an apple).
• Same as preceding activity, except that foods should be for a good dessert after a well-balanced meal somewhere else (e.g., an orange, an apple, or a piece of fruit pie and some milk).

Objective 1   The children will learn what to choose from the food machines for a nutritious snack.

Activities   • After a discussion of what makes a good snack, each child will show understanding by going to the classroom's cardboard food machine (see prerequisites section of this module) and purchasing a good snack. (Child should get coins back if he/she purchases the right combination.) The teacher operating the machine should say something complimentary.
• Each child will indicate an ability to select nutritious foods by purchasing an appropriate snack from the food machine after a puppet play (put on by the teacher) in which Rinky Snacker gets a toothache and stomachache from eating only candy from food machines, while Smart Snacker feels good all day because he purchased a nutritious snack.

Alternate Activities   *Simple Activity*
After a demonstration in which the teacher puts good snack items in a box decorated with a smiling face and poor ones in a box decorated with a frowning face, each child will demonstrate knowledge of a good snack by imitating the teacher under the teacher's supervision. (A small group activity.)

More Advanced Activity
To show understanding of what makes a good snack, each child will cut out a picture of one or two snacks and put them in the food machine for choosing at snack time.

Design your own activity to meet the needs of individual children.

Objective 2   The children will learn what to choose from the food machines for a nutritious lunch and/or dessert.

Activities   • After showing two items from each of the four basic food groups (items that could be found in food machines), each child will indicate an understanding of what to buy for a food-machine lunch by choosing one from at least three of the four groups.
• After discussing what food machine foods make good desserts, each

child will show an understanding by making a happy face for a good choice and a sad face for a poor choice when shown pictures of food-machine items.

Simple Activity
Given an array of good lunch and dessert items from food machines—except for one poor item—each child will indicate an understanding of what makes a good lunch and dessert by putting the good lunch items together, and then the good dessert items together, excluding the one poor item.

More Advanced Activity
The children will play charades to show their understanding of what makes a good lunch or a good dessert. (For example, if the item to be guessed is apple pie, the child claps hands twice to signal that it is a dessert, once for lunch. The child smiles and rubs his/her stomach to indicate that it is a good dessert, then picks apples off an imaginary tree to indicate that it is a fruit, and pretends to make a pie, putting it into an oven and taking it out. The other children have to guess what the food is.)

Design your own activity to meet the needs of individual children.

The postassessment is the same as the preassessment. After the postassessment, exit from the module or proceed to additional activities.

• After a review by the teacher and during a field trip where there are food machines, the children will show their knowledge of a good snack, by buying wisely from the food available.
• *The best machine in the world.* The children will show their ability to buy nutritious snacks, lunches, and desserts from food machines by playing this game: Each child is dealt seven cards (each card is a picture of a good food item or a bad food item). When it is a child's turn, that child must throw one bad food item into a garbage box in the center of the table. He must also let the child on the right draw one of his cards. The game continues until one child declares that he has a good lunch, snack, or dessert left in his hand.

Babbit, Natalie. *The Search for Delicious.* Farrar, 1969.
Borghese, Anita. *The Down-to-Earth Cookbook.* Scribner, 1973.
Childcraft, vol. 1. Field Educational Corp., 1974. (Poems and rhymes on food.)
Coff, Vicke. *Science Experiments You Can Eat.* Lippincott 1972.
Ferreira, Nancy. "Teacher's Guide to Educational Cooking in the Nursery school." *Young Children*, November 1973.
Goodspeed. *Let's Go to the Dairy.* 1956.
Green, Carla. *I Want to Be a Storekeeper.* Childrens Press, 1958.
Hinshaw, Alice. *The True Book of Your Body and You.* 1959.
Hope, John. *The Amazing Seeds.* Watts, 1965.
Kahl, Virginia. *The Duchess Bakes a Cake.* Scribner, 1955.

Alternate Activitis

Postassessment

Additional activities

Resources

Krauss, Ruth. *The Carrot Seed.* Harper and Row, 1945.

Lauber, Patricia. *Your Body and How It Works.* 1962.

Longstaff, John and Carol. *Shimmy Shimmy Coke-Ca-Pop!* Doubleday, 1973.

Meyer, Carolyn. *The Bread Book; All About Bread and How to Make It.* Harcourt, 1971.

Petersham, Maud and Miska. *The Storybook of Foods from the Fields.* E. M. Hale and Co., 1936.

Raskin, Edith. *World Food.* McGraw-Hill, 1971.

Rinkoff, Barbara. *Guess What the Grasses Do.* Lothrop, 1972.

Sawyer, Ruth. *Journey Cake, Ho!* Viking, 1953.

Schneider, Robert E. *Health and Growth.* Boston; Allyn and Bacon, Inc., 1967.

Selsam, Millicent. *The Apple and Other Fruits.* Morrow, 1973.

Skelsey, Alice, and Huckaby, Gloria. *Growing up Green—Parents and Children Gardening Together.* Workman, 1973.

The World Book Encyclopedia. (Latest edition.) See *nutrition* and *milk* for good background sections.

8.10 A Better breakfast

Rationale

Old or young, everyone needs a nutritious breakfast. There's no better way to get the morning going. Breakfast gives pep and energy to get the morning's work done. The question is, do some children eat a better breakfast than others? The purpose of this module is to help children learn to eat a better breakfast.

Prerequisites

Have on hand drawing paper, crayons, old magazines, coat hangers, yarn, construction paper, empty food containers (for a store), food and utensils for preparing a real breakfast; *A Right Breakfast,* by Hester Bland and Malcolm McLellan (a filmstrip by the American Medical Association), or a similar filmstrip on breakfast nutrition; "The Good Health Train" by Gloria Voorhees (*Grade Teacher,* October 1959), and "Alexander's Breakfast Secret."

Preassessment

Given magazine pictures of different kinds of foods, each child will show understanding of what constitutes a nutritious breakfast by choosing a breakfast from the pictures and including at least one item from each of the four basic food groups (milk group, vegetable-fruit group, meat group, and bread-cereal group).

Following the preassessment, exit from the module or proceed to the objective.

Objective

Each child will learn to choose a nutritious breakfast by choosing foods from each of the four basic food groups.

8.10 Buying a nutritious breakfast

Activities

• After the teacher reads the story "The Good Health Train" by Gloria Voorhees, each child will show understanding of a nutritious breakfast by making a good health train from construction paper, including an engine, caboose, and four cars on which pictures of foods from the basic four have been pasted (each car representing one basic food group).

• After each child has drawn a picture of his/her breakfast for that morning, each child will show an understanding of a nutritious breakfast by telling how many of the four basic food groups are included in or omitted from the picture.

• After viewing the filmstrip *A Right Breakfast* or a similar filmstrip on breakfast nutrition, each child will show an understanding of the concept of a nutritious breakfast by making a mobile (use a coat hanger, yarn, and pictures of food cut from magazines) and including at least one item from each of the four basic food groups in the mobile.

• After a discussion about the time lapse between the evening meal and breakfast (as compared with the lapse between breakfast and lunch), each child will show an understanding of how important a good breakfast is by counting and comparing the number of hours between dinner and breakfast and the number of hours between breakfast and lunch.

• Given a blank sheet of paper and crayons, each child will show an understanding of what a good breakfast consists of by making a breakfast menu that includes at least one item from each of the basic four. Have the children take their menus home and ask their mothers to prepare the breakfast the child's menu suggests.

• After children have cut from magazines pictures of different kinds of breakfast foods, each child will show an understanding of a better breakfast by pinning the pictures on a bulletin board subdivided to represent the seven days of a week.

197

• After reading the story "Alexander's Breakfast Secret," each child will show an understanding of how important a good breakfast is by reading and taking home a breakfast letter asking Mother to remind him/her to eat a good breakfast.

• After each child assumes the name of a breakfast food (John is an egg, Susan is a piece of bacon, Mary is a glass of orange juice) and is given a tag to wear to show what food is represented, each child will show understanding of what a nutritious breakfast consists of by grouping with others into nutritious breakfasts. (Teacher may want to use costumes and put on a small play.)

Alternate Activities

Simple Activity
Each child will demonstrate understanding of a good breakfast by learning the "Wow Breakfast Chant." (The chant is at the back of this module.)

More Advanced Activity
Given materials to make a booklet, each child will show understanding of a nutritious breakfast by making a full week's menus (seven breakfasts) and putting them into this booklet entitled, "Better Breakfasts." (Remember to have all food groups represented in each breakfast.)

Design your own activity for certain children according to their needs and learning styles.

Postassessment

The postassessment is the same as the preassessment. After the postassessment, exit from the module or proceed to additional activities.

Additional Activities

• Having brought into the classroom empty egg cartons, cereal boxes, milk cartons, orange juice cans, and other breakfast food containers, the children will show an understanding of a good breakfast by setting up a school store and using play money to purchase a balanced breakfast.

• After all preparations have been made (foods decided on and bought, committees set up to prepare food, and so on), each child will show an understanding of a nutritious breakfast by preparing and eating breakfast at school.

Sample Breakfast Menu

Scrambled eggs with ham
Toast and margarine
Orange juice
Milk

• After hearing "The King's Breakfast" by A. A. Milne (see resources), each child will show an understanding of a better breakfast by adding food ideas to bread and butter (mentioned in the poem) until a better breakfast for the king is designed.

Milne, A. A. *The World of Christopher Robin.* E. P. Dutton and Co., 1958.

Seuss. *Green Eggs and Ham.* Random House, 1958.

———. *Scrambled Egg Supper.* Random House, 1958.

Zim, Herbert S. *Your Food and You.* William Morrow and Co., 1957.

The Good Health Train*

Once upon a time there was a little black engine. He had big round wheels, a smokestack, and a window for the engineer to see out. He had a white flag and the flag said GOOD HEALTH TRAIN. He was so new that he had never gone any place at all. He had just been moved from the factory where he was built to the roundhouse where he would work.

He had heard the men talking and he knew that he was going to pull a train to the Town of Good Health. He was so excited that he could hardly wait to begin. Very early the first morning he looked around him and saw a bright red car with a flag over it. The flag said MEAT. "I just know that is the car I am to take to Good Health Town," he said. So he chugged over to the red car and hooked it on. Then he went chugging down the track toward Good Health. He felt so proud and happy!

Just before he came to the edge of the town, a big black engine came out to meet him. "Stop! Stop!" shouted the big black engine. "You can't come into Good Health Town with nothing but meat. It takes more than meat to get to Good Health."

"Oh, dear," said the little engine. "I'll have to go back. I didn't know there were any more cars for me to pull." And he turned around and went chugging back down the track the way he had come.

When he was back in the roundhouse he looked around. He saw a bright blue car which said GRAIN on its flag. "That's it! That's the one I need," he said. And he hooked the blue car on behind the red one. He chugged happily down the track toward Good Health.

Just before he came to the edge of town, he saw the big black engine again. "Stop! Stop!" the big black engine called. "You can't come into Good Health Town with only meat and grain products. It takes more than that to get to Good Health."

"Oh dear!" said the little engine, "I'll have to go back again. I didn't know there were more cars for me to bring." He felt a little discouraged, but he turned around and went chugging back down the track.

In the roundhouse he saw an orange car with a flag that said FRUIT AND VEGETABLES. "Of course," said the little engine. "I should have known I'd need fruit and vegetables." He hooked the orange car behind the red and blue cars and started back toward Good Health.

Just at the edge of town he met the big black engine again. "Stop! Stop!" shouted the big black engine. "You need meat and grain products and fruit and vegetables, but you need some more before you can come into Good Health."

---

*Reprinted from the October issue of *Grade Teacher* magazine with permission of the publisher. This article is copyrighted. c 1959 by MacMillan Professional Magazines, Inc. All rights reserved.

The little engine began to feel very discouraged indeed, but he turned around and went back down the track to the roundhouse.

In the roundhouse he looked around and he saw a yellow car. The flag on it said DAIRY. "There is the car I need!" said the little engine, and he hooked it behind the orange one. Down the track he went toward Good Health.

When he came to the edge of Good Health Town the big black engine was nowhere in sight. The little engine chugged right into Good Health Town. The station master came out on the platform. He looked at the little engine. Then he looked at the cars the little engine was pulling. "Well, well," said the station master. "Meat, grain products, fruit and vegetables, and dairy products. Looks like you have all the good food you need to come to Good Health Town."

The little engine tooted happily. He had made it. He finally had all the cars he needed to go to Good Health.

Now he goes up and down, up and down, up and down the track every day, taking cars loaded with good food to the Town of Good Health.

And if you will eat some food from every one of his cars, every day, you will get to Good Health, too.

—Gloria Voorhees

Poem   Wow Breakfast Chant

One, two,
One egg for me,
One egg for you.

Three, four,
I have some cereal,
I want some more.

One, two, three, four,
Orange juice and meat,
Fresh from the store.

One, two, three, WOW!
Energy, energy,
Look at me NOW!

200

9
Physical
Development

Young children do not develop physically just by eating properly. Like all other areas of the curriculum, physical development depends on experiences that enhance growth. Spodek (1972) advocates a program including large and small muscle movement, as well as balancing and moving through space.

Pulling, piling, lifting, climbing, riding, pounding, and throwing are some of the large muscle skills that the young child can learn through school experiences (Read, 1970). Read believes that small muscles can be developed through lacing, pouring, putting on boots, using eating utensils, buttoning, playing with objects such as cars, puzzles, and blocks, as well as painting and finger play.

Planned exercises should be included in the physical development program. Exercising with the total body builds strength and confidence. Unfortunately, there isn't much exercise in watching television or other quiet activities expected of children in most homes.

In this component on physical development, activities are given in all areas previously discussed so teachers can aid the development of all the muscles needed by a growing child. Other related modules that the teacher might want to consider in connection with this component are as follows:

3.12 Prewriting visual motor skills
3.13 Prewriting Sensory Training
3.14 Beginning (Premanuscript) Writing
3.15 Manuscript Writing
3.17 Drama—The Gestures
6.3 Machines Work For Us
The component on creative arts

The teacher will need to consider that no two children are at the same level of physical development at the same time. Some come to school knowing how to skip, hop, and cut with scissors, for example. Others may not know how to perform many of the physical skills. The solution is to accept the children as they are and to give them the experiences needed to learn the skill they lack.

Experience is the great teacher of us all. How many adults

(including teachers) say that they can't perform the simplest of dance steps? What they lack is a good teacher and some experience with these steps. Most do not lack coordination or adequate muscular development.

Teachers of young children are responsible for the initial training of Olympic stars and great painters as well as those of us who will never excel in sports or art. A total physical development program helps both the future athlete and the business executive.

The modules (units of learning) in the component on physical development are as follows:

9.1 Visual Dynamics—Large Muscles
9.2 Visual Dynamics—Small Muscles
9.3 Position in Space
9.4 Moving in Space
9.5 Balancing
9.6 Exercising

References

Read, Katherine H. *The Nursery School: A Human Relationships Laboratory.* 5th ed. W. B. Saunders Co., 1970.
Spodek, Bernard. *Teaching in the Early Years.* Prentice-Hall, Inc. 1972.

9.1 Visual Dynamics—Large Muscles

Rationale

Kinesthetic skills strongly influence visual dynamics that depend on all motor skills, both large and small. Bouncing, catching, throwing, passing, or tossing various objects are excellent means for developing large muscles. Large-muscle development is important for overall physical growth and coordination, which are, in turn, vital to the development of small muscles.

Prerequisites

You need balls of various sizes, deflated balloons, nylon net, styrofoam pieces, wooden dowels (may be bought at the lumber store), clothes hangers or other bendable wire, plastic lids or soft mason jar rims, lightweight cardboard, bean bags, cardboard fish and snowmen, feathers, and clothespins.

Preassessment

Given various types of balls and bean bags, the children will exhibit adequate coordination by bouncing them, catching them, throwing them, and hitting a designated target, 4 feet away, three out of five times.

After the preassessment, exit from the module or proceed to the objectives.

Objective 1

The children will learn to bounce, catch, and throw balls and bean bags.

9.1 Hitting a target

● Given a balloon to blow up, each child will bat it into the air, catch it, and then see how long he/she can keep it aloft, demonstrating catching ability.
● Standing in the center of a circle formed by the children, the teacher bounces a ball to a child who will catch it after the first bounce and then bounce it back, showing ability to bounce and catch.
● Using a medium-sized ball, the children will bounce the ball to each other with both hands.
● While standing in the center of a circle formed by the children, the teacher will throw a ball up and call the name of a child who, in catching the ball, demonstrates ability to catch the ball before it hits the ground. (Variation: child throws it back to teacher accurately.)
● After the teacher tosses the ball to a child, the child will toss the ball back, demonstrating ability to throw the ball in a certain direction accurately.

Alternate Activities

Simple Activity
Given a balloon to blow up, the child will bat it into the air, catch it, and then see how long he/she can keep it aloft.

More Advanced Activity
Standing in a circle, one child calls the name of another child and throws the bean bag to that child. The catcher throws the bean bag to a third child, and so on, demonstrating the skill needed to catch an object.

Design your own activity to meet the needs of individual children.

Objective 2   The children will hit a designated target with increasing accuracy.

Activities   • Children will keep their eyes on the target as they roll a ball into an overturned wastebasket, showing that they can hit a target accurately.
• After a demonstration of how to stand six erasers on end and "bowl" them from four to six feet away with a medium size ball, the children will indicate their understanding by repeating this activity with increasing accuracy.
• Given a wide-mouthed jar, the children will drop cardboard fish, snowmen, feathers or cothespins into the jar with increasing accuracy, demonstrating ability to hit a target.

Alternate Activities   *Simple Activity*
To demonstrate skill in hitting a designated target, each child will take a net (made of clothes hanger and nylon net) and catch at least three fish made of styrofoam that are floating in a tub of water.

More Advanced Activity
Given four soft mason jar rings and an upturned chair, each child will toss the rings onto the legs to demonstrate skill in hitting targets, each time standing farther away from the target.

Design your own activities to meet the needs of individual children.

Postassessment   The postassessment is the same as the preassessment. After the postassessment, exit from the module or proceed to additional activities.

Additional Activities   • Given a bean bag, the children will form two lines and throw it back and forth to each other across the lines, repeating twice, to show that they can throw in a specific direction.
• Using a fishing pole made of a pole, string, and a magnet, the children will catch cardboard fish with paper-clip noses, displaying their skill in hitting targets by catching more fish each time they play.
• Wire can be bent to resemble a tooth, a heart, a bell, and other objects. Each child will toss these at a wooden dowel in a stand of clay or plaster, exhibiting an ability to hit the target two out of five times.

Resources   Bentley, Wm. G. *Learning to Move and Moving to Learn*. Citation Press, 1970.
Hackett, Layne C. *Movement Exploration Games for the Mentally Retarded*. Peek Publications, 1970.
Orlick, Emanuel, and Mosley, Jean. *Teacher's Illustrated Handbook of Stunts*. Prentice-Hall Inc., 1966.
Porter, Lorena. *Movement Education for Children*. American Association of Elementary, Kindergarten, and Nursery Educators, 1962.
Pre-School-Kindergarten Handbook. Fort Worth, Texas: Fort Worth Public Schools, 1967.

Teacher Guide to Education in Early Childhood. California Department of Education, 1956.

Werner, P. "Physical Education During the Preschool Years." *Physical Educator* 29 (December, 1972):180 83.

9.2 Visual Dynamics—Small Muscles

Rationale

When a child enters first grade, certain degrees of skill in various types of activities are needed. Eye-hand motor skills for small muscles must be part of the experience curriculum in kindergarten. These skill experiences provide an excellent background for the reading, writing, and playing that a first-grade curriculum demands of the child.

Prerequisites

You need magazines, sponges, lightweight cardboard, hole punchers, string for lacing, scissors, glue, construction paper, blocks, and boards. Make blocks of milk cartons, cheese boxes, detergent boxes, or other similar containers, filled with sand, sawdust, or newspaper. Tape ends and cover with contact paper. Also needed are matchboxes, other small boxes, and thread spools.

Preassessment

• Given a shoe with eyelets and a shoe string, each child will lace it correctly to demonstrate small-muscle skill.
• Using a set of matchboxes, each child will build a simple structure to a height of twelve boxes or more, demonstrating small-muscle skill in stacking.
After the preassessment, exit from the module or proceed to the objectives.

Objective 1

The child will learn the correct procedure for lacing (a small-muscle skill).

Activities

• Given a cardboard punched with twenty holes and a string, each child will demonstrate the procedure of lacing in and out by doing it correctly three times following a demonstration by the teacher between each of the child's tries.
• After cutting and gluing magazine pictures to lightweight cardboard, each child will punch holes around the edge and lace the holes to show an ability to follow a pattern of going in and out correctly.

Alternate Activity

Simple Activity
Given cardboard with just two holes and string, the child will lace in and out correctly five times, displaying small-muscle skill. The teacher may demonstrate repeatedly if needed.

9.2 Lacing a shoe

More Advanced Activity
Following a demonstration of shoe lacing, the children will lace a shoe correctly by repeating the demonstration accurately. (Variation: Learn to tie the shoe.)

Design your own activities to meet the needs of individual children.

Objective 2 The child will become increasingly successful at stacking objects.

Activities
• Using tiny blocks, each child will construct a simple structure to exhibit skill in stacking.
• Using as many blocks as desired, the child will stack blocks waist high, showing skill in stacking.
• Using thread spools, the child will demonstrate skill in stacking by increasing the height of the structure in successive attempts.

Alternate Activities
Simple Activity
Using blocks of several small sizes, the child will show skill at stacking by building a house without having a single block fall.

More Advanced Activity
The child, using small blocks and small pieces of wood or tile, will build a complex structure, three to five stories high, exhibiting increasing skill in stacking. (Variation: use various small boxes—one-serving cereal boxes, match boxes, small salt boxes.)

Design your own activities to meet the needs of individual children.

The postassessment is the same as the preassessment. After the postassessment, exit from the module or proceed to additional activities.

• Given thread spools strung on a long cord, each child will display small muscle skill by stacking the spools as he/she removes them from the string.
• Using blocks, boards, and imagination, the child will construct a small two-story town, demonstrating skill at stacking.

Additional Activities

Corbin, C. B. *Inexpensive Equipment for Games, Play, and Physical Activities.* Wm. C. Brown, 1972.
Doll, E. A., ed. *Oseretsky, Tests of Motor Proficiency.* C-128 set of test equipment. American Guidance Service, Inc.
Matterson, E. *Play and Play Things for the Preschool Child.* Penguin Books, 1967.
Radler, D. H., and Kephart, N. C. *Success Through Play.* Harper and Row, 1960.
Starks. *Blockbuilding.* American Association of Elementary, Kindergarten, and Nursery Educators, 1970.
Todd, V., and Hefferman, H. *The Years Before School: Guiding Preschool Children.* Macmillan, 1970.

Resources

9.3 Position in Space

We cannot assume that all young children know where up, down, in, out, under, over, front, and back are. How can a child be expected to follow directions without these important word tools? These are just words to children until they can relate them to themselves and their environment and then transfer these relationships to other objects in the environment. It is hoped that this relating process can be facilitated by using the materials in this module. This aspect of physical development links the child cognitively to physical space.

Rationale

Have on hand inner tubes, boxes, chairs, tables, balls, balloons, cushions, ropes, flannel board and flannel objects, and playground slide.

Prerequisites

• Each child will show an understanding of the positions *up* and *down* by pointing to these positions three times when asked in random order.
• Using the flannel-board dog and doghouse, each child will show awareness of the related positions *in* and *out* by placing the dog in or out of the doghouse four times when asked to do so.

Preassessment

9.3 My position in space

● To demonstrate understanding of the positions *over* and *under*, each child will crawl over the table and under the table.
After the preassessment, exit from the module or proceed to the objectives.

Objective 1   Each child will have a physical knowledge of the positions *up* and *down*.

Activities   ● Given a ball, each child will show an understanding of the positions *up* and *down* by throwing the ball up or down as the teacher commands.
● Each child will hand-bat a balloon up in the air and down on the floor, upon request, demonstrating a knowledge of the positions *up* and *down*.
● The child will show knowledge of positions *up* and *down* by jumping up and falling down at the teacher's request.
● Using a flannel-board tree and cat, each child will place the cat in the tree and then show it climbing down the tree to show knowledge

208

of the difference between up and down. (Variation: the child will become the cat and pantomime climbing up and down the tree, or going up and down stairs.)

Simple Activity
While playing on the slide, each child will show understanding of the positions *up* and *down* by telling whether he/she is going up the slide or down.

More Advanced Activity
Given a color card, each child will show understanding of the positions *up* and *down* by standing up and sitting down when his/her color card is called and the teacher says "up" or "down." (Example: Teacher says, "Red up; blue down.")

Design your own activities to meet the needs of individual children.

Alternate Activities

Each child will become physically aware of the related positions *in* and *out*.

Objective 2

- After placing inner tubes on the floor, each child will demonstrate understanding of the positions *in* and *out* by jumping into the middle of the tube and jumping out several times, saying "in" or "out" appropriately.
- Given a big box, each child will show knowledge of in and out by climbing into and out of the box when Simon says to do so.
- While singing "Hokey Pokey," each child will show understanding of *in* and *out* by placing the correct parts in the circle or out of the circle as called for in the song. ("Hokey Pokey" can be found in almost any children's songbook.)

Activities

Simple Activity
Each child will demonstrate understanding of *in* and *out* by jumping into and out of a low box while saying "in" or "out" appropriately.

More Advanced Activity
Given a box of red and yellow blocks, each child will show understanding of *in* and *out* by taking the red blocks out and leaving all the yellow blocks in the box. (Variation: Take all the blocks out and put back only the yellow ones.)

Design your own activities to meet the needs of individual childern.

Alternate Activities

Each child will be able to demonstrate understanding of *over* and *under*.

Objective 3

- Using a rope held several inches from the ground, each child will demonstrate understanding of *over* and *under* by crawling under the rope several times. (Variation: Jump over the rope.)

Activities

● After a demonstration by the teacher and to show awareness of *over* and *under*, each child will roll a ball over the table and under the table as many times as necessary to understand the concept.

● After the teacher has drawn objects on the chalkboard, each child will show understanding of *over* and *under* by drawing straight lines over the objects and squiggly lines under the objects in response to teacher directions.

Alternate Activities

Simple Activity

Each child will demonstrate understanding of *under* and *over* by crawling under the table and holding a hand over the table upon request.

More Advanced Activity

To show understanding of *over* and *under*, each child will leapfrog over one child and crawl under another until at the other end of the line.

Design your own activities to meet the needs of individual children.

Postassessment

The postassessment is the same as the preassessment. After the postassessment, exit from the module or proceed to additional activities.

Additional Activities

● To show understanding of *up* and *down*, each child will bounce on a cushion for one minute when the teacher says "Go," calling out whether he/she is up or down.

● Given a laundry basket and ten sponges, each child will demonstrate awareness of *in* and *out* by throwing the sponges at the laundry basket and calling "in" when the sponge lands in the basket and "out" when it misses.

● Given a suspended piece of cloth to play peek-a-boo, each child will demonstrate understanding of *over* and *under* by looking over the cloth and under the cloth. The child on the other side says "Peek-a-boo" to the child peeking over and under.

Resources

Bentley, William G. *Learning to Move and Moving to Learn*. Citation Press, 1970.

Croft, Doreen J., and Hess, Robert D. *An Activities Book for Teachers of Young Children*. 2d ed. Houghton Mifflin Co., 1975.

Werner, P. "Physical Education During the Preschool Years." *Physical Education* 29 (December 1972): 180-83.

9.4 Moving in Space

Rationale

Children need to develop space awareness to help them understand their relationship to their environment. Space awareness, according to Croft and Hess, (1975), involves feeling space as it relates to the body, sensing spatial limits, and understanding the relationship of objects and space. The latter is covered in Module 9.3, "Position in Space." The other elements of space awareness are the topics of this module.

Space awareness is crucial to the athlete, dancer, artist, violinist, and the like. It is important to the rest of us because it pervades everything that we do and know. When we feel enriched, it generally is because we have experienced and understood a new spatial horizon. For the young child the enrichment might be the difference between running and skipping, the thrill of the big skip, the gallop, or the magical fun of spinning like a top. A cognitive spatial truth comes when the child discovers the space between words.

Ideally, space should be experienced in every conceivable dimension. This module will open up possibilities for the children and the teacher.

Moving in space involves moving from the simple, such as walking, to the complex, such as turning, hopping, jumping, galloping, and skipping. Skipping is the most difficult of the skills mentioned above because it combines a walk with a hop and changes feet very rapidly. It is best to move the child from the simple to the complex using as many experiences as necessary to help him to move well.

Prerequisites

Have on hand the poems and music mentioned in the activity sections, and a 10"-by-10" bean bag or pillow.

Preassessment

• The child will demonstrate understanding of space as it relates to the body by running in three styles (slow, slow motion, and fast); by jumping, hopping, and skipping (spatial movements involving height); and by turning while moving across the room on a diagonal.
• The child will show understanding of spatial limits by (1) walking until he/she has to stop (he should walk until he reaches a wall or a piece of furniture that he must go around) and (2) telling of three kinds of spaces that make him/her feel closed in (e.g., a dark room, an elevator, the inside of a box).

After the preassessment, exit from the module or proceed to the objectives.

Objective 1

Each child will learn about space as it relates to the body.

Activities

• Upon hearing the poem "The Four Friends" (see Milne in resources), each child will show an understanding of moving through space by running like Ernest, the elephant (slowly), Leonard, the lion (fast), George the goat (on tiptoe), and James, the snail (in slow motion).
• While learning the poem "Hoppity" (see Milne in resources), each child will demonstrate knowledge of hopping through space by hopping on one foot in one direction as the poem is read, and then, on the last four lines, turning around and around while hopping.
• As the poem "Shoes and Stockings" (see Milne in resources) is read, each child will indicate understanding of jumping by jumping up and down in place to the "hammers" and jumping across the room to the "chatters."
• To the tune of "Simple Gifts," a Shaker song found in many music books or folk song albums, each child will demonstrate knowledge of turning in space by turning in place to the music.

9.4 Hopping

• As the teacher reads "In the Fashion" (see Milne in resources), each child will show ability to turn in space by turning while moving on a diagonal across the room and wearing an imaginary animal tail on a band around the waist.

Alternate Activities

Simple Activities
Upon hearing the poem "Bananas and Cream" (see McCord in resources), each child will show knowledge of how to jump through space by jumping to the poem's obvious beat.
As the teacher reads "Scat! Scitten!" (see McCord in resources), each child will indicate skill in hopping through space by hopping through space to the obvious beat of the poem.
Upon hearing the poem "Busy" (see Milne in resources), each child will demonstrate skill in turning through space by turning while moving on a diagonal until the refrain that begins "Round About." At this point, the child will begin to turn very rapidly in place while listening to the refrain.

More Advanced Activities
While listening to the poem "Us Two" (see Milne in resources), each child will show ability to jump and hop through space by jumping on the word "Pooh" and hopping on the word "me."
While listening to some square dance music, each child will demonstrate ability to gallop through space by galloping to the music. (Move to the side instead of the front, doing a slide-together-hop.)

Design your own activities to meet the needs of individual children.

Objective 2

Each child will learn to sense spatial limits.

Activities

• Each child will show ability to sense spatial limits by walking blindfolded (with arms outstretched for feeling) until he/she bumps

212

into another child, and then returning to the original position. The child begins by standing on a large bean bag (10"-by-10") located in the center of a circle of children who are standing shoulder to shoulder. The child should tell how it felt to be closed in spatially by the darkness and to have restrictions on where he/she could walk.

• Upon hearing the poem "Vespers" (see Milne in resources), each child will demonstrate awareness of spatial limits by pantomiming the poem and then discussing with the teacher how it feels to be in a kneeling position crushed against the bed, and how it feels spatially to curl up small.

• While listening to the poem "In the Dark" (see Milne in resources), each child will indicate awareness of spatial limits by imitating the teacher who is pantomiming the poem and, later, by discussing with the teacher what it means spatially to (1) be in the dark alone, (2) play by oneself, (3) lie in a cave.

• After rowing with the arms and upper body to "Row, Row, Row Your Boat," each child will show understanding of spatial limits by telling why he/she couldn't run in the boat or row standing up. How was the space limited?

• After practicing jumping with both feet from one line to another, each child will show understanding of spatial limits by telling why he/she couldn't jump farther. The child will repeat jump as a leap to see that he/she can move farther this way.

Simple Activity
After trying toe touching and bending from the waist to touch the ground, eah child will discuss with the teacher why space was more limited one way, showing understanding of spatial limits.

More Advanced Activity
After flapping the arms like a bird and galloping like a horse, each child will indicate knowledge of spatial limits by telling why he/she can't fly like a bird or gallop as fast as a horse.

Design your own activities to meet the needs of individual children.

Alternate Activities

The postassessment is the same as the preassessment. After the postassessment, exit from the module or proceed to additional activities.

Postassessment

• Upon hearing the song "Goober Peas" (see Burl Ives record in resources), each child will show ability to hop through space by hopping first on the right foot, then the left, changing feet at the end of each measure. (Variation: Hop to the chorus of the music.)

• While listening to the song "Cool Water" (see Burl Ives record in resources), each child will demonstrate skill in skipping through space by skipping to the beat of the music.

• After sitting inside three boxes, each larger than the preceding one, the child will show an understanding of spatial limits by describing how he/she felt about the space in each box.

Additional Activities

213

Resources
Books

Cratty, Bryant J. *Movement, Perception, and Thought: The Use of Total Body Movement as a Learning Modality.* Peek Publications, 1969.

Croft, Doreen J., and Hess, Robert D. *An Activities Handbook for Teachers of Young Children.* 2d ed. Houghton Mifflin, 1975.

Glass, Henry. *Exploring Movement.* Educational Activities, 1966.

Hackett, Layne, and Jenson, Robert. *A Guide to Movement Exploration.* Peek Publications, 1967.

McCord, David. *Take Sky.* Little, Brown and Co., 1962.

Milne, A. A. *The World of Christopher Robin.* E. P. Dutton and Co., 1958.

Orlick, Emanuel, and Mosley, Jean. *Teacher's Illustrated Handbook for Stunts.* Prentice Hall Inc., 1968.

Porter, Lorena. *Movement Education for Children.* American Association of Elementary, Kindergarten, and Nursery Educators, 1969.

Records

Burl Ives' Greatest Hits MCA-114 (formerly DL7-4850) MCA Records Inc.

Carr, Dorothy. *Basic Concepts Through Dance.* Educational Activities, Inc.

Palmer, Hap. *Learning Basic Skills Through Music.* Educational Activities, Inc.

9.5 Balancing

Rationale

Body balance begins with correct posture. Learning to balance each body part, one on the other and keeping them in line with the pull of gravity is essential in good posture development. Once the children can stand, sit, and walk with correct posture, then other fundamentals of balance come easily as they move through space

Prerequisites

Read pages 11, 12, 26, 27, and 28 in *Physical Education: A Guide for Elementary Schools,* 1971. The book is free on request from the University of Arkansas, Department of Education, Little Rock, Arkansas.

Preassessment

The child, while balancing a book or small wooden board on his/her head, will walk ten feet, turn around, and walk back to the start without dropping or touching the book, demonstrating excellent balance and equilibrium. Also, the child will raise one leg front, side, and back (repeating with the other leg) without losing balance.

After the preassessment, exit from the module or proceed to the objective.

Objective

The child will learn to balance better by using good posture.

9.5 Balancing a paper cup on the head

Activities

• Using masking tape, make a 10-foot strip on the floor. Then each child will walk the tape while standing as straight as possible, demonstrating balance and proper posture. (A balancing beam could be used later.)
• Standing straight with the arms at the sides, each child will lift the right arm and leg for ten seconds, exhibiting skill in maintaining stability and balance.
• The child, to show bodily equilibrium, will stand with feet together and rock forward and backward as far as possible without tipping.
• To demonstrate balance, the child in a starting position with eyes closed, will jump up and down five times with arms at sides and three times with arms folded across chest.
• While balancing a paper cup on his/her head, each child will demonstrate balancing skill by walking in a circle as the teacher plays "Cool Water" (see Burl Ives record in resources).

Alternate Activities

Simple Activity
In a standing position, the child will balance on tiptoes with eyes opened and then closed to show skill in balancing.

More Advanced Activity
The child, in a standing position with eyes opened or closed, will balance on one foot and then jump and do a quarter turn, landing on two feet, thereby illustrating equilibrium and balance.

Design your own activities to meet the needs of individual children.

Postassessment

The postassessment is the same as the preassessment. After the postassessment, exit from the module or proceed to the additional activities

Additional Activities

• On hands and knees and with a straight back, the child will demonstrate good balance by crawling forward, backward, and sideways, going six feet in each direction.

215

• While on hands and knees, keeping back straight, the child will demonstrate body balance by raising one leg and one arm, holding the position for ten seconds.
• The above activity can be varied by holding up left arm and right leg, holding up right arm and left leg, holding up just one arm or leg, closing eyes and doing any of the above, holding the leg up to the side, or holding a leg up in the back.

Resources

Burl Ives' Greatest Hits MCA-114 (formerly DL7-4850) MCA Records Inc.

9.6 Exercise

Rationale

Young children receive less exercise than most adults realize. Television and staying indoors restrict physical activity. School is often a place where children have to sit quietly. It is true that children go out to playgrounds, but bad-weather days take their toll. Besides, some children simply stand around on the playground.

Few would dispute the relationship of exercise to good physical health and development. Many talk about it, like the weather, but they seldom put it into the young child's curriculum on a daily basis.

This module gives the teacher a beginning program in daily exercise. It is up to the teacher to create a more advanced program as the children master this one. (Check with the physical education teacher and the literature as to what to plan next.) A continuing program of daily exercise should involve as much of the body as possible.

Prerequisites

Have on hand some brisk marching music, some slow 4/4 time music, a mattress with a plastic cover on it, paper plates and cups, and some face masks on a stick to be held in front of the face.

Preassessment

• Each child will indicate skill in exercising the face, neck, shoulders, arms, wrists, and fingers by (1) making two faces that use most of the face muscles, (2) swiveling the neck farther than would be required to watch a tennis match, (3) hunching shoulders forward then back, (4) painting figure eights in the air with straight arms, (5) rotating wrists, (6) using fingers to climb like an inchworm, and (7) doing the seesaw (see activity under alternate activities).
• Each child will demonstrate skill in exercising the waist, back, legs, ankles, and feet by (1) doing somersaults on a mattress—both a forward and backward somersault, (2) making a table by positioning the back straight and parallel to the ground, arms stretched to the side (As child bounces with the back in that position, a paper cup and plate on his/her back do not fall.), (3) doing body twists with arms outstretched, feet apart on a line, swinging from the waist so that the child can identify the changing masks of a child standing about fifteen feet behind him/her, (4) bending over backwards from a sitting position on the floor, hands on the floor at sides, to identify an object held by another child high above his/her head (the other child is

standing about ten feet away), (5) rotating each foot, using the ankle both with toe pointed and then with heel thrust forward, (6) rocking up on tiptoes four times and walking in a circle on tiptoes.

After the preassessment, exit from the module or proceed to the objectives.

Each child will learn how to exercise the face, neck, shoulders, arms, wrists, and fingers.

• Each child will demonstrate knowledge of how to exercise the face, neck, shoulders, arms, wrists, and fingers by pretending to be a rubber soldier to the music of a march. Face grimaces, then relaxes; neck swivels so head faces right, then left, to the music; shoulders hunch forward then relax; arms bend one at a time from the elbow; wrists turn in, then out; fingers clench then extend one at a time). The teacher acts as the captain or leader of the soldiers.
• *Golf Pros.* Each child will indicate understanding of how to exercise the arms and shoulders by swinging like a golf pro to a slow 4/4 tempo. The child should stand sideways with feet apart, eyes on the imaginary ball, then swing straight arms back, then forward, and over the shoulder.
• *Baby Birds.* Each child will show knowledge of how to exercise the face, neck, arms, and wrists by trying to fly like a baby bird. (Child grimaces several times, swivels head and neck from side to side as well as down and up to see where bird might go; child puts arms out straight and flaps some, then rotates wrists like propellors; rotates, flaps, rotates, flaps, flaps, flaps; then takes off into the air.)
• *The Two-Handed Artist.* Each child will demonstrate skill in rotating the arms many ways by painting in the air with pretend brushes in each hand, making large circles, small circles, figure eights, slow and fast circles, and straight lines up and down.
• Each child will show ability to exercise fingers by making them crawl like a spider up an imaginary wall, like an inchworm on a log, and like claws of a tiger. Repeat eight to ten times.

Simple Activity
Two children at a time will show that they can exercise their shoulders, arms, wrists, and fingers by doing the "seesaw." (One child squats while grasping the hands of another child with straight arms. The standing child squats, pulling the other child to a standing position.) Repeat eight to ten times.

More Advanced Activity
Two children at a time will show that they can exercise their arms, shoulders, hands, and wrists by squatting together, holding hands and facing each other with arms straight. They pull each other up at the same time, keeping their arms straight.

Design your own activities to meet the needs of individual children.

Each child will learn how to exercise the waist, back, legs and ankles, and feet.

217

Activities

- To show knowledge of how to exercise certain muscles, each child will somersault forward on a mattress, touching first hands, then shoulders, then rounded back and then sitting up (chin on chest to protect head).
- On a mattress each child will somersault backwards, rolling onto a rounded back, then onto hands, then to a sitting position (chin on chest to protect head).
- *Set the Table.* While playing this game each child will indicate skill in exercising the back and waist by *not* allowing the objects on his/her back to fall down or off. (While one child with arms outstretched to the side lowers his/her back into a flat rather than a rounded position, another child puts a paper cup, plate, and plastic silverware on first child's back.) The child who plays the table must bounce four times in this position with no objects falling down or off. (Variations: turn body at waist to left or right side, and then become the table again.
- *Can You See Me?* While playing this game, each child will demonstrate ability to exercise by swinging the upper torso from the waist (arms at sides and feet apart), seeing the child behind, and identifying the mask the child is wearing. (Child behind changes the mask each time the other child swings.)
- Each child will show ability to exercise his/her back by sitting up straight on the floor with hands at sides and bending backwards until he/she sees an object held up by the teacher.
- *Toe circles.* Each child will show ability to exercise ankles and legs by rotating each ankle to music while sitting in a chair with leg outstretched and toe pointed. (Variation: Do the same thing with the heel instead of the toe thrust forward; do both toe circles and heel circles while lying on the floor with one leg pointing toward the ceiling.)
- *The Talking Foot Fist.* While playing this game, each child will show skill in exercising the foot by moving the toes into a fist, then relaxing; by moving only one toe to signify "yes" and making a fist of toes to signify "no"; by having the toes on one foot talk to the toes on the other foot or on another child's foot.
- *Rocking the Baby.* As this game is played, each child will demonstrate skill in exercising the feet by holding an imaginary baby and rocking up onto tiptoes and back on the soles of the feet to the music of Brahms' "Lullaby" or any other suitable lullaby. (Variation: Children carry imaginary babies and walk on tiptoes in a circle.)

Alternate Activities

Simple Activity
To demonstrate skill in bending and arching the back, each child will bend and arch the back while bending knees to Indian music (see resources), following the teacher who is acting as the leader.

More Advanced Activity
While listening to Indian Music (see "Sounds of Indian America" in resources), each child will show skill in exercising the ankles, feet, and legs by doing the following movements: toe-heel, toe-heel, and so on; step on one foot, then hop three times while lifting the other foot with knee bent and heel pointed toward the floor.

Design your own activities to meet the needs of individual children.

The postassessment is the same as the preassessment. After the postassessment, exit from the module or proceed to the additional activities.

• *Stuck in the Muck.*To show skill at exercising, each child will walk as though stuck in the muck by bending over to grasp ankles and walking in this position while the teacher tells a made-up story about a boy and girl who wanted to find a pot of gold. The story explains that they searched for the gold by running through the woods, up a mountain, through the muck, and other similar exertions.

• *The Long Puppy Walk.* Each child will show skill at exercising by doing the Long Puppy Walk after a demonstration by the teacher. (Lean over touching hands to floor. Walk forward until body is straight out and only toes and hands are touching the foor. Raise one leg and then the other as the hands walk forward.)

Bentley, William G. *Learning to Move and Moving to Learn.* Citation Press, 1970.

Corbin, C. B. *Inexpensive Equipment for Games, Play, and Physical Activities.* Wm. C. Brown, 1972.

Glass, Henry. *Exploring Movement.* Educational Activities, Inc., 1966.

Matterson, E. *Play and Playthings for the Preschool Child.* Penguin Books, 1967.

Orlick, Emanuel, and Mosley, Jean. *Teacher's Illustrated Handbook of Stunts.* Prentice Hall, Inc., 1966.

Stecher, M. "Expressing Feeling, Facts, and Fancies Through the Movement Arts," *Childhood Education.* January 1975, pp. 123-27.

Carr, Dorothy. *Basic Concepts Through Dance.* Educational Activities, Inc.

Sounds of Indian America: Plains and Southwest. Indian House, 1970.

10
Career Awareness

The young child usually is aware that Daddy goes off to work and that Mother has the responsibility of being a homemaker and/or a career woman. Often the child may not know details of the careers but is developing an awareness of the world of work. The child has many years ahead before making a decision about his/her life's work. However, this does not preclude experiences that will help the child understand the dignity of many kinds of work and the interdependence of jobs within an institution such as a school and within a team, such as a football squad.

Not all boys must grow up to become doctors. The health professions include hundreds of varied, interesting, and important jobs. Similarly, girls are no longer limited to becoming teachers, nurses, secretaries, stewardesses, librarians, or housewives. Because boys and girls live in a society that offers them an almost infinite number of career possibilities, they should learn about some of these areas early in a setting that attaches importance to all contributing careers. The auto mechanic is as vital and worthwhile a member of the auto industry as is the president of an automobile company. Each is an important contributor of services.

The teacher using this component will need to examine his/her own biases about certain careers so that the children don't receive the teacher's own values. A school (an example of a job cluster) needs all its personnel to function well. Teachers are not superior to janitors nor inferior to principals in the job cluster. Each is very important in the operation of a school.

The modules in this component discuss sports, health, government, manual service, and grooming occupations. These are only a small sampling of career possibilities. The creative teacher needs to add modules about other occupational clusters, especially unusual occupations and those of interest to the children. The modules in this component are as follows:

- 10.1 Football
- 10.2 Health Helpers
- 10.3 The Mail Carrier
- 10.4 Builders

10.4 Awareness of what a carpenter does

10.1 Football

Rationale

Some of the highest-paying occupations are in sports and recreation. Even though an individual might not play a sport professionally, he/she may enter any of a number of activities related to his/her "interest area" sport. Such jobs as coach, assistant coach, trainer, announcer, official, sports writer, narrator, manager, and sportswear salesperson, to mention a few, are all important to a sport. With the expansion of the different leagues of professional players, the emphasis on sports in schools, and the increased amount of leisure time, the number of jobs in the sports area is constantly expanding. This module is designed to help young children become aware of one sport and of its career and recreational possibilities.

Prerequisites

Gather some football equipment such as footballs, helmets, shoes, pads, mouth and chin protectors, and an official's shirt and whistle. Pictures of players, coaches, popcorn sellers, managers, trainers, ticket takers, and cheerleaders, and of any football scenes will be most helpful. Buy an NFL football parlor game (available in most department stores). Make arrangements for field trips to training facilities, first-aid and equipment rooms, a football game, and a football field.

Preassessment

• Given a sampling of football equipment (both playing and wearing equipment), each child will show knowledge of football equipment by selecting five objects, telling what they are, and how they are used in football.
• Given a set of occupational pictures, each child will demonstrate knowledge of football personnel by pointing to the pictures and naming five occupations associated with football.
After the preassessment, exit from the module or proceed to the objectives.

Objective 1

The children will learn about football players and the equipment they use.

Activities

• Each child will identify each piece of equipment by saying the name aloud to show knowledge of the names of equipment and by correctly putting on the equipment after a demonstration by the teacher.
• After discussing why players wear pads, special shoes, helmets, and mouth and chin protectors, each child will demonstrate understanding by telling what these items protect.
• After discussing why it is important to wear this special equipment, each child will demonstrate understanding by telling what would

10.1 Teacher dressed as a football trainer and leading jumping jacks

happen if it is not worn. (Variation: Role play what can happen without a certain piece of equipment.)

Simple Activity
Given a football parlor game, each child will demonstrate awareness of what football players do by picking out the players, ball, helmet, and playing field.

More Advanced Activity
Given a football parlor game, each child will demonstrate awareness of football by picking out some of the playing positions (center, quarterback, tailback, lineman) and playing these roles in the course of the game.

Design your own activities to meet the needs of individual children.

The children will learn about some of the football personnel other than players.

Alternate Activities

Objective 2

Activities

• Using part of the classroom as a press box, each child will demonstrate growing awareness of personnel connected with football by starting and stopping the clock, running the scoreboard, and speaking over the P.A. system (as announcers do).

• While some students role play the coach, assistant coach, and trainers, the other children will follow their instructions in leg-lift exercises, demonstrating awareness of football personnel.

• Using a football and kicking tee, the teacher will act as an official, wearing an official's shirt and whistle. Each child will take turns demonstrating a further awareness of personnel involved with football by kicking the ball, acting as a ball boy/girl, and keeping up with the ball. Others will act as cheerleaders leading cheers.

• Given cookies and punch, the children will become aware of the personnel involved with a concession stand by setting up their own concession stand, serving refreshments after the third activity.

• After refreshments, each child will demonstrate awareness of how football facilities are kept clean and attractive by picking up the trash and putting it in the trash barrels.

• After taking a tour through the training facilities and the first-aid and equipment rooms, the children will attend a football game. Following the game, each child will demonstrate awareness of personnel connected with football by identifying photographs taken by the teacher when the team was on tour. (The local high school is a good place for a tour.)

Alternate Activities

Simple Activity
After looking at pictures of a football game, each child will demonstrate awareness of personnel connected with football by picking out the security guard, the popcorn seller, and the scorekeeper and by role playing their occupations.

More Advanced Activity
After being shown the correct way to do the exercises, each child will demonstrate an understanding of what it means to be a football player by doing some more advanced football warm-up exercises, such as jumping jacks, push-ups, and deep knee bends, led by student coaches and trainers working with the teacher.

Design your own activities to meet the needs of individual children.

Postassessment

The postassessment is the same as the preassessment. After the postassessment, exit from the module or proceed to additional activities.

Additional Activities

• Have a game of touch football, using as many occupations mentioned in the module as possible so that the children are aware of these occupations.

• Using the NFL football parlor game, each child will demonstrate knowledge of occupations associated with football by naming personnel associated with the team (coach, trainers, assistant coaches, others).

After this, the postassessment should be given again. If a child does not pass the postassessment after doing the additional activities, the teacher should individualize the instruction and help the child in the area of his/her weakness.

10.2 Health Helpers

Because it is important that we be healthy both in mind and body, millions of individuals have devoted their lives to the health-related occupations. It takes very special persons to work in this area because they must possess a desire to better mankind and be willing to work long hours without seeing immediate results. Because of these special requirements, few people enter health occupations. Therefore, people are needed in this area. This module is designed to help young children become aware of some of the careers in the health fields.

Rationale

Items needed for this module include models or dolls of a doctor, a nurse, a custodian, and a medical secretary; a mop and bucket, and a flannel board; pictures of equipment used in the medical field, such as stethoscope and a thermometer; several small dentist's mirrors, pictures of healthy and bad teeth and gums, and a film about a visit to the dentist. Arrangements should be made for a visit to a drugstore and the school nurse's office. For the research unit, collect three microscopes, water that has been boiled, water from the tap and from a road ditch, one loaf of white bread, test tubes, cotton, and beans.

Prerequisites

• Given samples of the equipment used in a doctor's office, each child will demonstrate knowledge of occupations in the doctor's office by correctly matching the equipment used in each of the following occupations with a miniature model representing a doctor, a nurse, an aide, a cleaning lady, and a medical secretary.
• Provided with pictures of dental personnel doing their jobs, each child will demonstrate awareness of these personnel by correctly identifying their occupations.
• To show awareness of careers in research, each child will identify the funny color on bread as mold, and the ditch water under a microscope as being unsafe to drink.
After the preassessment, exit from the module or proceed to the objectives

Preassessment

The children will become aware of careers connected with the doctor's office.

Objective 1

• After a "show and tell" of personnel who work in the doctor's office, using appropriate miniature models and objects of the professions, each child will demonstrate knowledge of these professions by telling

Activities

225

what person each model represents and some of the jobs assigned to that person in the doctor's office.

• Given "play" doctor's office equipment, each child will demonstrate knowledge of occupations in the doctor's office by role playing a particular part—doctor, nurse, custodian, medical secretary.

• After a visit by the school's dietitian, each child will demonstrate awareness of a health career by telling some of the things a dietitian does.

Alternate Activities

Simple Activity
Given dolls dressed as doctors, nurses, custodians, and the like, each child will demonstrate knowledge of personnel connected with the doctor's office by telling the name of the occupation they represent and why they are dressed the way they are.

More Advanced Activity
Using a flannel board, each child will demonstrate knowledge of health occupations by matching objects related to specific health fields to the field; for example, doctor—stethoscope; nurse—thermometer or scales.

Design your own activities to meet the needs of individual children.

Objective 2

The children will learn some occupations associated with dentistry.

Activities

• After watching a film about a visit to the dentist, each child will demonstrate knowledge of occupations associated with dentistry by naming them when they are pointed to by the teacher. The film may need to be shown several times.

• After a class visit to a dentist's office, each child will demonstrate awareness of occupations associated with dentistry by telling three things done at the dentist's office by the dentist, the dental assistant, the receptionist, and the dental hygienist.

Alternate Activities

Simple Activity
Given mirrors, the children will demonstrate awareness of dental jobs by checking each others' teeth as the dental hygienist does.

More Advanced Activity
After comparing "healthy" teeth and gums with "sick" teeth and gums, each child will demonstrate awareness of dental careers by telling what the dentist would probably do for the patient.

Design your own activities to meet the needs of individual children.

Objective 3

The children will become aware of the field of research as a source of health careers.

Activities

• Using pieces of white bread, half the children will dampen their piece of bread, leave it in the air, redampen if necessary, wrap it in plastic. The other half of the class will wrap their bread in plastic. On the third or fourth day, each child will demonstrate awareness of what it means to be a researcher by examining the bread and telling what happened to it (whether mold formed or not). The teacher can enrich children's understanding by helping them to understand that from mold research came medicines like penicillin.

• Provided with boiled water and with water from a road ditch and a sink, and using microscopes sharply focused, the children will demonstrate awareness of what a researcher does by telling what they saw after looking at each type of water under the microscope. Children should discuss which would be the safest for drinking.

Alternate Activities

Simple Activity
The class will be divided into three groups. Using test tubes containing a bean and filled with cotton, Group A will not add water to the bean in their tubes; Group B will add a little water—just enough to sprout the bean; Group C will add water to sprout, and will continue to water the bean when necessary. In attempting to sprout his/her bean, each child will demonstrate awareness of what researchers do by examining and marking growth each day on the test tube.

More Advanced Activity
After a visit to the drugstore, where the druggist discussed some harmful medicines and the danger of taking medication not prescribed, each child will demonstrate knowledge of what researchers contribute by role playing discovering a new medicine, which will consist of small bottles, eye droppers, food coloring, and water.

Design your own activities to meet the needs of individual children.

The postassessment is the same as the preassessment. After the postassessment, exit from the module or proceed to additional activities.

Postassessment

• The children will play "Who Am I?" using the appropriate dress and equipment of the different health occupations and pantomiming one occupation before the class, demonstrating their knowledge of health fields.

• After a visit to the school nurse's office, each child will demonstrate knowledge of the nurse's duties by reenacting these in a puppet show. After this activity, the postassessment should be given again. If a child does not pass the postassessment, the teacher should individualize the instruction and help the child in the area of weakness.

Additional Activities

10.3 The Mail Carrier

Since the government employs more people than private enterprise, often at higher salaries, many people are turning to government positions for their vocation. Government positions include city

Rationale

managers, mayors, city employees, all county officials, state government officials such as legislators, agency and department personnel, national guardsmen, and highway department employees. The national government employs civil service workers, armed forces personnel, national legislators, the diplomatic corps, regulatory agency people, the president, and cabinet officers. Such jobs are vital to the functioning of our country, and students should have the opportunity to learn about these positions. A good starting point for your discussion of government positions is an employee that children might see frequently—the mail carrier.

Prerequisites

The teacher should become aware of governmental occupations through research: visiting local governmental offices and officials; obtaining booklets, literature, and filmstrips from local, county, state and federal agencies, and arranging for tours and for visits from local governmental officials. The teacher should have materials such as pictures and miniature models of all governmental officials, buildings, and uniforms, as well as items that would be used in a post office and by post office personnel (new and used stamps, letters with canceled stamps, postage meters, a mailbag, a mail cart, mailboxes, mail vehicles, and a large neighborhood map).

Preassessment

• Given pictures and models of post office buildings, each child will demonstrate knowledge of the post office by placing these articles on a large neighborhood map, showing the relationship or location of the post office and post boxes to home and school.
• Using pictures, hats, uniforms, models of mailboxes, and mail transportation, each child will show knowledge of the uniform and equipment of the mail carrier by correctly placing these items with a large picture of a mail carrier. Also present would be large pictures of a fire fighter, a policeman, and a garbage collector.
    After the preassessment, exit from the module or proceed to the objectives.

Objective 1

Each child will learn to identify the mailboxes and post office building in the neighborhood.

Activities

• Using a tabletop model of the neighborhood, the teacher will use models to show where each mailbox and the post office is. Provided with a miniature house with his/her initials on it, each child will put the house where it belongs on the table and show how to get to the post office and mailbox nearest the house.
• Provided with materials, the children will make a post office in a corner of the room, showing their awareness of what a post office is. Each day they can take turns playing postmaster or -mistress, clerk, mail sorter, mail carrier, etc.
• Using paper, each child will make his/her own letter, envelope, and stamp to show knowledge of post office procedure.
• With access to a mailbox, each child will walk to the mailbox and drop in his/her own real letter with real stamps, demonstrating awareness that the mailbox is an extension of the post office.

228

Simple Activity
Given pictures of three buildings (a school, a firehouse, and a post office), each child will point to the post office to show awareness of what a post office looks like. The teacher will have discussed the differences in the appearance of these buildings.

More Advanced Activity
Using slides of local governmental buildings, each child will identify the post office to show that he can discriminate between governmental buildings.

Design your own activities to meet the needs of individual children.

Each child will learn to identify the mail carrier, the mail carrier's uniform and equipment, and mail vehicles in the community.

Objective 2

• Using pictures of the mail carrier and other uniformed employees (male or female), each child will distinguish the mail carrier from among other individuals in the community after the teacher has pointed to the differences on the pictures.
• The teacher will select a child to play the role of a mail carrier—in dress, delivering mail, and so on, for the other children, showing awareness of the dress, equipment, and function of the mail carrier.
• Given paper and cloth, each child will make a mailbag and a mail carrier's hat to demonstrate awareness of the mail carrier's dress and equipment. (Pictures of these should be available for children to look at.)
• Provided with blocks and chairs, and prepared in a discussion, each child will make a mail cart, truck, plane, and train to demonstrate awareness of what mail vehicles are.

Activities

Simple Activity
Make arrangements for a mail carrier(s) to visit the class and deliver mail, so that the children will be faced with the actual uniform, mailbag, and articles of mail.

More Advanced Activity
Provided with materials, each child will make a mailbox from a cardboard carton and paint it to resemble a mailbox he/she has seen, showing an awareness of what a mailbox looks like. (The child can use it to send messages to other children and the teacher.)

Design your own activities to meet the needs of individual children.

Alternate Activities

The postassessment is the same as the preassessment. After the postassessment, exit from the module or proceed to additional activities.

Postassessment

• After a field trip to the post office, each child will demonstrate knowledge of how the post office operates by telling who was seen and what each person was doing.

Additional Activities

• After a visual demonstration by the teacher, each child will make a stamp from colored paper to show ability to identify a postage stamp from other types of stamps that the teacher has available.

• With access to stamps, envelopes, and letters with canceled stamps, each child will collect items for a scrapbook to show that he/she knows what a post office handles.

10.4 Builders

Rationale

Buildings of all kinds are constantly under construction around us. People of all ages, especially young children, are fascinated by the process of building. For children the process of building is not only interesting, but also an important part of their basic knowledge. Occupations in the building industry include carpenters, painters, electricians, bricklayers, and plumbers. These positions are increasingly vital because the number of businesses and homes being built in this country is on the rise. The children should have an opportunity to become aware of the satisfaction gained from working in these positions. (Girls as well as boys will want to explore these interesting and rewarding occupations.)

Prerequisites

The teacher should become aware of manual occupations involving construction of buildings by researching pictures showing various kinds of construction, including blueprints, by observing construction that is most easily accessible to the school and by arranging for some of the children's fathers who are contractors or construction workers to visit the room or to be special trip guides. The teacher should have materials such as scrap lumber, nails, saws, hammers, water-base paint, paintbrushes, short ladders, electrical wire, conduit pipes, bricks, sand, plumbing tools, water pipes, and a cut-away model of a house showing the items needed in construction.

Preassessment

• Given blueprints, paper, crayons, materials and equipment used by construction personnel, and pictures of construction personnel, each child will show knowledge of the construction jobs by using a simplified blueprint as a guide to draw what will be constructed and then, using blocks, building what was planned.

• Each child will demonstrate ability to identify the personnel involved in the construction of a building by correctly placing pictures of workers with the appropriate job-site pictures and by telling, showing, or singing one thing he knows about each construction worker.

After the preassessment, exit from the module or proceed to the objectives.

Objective 1

Each child will learn about the jobs related to the construction of a building.

- Using a simplified blueprint, the teacher will point out how a one-room building is drawn. Provided with paper and crayons, each child will draw a room in a house to show awareness that a plan is used to make a building come out right.
- Provided with materials and equipment used by carpenters, painters, electricians, bricklayers, and plumbers, each child will demonstrate awareness of the jobs related to construction by role playing these after seeing pictures of each worker doing his/her job. (Role playing should occur at the time the teacher shows the picture and says who the worker is.)

Alternate Activities

Simple Activity
One child will role play a carpenter for the other children in the class, demonstrating what a carpenter does by measuring, sawing, and hammering. (Variations: Demonstrate plumbing, wiring, or other construction activities.)

More Advanced Activity
Provided with a building kit, each child will work with others to build a small house, demonstrating knowledge of construction.

Design your own activities to meet the needs of individual children.

Objective 2

Each child will learn to identify the personnel involved in the construction of buildings in the community.

Activities

- Using pictures, each child will identify the carpenter, electrician, bricklayer, plumber, and painter to show ability to distinguish these personnel from other workers in the community, placing models of each worker with the correct picture and naming the models.
- Placed in a group, each child will show, tell, or sing one thing about a builder, showing awareness of what the builders look like and what they do.

Alternate Activities

Simple Activity
After a visit to a construction site to see construction personnel working, each child will demonstrate knowledge of the personnel by picking out pictures of construction workers from pictures of workers in many other occupations. (The teacher has photographed these workers ahead of time.)

More Advanced Activity
Using crayons or paint, each child will demonstrate knowledge of construction personnel by coloring or painting a picture of a builder or builders doing their jobs.

Design your own activities to meet the needs of individual children.

Postassessment

The postassessment is the same as the preassessment. After the postassessment, exit from the module or proceed to additional activities.

Additional Activities

- After a trip to another construction site, the children will demonstrate knowledge of personnel by describing the different activities. (Tape record at the site so that children can play back sounds and remember. Video taping would be even better.)
- After hearing and seeing a series of picture book stories about construction workers, such as "Mike Mulligan and His Steam Shovel," each child will indicate awareness of what a construction worker does by building with equipment in a sandbox.

10.5 The Fire Fighter

Rationale

Even though children hear a lot about fire fighters, and most little boys think they want to be one when they grow up, they need to be made aware of fire fighters as more than just persons with exciting jobs. The children need to learn what the job is, the training he or she goes through, what kind of clothing is worn and why, as well as the kind of equipment used.

Some women are successful filling the roles of fire fighters. Girls will be interested in this and will want to know what is involved. Also, members of fire departments in some communities are trained as drivers of emergency vehicles and as paramedics. Young children are fascinated by these workers who serve so well.

Prerequisites

Have these materials on hand: pictures, films, filmstrips, books, records, a list of resource people, dress-up clothes (complete fire fighter suit), some equipment, materials with which to conduct experiments (two candles, matches, jar), art materials such as crayons and newsprint. Contact people to visit the classroom, and make arrangements to visit a fire station when a knowledgeable person is available to answer questions. Be sure to ask these resource people to talk not only about fire fighting but about their jobs as paramedics.

Preassessment

- Given a picture of a fire fighter, a policeman, and a mail carrier, each child will show knowledge of fire fighters by selecting the fire fighter picture and telling five things the fire fighter does.
- Given clothing and tools used by fire fighters, each child will demonstrate knowledge of clothing and tools by naming three pieces of clothing and four pieces of equipment, and telling how each is used. After the preassessment, exit from the module or proceed to the objectives.

Objective 1

The children will learn what a fire fighter is called and what he or she does.

Activities

- After a visit to a fire station, each child will show knowledge of a fire fighter by making an experience chart with the teacher.

232

• Given a set of pictures showing different occupations, the child will show knowledge of the fire fighter by pointing to the correct picture when asked to do so by the teacher. The child will also tell the teacher what a fire fighter does. (Pictures of male and female fire fighters are needed.)

Simple Activity
After a visit by a fire fighter dressed as Smokey the Bear, the children will show understanding of what a fire fighter does by discussing with their teacher how fire fighters teach children about fire prevention.

More Advanced Activity
Given two candles, a jar, and a match, each child will show or simulate how a fireman puts out a fire by placing a jar over one lit candle. (Follow this experiment with a discussion of fires and the many ways fire fighters can put out fires.)

Design your own activities to meet the needs of individual children.

The children will learn the names and uses of the uniform and tools used by the fire fighters.

• After a resource person has visited the classroom and shown a film on fire fighters, each child will demonstrate knowledge of clothing and tools by naming three pieces of clothing and four pieces of equipment (that are on display) and by telling how each is used.
• After seeing a filmstrip on fire fighters, the children will make up a song, sing it, and act it out, demonstrating knowledge of what a fire fighter wears and does. (Example: "This Is What the Fire Fighter Does, Wears, and Uses.")

Simple Activity
Each child will show knowledge of two tools to use for extinguishing fires by building an imaginary fire in the sandbox and by using water and dirt (or sand) to put it out.

More Advanced Activity
The children will demonstrate the uses of the fire fighter's uniform and equipment by role playing how these are used at a fire.

Design your own activities to meet the needs of individual children.

The postassessment is the same as the preassessment. After the postassessment, exit from the module or proceed to additional activities.

• Using crayons and newsprint, each child will show knowledge of fire fighter's clothes by drawing a picture of the uniform and telling other children about it.

Alternate Activities

Objective 2

Activities

Alternate Activities

Postassessment

Additional Activities

233

• Using a blanket or a towel, each child will show how to put out a fire (when someone's clothing is on fire) by smothering the imaginary fire with the blanket or towel, or by rolling on the ground. (Always stress—DO NOT RUN.)

10.6 Beauticians and Barbers

Rationale

In this day of the "beautiful people," everyone is or should be conscious of his or her appearance. Many times one's appearance has a bearing on how one feels and how others see him/her.

Young children go to beauty shops and barber shops with their parents as a routine thing, but they need to be made aware of the beautician, the manicurist, the barber and the shampooer as people who perform an important service for others. Care should be taken not to sex stereotype these occupations. There are lady barbers and male beauticians.

Prerequisites

Have on hand equipment used by each person, such as combs, brushes, curlers, scissors, clippies, fingernail polish (tempera paint); art materials such as newsprint and crayons; old shoes; pictures, films, and books; and a list of resource people and a complete set of uniforms relating to each occupation. Make arrangements for field trips.

Preassessment

• Given a set of pictures of the beautician, barber, manicurist, and shampooer, each child will name the occupation of the person shown in each picture and tell what each does and how each helps to improve appearance.
• When shown different uniforms, tools, and items used in each occupation (display items on a table), each child will group the tools and items according to the occupations they are used in.
• When asked by the teacher, each child will be able to tell the different steps a person goes through when getting a haircut, a hairset, a manicure, or a shave.
After the preassessment, exit from the module or proceed to the objective.

Objective 1

The children will learn the names of the occupations of the beautician, the manicurist, the barber, and the shampooer, what each does, and how each helps improve personal appearance.

Activities

• After a visit to a beauty shop and a barber shop, each child will show knowledge of the occupations involved by using an occupational Lotto game—matching the right picture of each person with the right background.
• After the teacher demonstrates what beauty people do, each child will indicate what he/she has learned by dressing the hair and nails of dolls correctly. (Variation: Give dolls a shave.)

10.6   Fingernail painting

Simple Activity
After a visit to the beauty shop and the barber shop, the children will make an experience chart, giving the name of each occupation and what the person in that occupation does. (The children might also want to list the ways these people help us improve our appearance.)

More Advanced Activity
After visiting a beauty shop and a barber shop, the children will show their knowledge of the occupations involved by building "The Beautiful Place" (a beauty/barber shop) in the classroom to role play in daily.

Design your own activities to meet the needs of individual children.

Alternate Activities

The children will learn what each person in each occupation wears (uniform) and the tools or items used in each occupation. The children will also learn the different steps a person goes through in getting a haircut, a manicure, a hairset, or a shave.

Objective 2

• After seeing a video tape (taken by the teacher) of each of the beauty people at work, and after hearing about the tools the worker uses in the particular occupation, each child will show knowledge of tools used in each occupation by going to the display table and grouping the tools according to occupations (pictures).
• After a resource person from each occupation has demonstrated or actually given a manicure, a haircut, or a mock shave to one or more

Activities

of the children, each child will indicate knowledge of the steps involved by demonstrating three steps in each operation in "The Beautiful Place."

Alternate Activities

Simple Activity
The children will show their knowledge of the tools used in each occupation (and the uniform worn by each person) by role playing—dressing in the proper uniform, using the correct tools and equipment, and working in the right area of "The Beautiful Place."

More Advanced Activity
The children will demonstrate their knowledge of the steps involved in each operation (haircut, hairdo, manicure, shampoo) by making a flowchart (with the help of the teacher) of each operation.

Design your own activities to meet the needs of individual children.

Postassessment

The postassessment is the same as the preassessment. After the postassessment, exit from the module or proceed to additional activities.

Additional Activities

● Using wigs and wig stands, the children will demonstrate their knowledge of the basic steps in a hairset by washing and setting wigs.
● Using crayons and newsprint, the children will create pictures of the occupations they have learned about to demonstrate their understanding of these careers.

11
Number
Concepts and
Skills

The young child, mathematically speaking, is very much tied to the real world of concrete objects (Sharp, 1969). He/she is still struggling with the realization that quantity and number do not necessarily change in mysterious ways when appearances are altered. Young children may think that one straw is longer than another one simply because one has been moved a little to the left of the other. They also have problems perceiving the parts of a whole if the whole isn't present at the time. They seem to be able to think about one only by forgetting the other.

These problems of conservation require, according to Piaget (1953), an understanding that the individual's mental development is dependent upon experiences in the environment. The teacher is the one who plans the kind of mathematical experiences young children will have. The teacher following Piaget's thinking will plan most of the curriculum using manipulation of concrete objects. Only after children have shown real understanding at this concrete level will the teacher move them to the semiabstract or pictorial level of abstraction. If the children are learning about sets, the teacher will have them experiencing, manipulating, and counting many kinds of objects in boxes or bags representing sets before giving a flannel board demonstration or a ditto sheet with the pictures of these sets.

The young child can function at the semiabstract (pictorial) level in sets and perhaps even at the transitional level of abstraction (pictures matched with symbols) in counting but still have to function at the concrete (manipulative) level in terms of physical dimensions (e.g., length, depth). And this same child might also be able to function at the abstract level (numerals and other math symbols, such as plus, minus, and equals, without pictures) in some other area of math. Mental development in the area of math is an individual affair, and each child varies in terms of the level of abstraction he/she can apply to the mathematical concept being experienced.

Therefore, it is better for the teacher to start each child at the concrete level of abstraction in math. The only exception to this would be the mathematically gifted child, who can begin functioning at the semiabstract or the transitional level with a minimum of frustration.

If the teacher starts all the young children at the semiabstract or abstract level when introducing a concept such as counting, the children learn very little math. Math might as well be Greek; the level is too abstract to be understood. They do learn that math is hard and not much fun, however. Starting at the concrete level and remaining there until children are fluent with each concept allows children to understand what they are learning and to grasp the concept. It also makes math more enjoyable.

There are other modules in this book that should be considered part of the math curriculum even though they are not in this component.

They are as follows:

2.3   Medium of Exchange
2.4   Our Money
3.11 Visual Discrimination
5.1   Measuring and Stirring
5.4   A Slice of Bread
5.5   An Egg by Any Other Name
7.1   Shapes
7.2   The Container with Six Sides

These eight modules plus the seven in this component are a beginning curriculum in math for the young child. The modules in the component on number concepts and skills are as follows:

11.1 Counting and Recognizing Numbers
11.2 Number Sequence
11.3 Centimeter and Meter Are Sweeter
11.4 One-to-One Correspondence
11.5 A Matter of Weight
11.6 Greater Than, Less Than, and Equal To
11.7 A Set for You

References

Piaget, J. "How Children Form Mathematical Concepts." *Scientific American*, November 1953.
Sharp. E. *Thinking Is Child's Play*. Avon Books, 1969.

11.1 Counting and Recognizing Numbers

Rationale

Children can learn to rote count, but a real understanding of numbers is something they must develop out of their own experiences. Classifications and ordering activities are prenumber experiences that all children need if they are to develop an understanding of numbers. Classification is being able to group objects according to likenesses and differences. Ordering calls for arranging objects in a specified series.

In the early curriculum, the young child should be given many opportunities for classifying and ordering concrete objects from the simple to more complex. Many activities involving the tactile, visual, and other senses develop these concepts in young children. The main goal of the activities in this section is understanding. The child will handle concrete objects and make sets that can actually be seen, manipulated, and counted.

Before (and during) the following unit, the teacher should give the students experiences involving the classification and ordering of objects.

The teacher should now assemble all the materials required for each of the activities.

Prerequisites

Materials needed: clothespin stands (made by gluing half a clothespin to the bottom of a complete one), cards for writing sets of dots and numerals, one-inch cubes, and containers for the cards and cubes.

Given sets of dots on cards (one dot on the first card, two dots on the second, and so on through ten), the child will demonstrate an ability to count and recognize numbers by counting the dots correctly, placing the corresponding numeral cards on the clothespin stands and setting aside the correct number of cubes.

After the preassessment, exit from the module or proceed to the objective.

Preassessment

The children will learn to count, to recognize the numerals 1 through 10, and to relate those numerals to appropriate sets.

Objective

• After setting up a fruit market or a play store with empty containers, each child will demonstrate an ability to count and make sets by going to the store to look for sets or groups of items that can be counted, bringing them back to the table, then arranging his/her counters to indicate numbers found, such as four (4) counters to show that four cans of soup were found on the shelves.
• Materials needed: empty milk cartons covered with construction paper, hinged numeral cards with number dots underneath—attached to top of milk cartons, ten small plastic cars with dots on top (1-10).

The child will show an ability to count and recognize numbers by counting the dots on each car and matching that number with the corresponding numeral on the garage (milk carton) and then "driving" the car into its garage. The car with five dots should be in the garage with the number 5 on the door, etc. The child checks himself or herself by flipping the hinged top to the garage and matching up one-to-one the dots on the garage and the dots on its car.
• Materials needed: 5"-by-5" cardboard squares with large felt numerals and felt circles to represent sets—laminated if possible—and large paper clips.

The child will demonstrate skill in counting, recognizing numbers, and making sets by correctly counting and clipping the number of paper clips to each square shown by the felt numeral.

Activities

Simple Activity
The child will tell how many times the teacher dropped beads in a can, tapped on a table, or rang a bell. Next, the child will hold up the appropriate numeral upon hearing the sounds. The child will demonstrate ability to recognize and count numbers by giving correct

Alternate Activities

responses four out of five times. (If numeral cards are too abstract, revert to cards with dots.)

More Advanced Activity
Materials needed: eight to ten hosiery boxes, a written label stating "I counted," paper and pencil, various sets of ten objects—nuts, pencils, blocks, crayons—each set in a labeled jar.

Given the above materials, the child will show an ability to recognize and count numbers by taking out the boxes and placing in each some objects from the jars. Then the child will take a piece of paper and write the number of objects put into each box, copying the label on the container to show he/she counted ("I counted 4").

Design your own activities to meet the needs of individual children.

Postassessment
The postassessment is the same as the preassessment. After the postassessment, exit from the module or proceed to the additional activity.

Additional Activity
Materials needed: ten flash cards with dots one through ten.

Given the group of flash cards on the chalk rail and a leader who will clap his hands a number of times, the child will show an ability to count and recognize numbers by picking the numeral card which represents the number of claps. (If the dots are too abstract for children, use concrete objects.

Resources Books
Dumas, Enoch. *Arithmetic Learning Activities.* Fearon Publishers, 1967.
Lorton, Mary Baralta. *Workjobs.* Addison-Wesley Publishing Co., 1973.
Sharp, Evelyn. *Thinking Is Child's Play.* Discus Books, 1969.

Record
Learning Basic Skills through Music. Kimbo Records. Educational Activities, Inc.

11.2 Number Sequence

Rationale
A most important goal of any good math program for young children is to remember that children develop their learning abilities through experiences with concrete objects. Young children need to use manipulative materials for their own firsthand experiences involving numbers.

The concept of number sequence can be acquired through active involvement with concrete and familiar materials. Children need the experience of learning activities involving counting, forming sets of objects, and then ordering numerically as a basis for understanding numbers.

Prerequisites
Before the following unit of learning is presented, the teacher should

give the students learning experiences involving counting and recognizing the numbers 1-10. An ability to count and recognize numbers is basic to understanding number sequence and value. Also, the children should understand the concepts of greater, less, and equal to as these terms will be used in teaching numerical sequence. The teacher should assemble all needed materials before beginning the activities.

Materials needed: blocks of foam rubber glued to cardboard with the numerals 1-10 written on them, fifty-five large-headed straight pins.

Given pin cushions and pins, the child will demonstrate an ability to form sets of objects and order them numerically by putting the appropriate number of pins into the pin cushions and ordering them from 1 through 10. (Use pins with large, colored heads.)

After the preassessment, exit from the module or proceed to the objective.

Objective

The children will learn how to form sets of objects and order them 1 through 10.

Activities

• Material needed: ten clothes hangers, plastic clothespins, tagboard with numerals 1-10 stapled to each clothes hanger, dowel or hook to support clothes hangers.

Given ten labeled clothes hangers and the clothespins, the child will demonstrate an ability to form sets of numerical sequences by counting out the appropriate number of clothespins for each hanger and putting them on each hanger, and then ordering the hangers from one to ten.

• Materials needed: ten small Easter baskets—butter cartons filled with grass and labeled 1-10, paper cups filled with sugar-coated colored cereal to look like Easter eggs.

Given the baskets and a cup of cereal, each child will demonstrate skill in forming sets and numerical ordering by filling each basket with the appropriate number of eggs, and then arranging the baskets in order one through ten.

• Materials needed: ten labeled baby food jars (1-10) and a jar of counters.

Given ten labeled baby food jars (1-10) and a jar of counters, the child will demonstrate skill in numerical ordering by placing the correct number of counters into each jar and then ordering the jars in correct numerical sequence.

Alternate Activities

Simple Activity
Materials needed: small counters, one larger milk carton made into a train engine, and ten small empty milk cartons covered with paper and labeled with the numerals 1-10 on one side and the corresponding number of dots on the other.

Given the milk cartons and counters, each child will show an ability to form sets and order them numerically by filling each car with the appropriate amount of "cargo" and then ordering the cars correctly into a train.

More Advanced Activity

Materials needed: old magazines, paper booklets, numeral names 1-10.

Given the booklets following a discussion of the numeral names for 1-10 and their visual presentation, each child will show skill in forming sets and numerical sequencing by constructing a number booklet allowing one page for each number and its accompanying name. The children then cut out and paste into the book a picture of each number.

Design your own activities to meet the needs of individual children.

Postassessment

The postassessment is the same as the preassessment. After the postassessment, exit from the module or proceed to the additional activity.

Additional Activity

Materials needed: ten pictures of cars cut from magazines and glued to cardboard with one of the numerals 1-10 on the car and the appropriate number of dots on the back of the cardboard, a stand for each cardboard made from a block of wood and glued to each cardboard car.

Given the ten labeled pictures of cars, each child will demonstrate understanding of sets and numerical order by correctly putting the cars in order.

Resources

Brock, J,. and Heath, S. "Piaget Is Practical." *Science and Children,* October 1971.

Curriculum Guidelines for Kindergarten Activities. Magnolia, Arkansas: Magnolia School District.

Friedman, F,. and Fink, B. "Piaget in the Classroom." *Science and Children,* September 1972.

Lorton, Mary Baralta. *Workjobs.* Addison-Wesley Co., 1973.

11.3 Centimeter and Meter are Sweeter

Rationale

The United States was the only major industrial nation that was not using the metric system (SI) at the end of 1976. To remain competitive in world trade markets, the United States must eventually convert to SI.

Young children in other countries have been using SI for a number of years. Many school systems throughout the United States are incorporating SI into their curriculum. At the end of 1976, school children in California and Maryland were taught only metric measures.

Prerequisites

Children should have a knowledge of the measuring concepts longer than, shorter than, and the same length as another object.

Have on hand items to measure, such as soda straws, popsicle sticks, plastic spoons, ribbons, old ties, combs, clothespins, pencils, erasers, crayons, tissue boxes, jello boxes, and similar objects. You will also need eight to ten empty 6 ounce orange juice cans; a stick of gum for each child; red, green, orange, yellow, and purple lollipops (approximately two for each child); a 20 cm rule and a meter stick for each child. These may be purchased or constructed from oak tag. The children will need three classroom charts to record their data.

Preassessment

Establish two lollipop trails by using masking tape between two inverted orange juice cans on which a lollipop has been secured. The first trail which is between two red lollipops will be 25 cm long. The second trail (green) will be 2 m.

    Given a variety of objects such as a meter stick, a pencil, an eraser, a crayon, a 20 cm rule, each child will demonstrate ability to measure the red lollipop trails by doing so with each of the objects given him or her. Each child will be given a lollipop after measuring with the meter stick and the rule because the centimeter and the meter are sweeter (easier to use).

    After the preassessment, exit from the module or proceed to the objective.

Objective

The child will develop an understanding of the centimeter and meter used as standard units of measuring.

Activities

• Each child will be given an opportunity to measure the distance on the green lollipop trail using whatever objects or body parts he or she chooses as a measuring device. Each child will record the data on the classroom chart as an awareness experience on the use of the centimeter and meter.
• After much discussion, the children will discover the variety the class has in measuring the green lollipop trail by using different sized feet, straws, erasers, and so on. When the children have discovered a need for a standard unit of measure, each child will be given a meter rule. At this time the teacher will introduce the meter stick and demonstrate its use in measuring so that the children can learn that the centimeter and meter are easier to handle and more useful.
• Using the meter rule, each child will demonstrate skills in measuring various items in the room, such as the table, desk, bookcase, window, or door to find out whether the item is longer or shorter than a meter stick.
• As the child discovers the need to measure items that are longer than the meter rule, the child will discover by joining his/her meter stick with a friend's meter stick, that they can measure longer distances. The children will demonstrate their skill in measuring tables, desks, bookcases, doors, or windows by joining meter sticks.
• Each child will demonstrate ability to measure the green lollipop trail by combining meter sticks. Each child will record his/her data on the classroom chart.
• To give the children additional practice in using the meter as a standard unit of measure, construct three additional lollipop trails. The purple will be 4 meters in length; the orange, 6 meters in length; and the yellow, 7 meters. Each child will practice using the meter as a

standard unit of measure. Each child will record the data on a personal chart. Reinforcing the concept that a "meter is sweeter," each child will enjoy a lollipop after completing the measuring.

• After each child receives a stick of gum, the class will consider the idea of measuring the stick of gum with meter sticks. If the children find the meter stick is too long, they will consider measuring the stick of gum with various objects such as crayons, chalk, beads, or various parts of the body, such as fingers, knuckles, or tongues. Each child will record the data on the classroom chart.

• After much discussion, the children will discover they need a standard unit of measure to measure a stick of gum. Each child will be given a 20 cm rule. After a demonstration by the teacher in using the 20 cm rule, each child will use his/her skills to measure the stick of gum. After recording the data on the chart, each child will enjoy chewing the gum, remembering that the centimeter is sweeter.

• Using a measuring table (the items may be those listed in the prerequisites section and other items the children would like to contribute), the children will enrich their awareness of measurements and increase their skills in measuring by experimenting.

• Invite the school nurse to bring the individual height records for each child to the class. (These will be in centimeters). Each child, assisted by the school nurse, will measure another child. Each child will record his/her new height on the record.

• After viewing the filmstrip *Metrics from the Start* or *What Is Measurement?* each child will demonstrate an understanding of metric measurement by measuring with either the 20 cm rule or a metric stick. (The filmstrips show that the meter is used to measure objects of greater length and that the centimeter is used to measure objects of smaller length.)

• To show their understanding of using standard units of measure, the children will use their 20 cm rules and meter sticks to measure items on the playground. Items which the children may measure are seats of swings, steps on the slide, the distance between posts of the playground fence, segments of sidewalks, steps to the school building, distance between windows, and so forth.

Alternate Activities

Simple Activity
After each child has traced around his/her hand on a sheet of paper, he/she will use a 20 cm rule to measure the width of his/her thumb and the length of one finger to show knowledge of measuring by centimeters. This activity should be repeated as often as necessary for individual children using different fingers.

More Advanced Activity
Establish additional lollipop trails. these will be irregular trails winding around tables or chairs.
Each child will practice measuring both in centimeters and in meters using these new trails. Each child will record the data on a personal chart.

Design your own activities to meet the needs of individual children.

Postassessment

The postassessment is the same as the preassessment. After the postassessment, exit from the module or proceed to additional activities.

- Using a 20 cm rule, each child will use crayons to color each centimeter on the rule a different color, reinforcing his/her perception of the units.
- Using the colorful centimeter rule, each child will demonstrate measuring skills by measuring his/her shoe.

Additional Activities

Resources
Books

Branley, Franklyn. *Think Metric!* Thomas Y. Crowell, 1972.

Glazer, Anton *Neater by the Meter.* Glazer, Inc., 1974.

Ferguson, Thomas A,. and Repass, Susan. "Developing a Measurement Unit for Primary Children." *Science and Children* 12(March 1975):6.

Gilbert, Thomas F,. and Gilbert, Marilyn B. *Thinking Metric.* John Wiley and Sons, Inc., 1973.

Higgins, Jan L. *A Metric Handbook for Teachers.* National Council of Teachers of Mathematics, 1974.

Hughes, Rowland. "Teaching Measurement and the Metric System." *Science and Children* 12(March 1975):6.

Iona, Mario. "Making Comparisons of Rulings for Metric Measuring Devices." *Science and Children* 12(March 1975):6.

Johnson, H., and Roberson, M. *Experiences in the Metric System.* Amidon and Associates, 1974.

Kapel, David; Resnick, Harold; and Wilderman, Ann. *Metric Measure Simplified.* Prindle, Weberand, Schmidt, Inc., 1974.

Schultz, Klause. "Do-it-Yourself Metrication." *Science and Children.* 12(March 1975):6.

Turner, L., and Stronck, D. "Making Measurements and Metric Units." *Science and Children.* 12(March 1975):6.

Walker, Margaret. "Metric in the Kindergarten." *Science and Children.* 12(March 1975):6.

Wilderman, Ann. "The Metrics Are Coming." *Early Years.* 5(April 1975):8.

Willert, Frederick. "Centimeter by Centimeter." *Early Years.* 5(April 1975):8.

Willert, Frederick. *My Metric Measurement Manual.* Pauper Press, 1973.

Chart

Metric Chart (free)
Hayes School Publishing Co., Inc.
321 Pennwood Avenue
Wilkinsburg, Penn. 15221

Filmstrips

Metrics From the Start, Clearvue, Inc., 1975.

What Is Measurement? Baker & Taylor Co., Audio Visual Services Division, 1974.

Record and Cassette

"The Metric System of Measurement." Learning Resources Company, Dept. 45, 202 Lake Milam Drive, Lakeland, Florida 33803.

Task Cards

Primary Math: Metric System DPR Publishers, Inc., Box 1000, Newfield, New Jersey 08344.

Activity Booklet

Miller, Mary Richardson, and Richardson, Toni Cresswell. "Making Metric Maneuvers." Activity Resources Co., Inc., Hayward, California.

Kit "Welcome to the World of Metrics." Listener. 6777 Hollywood Blvd., Hollywood, California. (Full year program.)

11.4 One-to-One Correspondence

Rationale

Before the child counts meaningfully, he/she must have a grasp of one-to-one correspondence (Sharp 1972). The purpose of this module is to give the child many concrete experiences with one-to-one correspondence. Some experiences at a semi-abstract level are provided, too.

The teacher needs to keep in mind that conservation of numbers may be a problem for some young children. It is hoped that with experience each child will conserve (be able to understand without one-to-one correspondence).

Prerequisites

Have on hand sets of twenty of each of the following materials: identical buttons, bottle caps, poker chips, checkers, coasters (identical in size and shape), pennies, felt circles, squares, triangles, ducks, boats, cups and saucers (each set identical in size), and a flannel board. Also have enough swords, hats, capes, and mustaches for each child to have one of each.

Preassessment

• Each child will demonstrate understanding of one-to-one correspondence by matching a row of four buttons. He must place them one directly under the other as illustrated below.

0 0 0 0 Teacher's row
0 0 0 0 Child's row

The child should then tell which row has more members.
• Each child will demonstrate understanding of one-to-one correspondence by making a row of six buttons and answering the teacher's questions correctly. (The teacher puts six buttons directly under the child's and asks, "Which row has more?" Answer: "Both have the same." then the teacher moves his/her buttons farther apart and asks, "Which row has more?" Answer: "Both have the same number of buttons."

Repeat this test twice. If the correct answer is not given, proceed to the objective; otherwise, exit from the module.)

Objective

Each child will learn to do a simple one-to-one correspondence.

Activities

• After a demonstration by the teacher, each child will show understanding of one-to-one correspondence by matching checkers to checker cards (cards with checkers glued on in certain row patterns such as three evenly spaced in a row, four in a row, five to ten in a row), and counting what he/she has done. (Variation: same patterns but not evenly spaced.)

246

11.4 Cups and saucers—showing one-to-one correspondence in math

- After each child has chosen any number of cups, he/she will indicate knowledge of one-to-one correspondence by choosing the correct number of saucers to put under the cups.
- Same as preceding activity, except that the child is asked to put a sugar cube in each cup.
- Given five bottle caps in a row, and five felt circles, each child will show understanding of one-to-one correspondence by putting the same number of felt circles on the flannel board as he/she has bottle caps in front of him/her.
- Given five felt circles and five felt copies of the numeral one (1) and a demonstration by the teacher, each child will show understanding of one-to-one correspondence by putting the numeral 1 under each circle and counting up to five.

Alternate Activities

Simple Activity
At the teacher's command, each child will demonstrate understanding of one-to-one correspondence by selecting a partner to play a game with.

More Advanced Activity
The Three Musketeers Game. While playing this game the child will indicate understanding of one-to-one correspondence by getting one of each of the items needed for him/her to be a musketeer. The children are divided into groups of three and told that each musketeer needs to make or get the following: a sword, a hat, a cape, a mustache, and a secret weapon.

Design your own activities to meet the needs of individual children.

Postassessment   The postassessment is the same as the preassessment. After the postassessment, exit from the module or proceed to additional activities.

Additional Activities   • After the teacher has arranged five coasters in a row, each child will show knowledge of one-to-one correspondence by putting a coaster on top of each of the teacher's coasters and counting them with the teacher. (Variation: The teacher moves the top coasters between each of the other coasters and asks, "Do we still have the same number of coasters?" Children take turns counting as each puts a coaster on top of each of the ones already there.)
• After the child has made a row of buttons, he/she will demonstrate understanding of one-to-one correspondence by putting an identical number of buttons in a row directly underneath the first row. He/she counts the number in each row to see if each row has the same number of buttons. Then the child puts another identical row underneath if he has enough buttons.

Resources   Piaget, J. "How Children Form Mathematical Concepts." *Scientific American.* November 1953.
Sharp, E. *Thinking Is Child's Play.* Avon Books, 1969.
Suppes, P. "Mathematical Concept Formation in Children." *American Psychologist,* February 1966.
Wagner, G., et al. *Arithmetic Games and Activities.* Macmillan Publishing Co., Inc., 1970.

11.5 A Matter of Weight

Rationale   The purpose of this module is to provide experiences concerning weight while encouraging children to use a vocabulary appropriate for describing what they experience. The focus is more on how to say it than on accurate measurement. Young children need to start with gross differences and move toward fine differentiations.

Prerequisites   Have on hand several sets of scales (each with two balancing surfaces on which the teacher has covered the indicator face with a simpler metric scale reading zero when balanced), a cardboard box, bricks, rocks, a large feather, several paper cups, golf balls, 227 grams of rice, a pair of shoes, a large hat, bananas, a gram scale, dinner knives, ballpoint pens, tennis balls, saucers, flour, beans, cotton.

Preassessment   Each child will demonstrate understanding of gross differences in weight by answering the teacher correctly when asked, "Which is heavier
• a cardboard box [larger than a brick] or a brick?" (Ans: Brick)
• a rock or a large feather?" (Ans: Rock)
• a large paper cup or a golf ball?" (Ans: Golf ball)

• 227 grams of cheese or 227 grams or rice?" (Ans: Same, or I can't tell without scales.)
• a pair of shoes or a large [but lightweight] hat?" (Ans: Shoes)
After the preassessment, exit from the module or proceed to the objective.

Each child will learn to measure objects in terms of gross differences in weight.

• Given some scales, several sizes of paper cups, a large feather, and some rocks, each child will show knowledge of gross differences in weight by experimenting with the objects, placing them on the scales to see which is the heaviest. Children will share their findings with the teacher.
• Given some scales, a brick, a box, and a pair of shoes, each child will indicate understanding of gross differences in weight by stacking the heaviest object on the bottom, then the next heaviest, and so on, after weighing or feeling for weight.
• Given some scales, a golf ball, a large paper cup, a large hat and a pair of shoes, each child will show understanding of which is heavier by attempting to balance the scales (getting the indicator to read zero or close to it).
• Given some scales, 227 grams (½ lb.) of cheese, 227 grams of grapes, 227 grams of rice, and 227 grams of rocks, each child will demonstrate knowledge of gross differences in weight by showing ability to put two of the items on one side of the scale and two on the other side of the scale, thus balancing the scales at zero. The child can report on other combinations.

Simple Activity
Given a banana, a large rock, and a large feather, each child will indicate understanding of gross differences in weight by feeling these in his/her hands, two at a time, and telling which is heavier and which heaviest. (Variation: Have child tell which is lighter and lightest.)

More Advanced Activity
Given a dinner knife, a ball-point pen, a tennis ball, and a saucer, each child will show knowledge of weight by estimating which will be heaviest, which will be lighter than the first but heavier than the third, and so on and then weighing each on a gram scale to check correctness.

Design your own activities to meet the needs of individual children.

The postassessment is the same as the preassessment. After the postassessment, exit from the module or proceed to additional activities.

• Given an array of rice, cotton, beans, and rocks and a gram scale with a red arrow (attached by teacher) marking the 454 gm mark (1

11.5 Weighing a banana and a feather

lb.), each child will experiment to see how much of each item placed on the scale will make the arrow read 454 grams, indicating understanding of weight and its relationship to the size or amount of an item.

• Given 227 grams of rocks on one surface of a set of scales, each child will show knowledge of weight by placing on the other surface some items mentioned in the prerequisites, continuing to do so until they overbalance the rocks.

Resources   Refer to the extensive resources section in Module 11.3.

11.6 Greater Than, Less Than, and Equal To

Rationale   A great deal of what the young child needs to learn is in the area of math vocabulary. That is, how do we express ideas mathematically? We say such things as *how many, a set of, heavier than, the longest,* and *regroup,* for example. Usually we speak of the terms *greater than, less than,* or *equal to* when comparing the members of two sets.

To avoid later confusion, it is important that young children be taught to express themselves in mathematical terms relative to the concepts they are experiencing. It is the purpose of this module to teach three of these terms.

Prerequisites   Have on hand twenty cardboard cards with pieces of wrapped candy fastened to each (one to ten pieces on any card), several boxes of checkers, an assortment of bracelets, felt funny face characters and a flannel board, two sets of number cards from one to ten, spinners numbered from one through ten, several decks of playing cards, ten unequal groups of pencils (with a rubber band holding each group).

Using the candy cards (described in the prerequisites), each child will demonstrate understanding of the terms *greater than, less than,* and *equal to* by responding appropriately when the teacher asks: (1) Is your candy greater than mine? (2) Is your candy the same as mine? (3) Is your candy less than mine? (This questioning occurs five times as follows: the teacher draws a card, the child draws a card, the teacher and the child compare cards, and then the teacher asks a question.)

After the preassessment, exit from the module or proceed to the objective.

The children will learn to use the terms *greater than, less than,* and *equal to.*

• Given a handful of checkers and a small box, each child will indicate understanding of comparative terms by hiding some of his/her checkers in his/her box (the rest stay in his/her lap), and when it is the child's turn, telling whether his/her number is greater than, less than, or equal to another child's. The game is played by two people who dump their checkers from the box onto a table for comparison. If the child uses the right comparison term, that child gets both his/her checkers and the partner's at that time. When all the checkers have been used, the child with the most checkers wins. (Variation: Use bottle caps instead of checkers.)

• The teacher, wearing three bracelets on one arm, gives the children a box of bracelets. Each child will show understanding of comparative terms by choosing the number of bracelets to wear according to the teacher's command: (a) Choose the same number as I have, a number equal to mine. (b) Choose a number greater than mine. (c) Choose a number less than mine.

This is a small group activity for the teacher and four or five children. (Variation: Teacher changes the number of bracelets on his/her arm, and the game begins again.)

• The Detective Game. The teacher puts three funny faces on the flannel board, telling the children that Colonel Mustache is having a party for his friends. So far Betty Bad and Clara Clunk have come. "If Larry Lucky comes," the teacher asks the children, putting Larry on the flannel board, "will the number at the party be greater than, less than, or equal to the number there before? You be the detective and tell us." Continue the game having characters come and go. (Variation: Play numerals to correspond with the number present at any one time.)

• Given two sets of number cards from one to ten turned face down, each child will show understanding of comparative language by challenging another player (when it is his/her turn) by saying, (a) "My number is greater than yours," (b) "My number is less than yours," or (c) "My number is equal to yours." Then both players turn their top card face up. If the challenger has correctly guessed the relationship of the two cards, he/she keeps both cards. Both players choose another card from the pile. At the end, the player with the most cards wins.

Simple Activity
Playing with two hands doubled into fists, each child will show

understanding of comparative terms by extending fingers from either one or both hands simultaneously with a partner while another child (referee) sits with his/her back to the game and calls out "equal to," or "less than," or "greater than." If the referee says "greater than," the child with the higher number of fingers extended wins a point. If the referee says "less than," then the child with the fewer number of fingers extended wins. If the referee says "equal to" and the finger counts are equal, both players get a point. If the finger count is unequal when "equal to" is called, then neither player gets a point. (Instead of points you can use small candies or raisins.)

More Advanced Activity
Using a spinner with numbers from one to ten on it, each child will indicate knowledge of comparative terms by calling out a number and then spinning to see if the spinner will land on one greater than the one called out. Player loses turn when he/she spins a number less than the one called out at the beginning of the turn. (This game is for two to four players.)

Design your own activities to meet the needs of individual children.

Postassessment

The postassessment is the same as the preassessment. After the postassessment, either exit from the module or proceed to additional activities.

Additional Activities

• Given a pack of playing cards, a child will demonstrate knowledge of comparative terms by putting out several cards and asking his/her partner to put out cards (on a row below first players) either (a) equal to, (b) greater than, or (c) less than the number in the first row. If the partner does this correctly, he gets all of the cards used in that turn and it becomes the partner's turn. (Each child starts with a pack of cards.)
• Given ten rubber-banded groups of pencils and a partner, each child will show understanding of comparative terms by following these directions: (a) Find all the groups greater than two and put them here. (b) Find all the groups less than two and put them here. (c) Find all the groups equal to two and hold them in your hand. (d) Take the rubber bands off and regroup the pencils to play again. (Variation: The teacher chooses a different number such as three or five. Two children and the teacher work well in this exercise.)

Resources

Croft, D. J., and Hess, R. D. *An Activities Handbook for Teachers of Young Children.* 2d ed. Houghton-Mifflin Co., 1975.
Wagner, G., et al. *Arithmetic Games and Activities.* Macmillan Publishing Co., Inc., 1970.

11.7 A Set for You

Rationale

Sets and subsets underlie much of elementary school through college math. When we add, subtract, multiply, or divide, we are dealing with numbers of sets and set members.

The young child needs to begin familiarity with sets at the concrete (manipulative) level. He or she needs to have numerous experiences with different kinds of sets, classifying by subsets, and counting set members before even as fundamental an operation as addition (the union of sets) can begin to hold meanings for him or her.

Inherent in this process is the young child's problem of dealing simultaneously with the whole and its parts. A child can have difficulty understanding that a string of red and yellow beads together forms a set and that the red beads are a subset of the whole set of beads. It takes a patient, creative teacher who can bring the concept of the whole's relationship to its parts into a significant focus for each child. The purpose of this module is to help the child identify with sets.

Prerequisites

Have on hand several sets of toy cars, trucks, and buses; blocks of different sizes and shapes; six bananas, one orange, two pears, three plums, three grapes; a size assortment of nuts, bolts, nails, and screws; twenty cups and saucers varying in size and color; and twelve to fifteen thread spools varying in size and color.

Teach children to count up to twenty before doing this module.

Preassessment

Given a set of toy cars, each child will show understanding of the basics of sets and subsets by answering three of the four following questions correctly:
• I have a set of cars. How many members are in the set? (Child counts and tells how many cars there are all together.)
• I want to park cars that are alike together. This would be a subset of cars. Can you park the cars that are alike over here? Are there any others alike? Do we have any other subsets? (The child should park or classify by color and by make or model.)
• If I were to drive some trucks into a parking lot, would these trucks be a subset of the set of cars? (Answer: No).
• If the parking lot was for cars, buses, and trucks, what could we call this set? (Possible answers: four-wheelers, transportation, or vehicles.)
After the preassessment, exit from the module or proceed to the objective.

Objective

Each child will learn some of the basics of sets and subsets.

Activities

• Given twenty poker chips of different colors, each child will demonstrate knowledge of sets and subsets by counting all the poker chips to determine the set number and by sorting and counting chips into subsets of color.
• Using a set of twenty cars, each child will indicate understanding of sets and subsets by counting all the cars to determine the set number and by sorting and counting subsets of cars determined by the model (two-door or four-door), or color.
• Given a set of fifteen blocks (all the same shape but varying in size), each child will show knowledge of sets and subsets by counting all the blocks to determine the set number and by sorting and counting

subsets by sizes. (Variation: Same activity but with the size of the blocks constant and the shape varied.)

Alternate Activities

Simple Activity
Given a set of six bananas, one orange, two pears, three plums, and three grapes, each child will show understanding of sets and subsets by answering the following:
• How many members are in the set of fruit?
• How many subsets can you show me?
• If I eat the orange how many members do I have in the subset of oranges?

More Advanced Activity
Given an assortment of nails, nuts, bolts, and screws (each item varying in size from others in a given subset), each child will demonstrate knowledge of sets and subsets by counting the total in the set of fasteners and by sorting and counting subsets by kind and by size.

Design your own activities to meet the needs of individual children.

Postassessment

The postassessment is the same as the preassessment. After the postassessment, exit from the module or proceed to the additional activities.

Additional Activities

• Given a set of ten cups and saucers, each child will demonstrate knowledge of sets and subsets by counting the members of the set (twenty) and by sorting and counting by subsets (size, some are cups and some are saucers, color, etc.)
• Given a set of twelve thread spools, each child will indicate knowledge of sets and subsets by counting the members of the set of spools and by sorting and counting by subsets according to size and color.

Resources

Andrews, R. E. *Numbers, Please.* Little, Brown & Co., 1961.
Crescimbeni, J. *Treasury of Classroom Arithmetic Activities.* Parker Publisher Co., Inc., 1969.
Dumas, E. *Arithmetic Games.* Fearon Publishers, Inc., 1956.
Durr, W. K., and Manning, W. *Arithmetic Aids for All the Grades,* books 1-4.
Flavell, J. H. *The Developmental Psychology of Jean Piaget.* D. Van Nostrand Co., Inc., 1963.
Piaget, J. *The Child's Conception of Number.* Humanities, 1952.
Sharp, E. *Thinking Is Child's Play.* Avon Books, 1969.
Suppes, P. "Mathematical Concept Formation in Children." *American Psychologist,* February 1966.
Turner, E. M. *Teaching Aids for Elementary Mathematics.* Holt, Rinehart and Winston, Inc., 1966.
Wagner, G., et al. *Arithmetic Games and Activities.* Macmillan Publishing Co., Inc., 1970.

12
Teaching Solo

Learning is largely a personal matter and is a function of perception or of how the learner sees the situation. Since each individual's perceptions depend upon the physical organism he possesses, how long he has lived, his experiential background, his goals, values and recognized needs, how he feels about himself and others, and his freedom from threat—his perceptions differ. Teaching becomes primarily a task of helping children perceive differently and discover personal meaning in what is to be learned. To do this, the teacher must know each learner well and see him and his world as he sees them.

> —*Lavone Hanna.* "Meeting the Challenge," in E. Short and G. Marconnit. *Contemporary Thought on Public School Curriculum,* 1968, p. 70.

Teaching solo means teaching alone rather than team teaching or working with the help of aides in the classroom. The ideal arrangement for individualizing instruction is an adult for every ten to fifteen children, but sometimes the teacher has no help and must operate solo.

The curriculum in this book has individualization built in so that the teacher does not have to worry about adapting the curriculum to the needs of the individual child. However, the solo teacher does have to adapt the curriculum somewhat to meet the needs of a lively group of five-year-olds.

Selecting Modules and Beginning

To organize the curriculum for solo teaching, start by selecting two modules from one chapter. One module should require more teacher interaction with children than the second module does. Module 3.2, "Listening for a Purpose," requires that interaction. Module 3.5, "Let's Look!" would be a good second choice because it leaves the teacher freer. The materials (which the teacher has set up ahead of time) do the teaching.

The plan would be to begin with one module, such as 3.2, and those who could test out of it could go into 3.5.

Preassessment

The solo teacher should choose a time to preassess each child when the rest of the children are busy—perhaps during free play and outside play. If done indoors, the preassessment for Module 3.2 could be given (one child at a time) as it appears in the book. If done outside, it could be modified by giving five consecutive directions. (In this case, directions such as run to the fence, pick up some grass, hop to the swings, throw the grass down, and walk back to the teacher.)

If the teacher is in a school that includes fifth or sixth graders, two of these young people could be invited to the class on days that the teacher wants to preassess. While the teacher preassesses individuals one of the older children could read stories and watch children while they use clay or draw, while the other could tell a story and help children at a listening center equipped with headsets and tape recorded instructions of what to do with a set of objects on a table or a ditto sheet.

During the preassessment the teacher should be recording which children pass or test out, which have some success, and which have little or no success. No teacher should simply look at a preassessment and say that he/she doesn't have to test because it's obvious which children would pass. The preassessment must be given.

The preassessment in 3.2 will divide the children into two groups: those who demonstrate their ability to listen for a purpose and those who cannot. Those who cannot or who have only partial success are the children the teacher will take through Module 3.2. The rest will be preassessed for 3.5.

The solo teacher can save time by having the materials set up for preassessing for 3.5 and, as a child tests out of 3.2, preassessing that child immediately for 3.5. The number that test out of 3.2 at age five is usually small. If almost all test out of 3.2, the teacher should consider himself/herself fortunate to be the teacher of children with such fine listening skills. However, before abandoning 3.2, it would be wise to preassess with five directions more difficult than those in the preassessment. (Do not, however, do this the first time around.)

At this point the teacher has identified the starting point for each child. Recording how much difficulty each child had who did not pass the preassessment helps the teacher decide who needs the simple activities and who the more advanced activities when that section of the module comes up.

A recording sheet might look like this:

Module 3.2 Preassessment

Name	No. Followed	Passed	Did Not
Mary Smith	3		X
John T.	4		X
Bob R.	1		X
Alice K.	5	X	
Robin O.	5	X	
Jack J.	2		X

The teacher can tell from the above recording that Alice and Robin

Stringing beads for ornamental clothing

do not need to go through Module 3.2. They can go on to 3.5 or another module. Mary (3) and John (4) had some success with 3.2 and will do the more advanced activities in 3.2 later. Bob (1) and Jack (2) had real problems with listening for a purpose and will probably need to do the simple activities later in 3.2

It is best to take all the children (as a group) who did not pass the preassessment through all of the situations labeled "Activities" under the "Objective" in the module. In Module 3.2 are three. In some modules the teacher will see that the order of the activities is sequential and should be followed. An example of this would be Module 5.2 "Stone to Bone Soup." Because the activities follow the steps in the recipe, they are sequential.

On the first activity day, Mary, John, Bob, and Jack will be in a group with the teacher, doing the first activity in Module 3.2. Meanwhile, Alice and Robin (who did not test out of 3.5) are busy working at a table. Each has several sets of animal shapes to match on ditto sheets as to shape, size, and position. If they finish, they can trade sets and sheets. This is the first activity in Module 3.5.

Both groups of children should be at their activities for about fifteen minutes. The solo teacher who usually has trouble in this situation either has not planned for a reasonable learning period (fifteen minutes) or has not prepared enough materials for the 3.5 group.

Setting up and Doing Activities

Planning to pace a lesson well within a reasonable time and planning interesting and adequate materials are essential to good discipline. The solo teacher who keeps children at an activity too long is encouraging them to become tired, restless, and irritable. Even ten minutes at an activity is long enough for some five-year-olds.

The solo teacher, when first using this book, should plan for only one activity each day in 3.2 and one in 3.5 (if these particular modules are selected for the beginning.) The teacher needs the opportunity to get used to the curriculum and to planning.

When the teacher feels ready, he or she can expand to a daily plan like the following:

Half-day Plan

8:30-8:45	3.2	Third activity—Mary, John, Bob, Jack
	3.5	Third activity—Alice, Robin
8:45-9:00	7.9	First activity— John, Alice, Bob, Jack
	7.10	Third activity—Robin, Mary
9:00-End of Session		Activities planned by teacher including free play and outside play.

The above plan allows the teacher to plan for only two groups at a time but to work from four modules on the same day.

The teacher is concerned with each child and that child's learning, not with covering every module or activity in this book. When the solo teacher feels that he/she and the children can handle more, the plan may be expanded to include another subject. The teacher should remember that he/she might have to plan for two groups in each of two modules in a half-day session. The plan must never be so full of modular activities that elements such as free play, outside play, and snack time are excluded.

Two half-day plans are necessary if the solo teacher teaches one group of children in the morning and one in the afternoon. Care must be taken to plan for the afternoon group as individuals. Suppose that all the afternoon group test out of the preassessment on module 3.2 and 3.5 but that the morning group is still working in 3.2 and 3.5. This means extra planning. All individualized instruction means more work in planning and in preparing materials. Nevertheless, teachers will find individualized instruction well worth the effort, as they achieve meaningful rather than superficial learning for the children.

Simple and More Advanced Activities

If the solo teacher is operating out of two modules, the number of groupings for instruction will increase to four. That is, in each of the two modules some children will have the simple activity and some the more advanced activity. These two kinds of activities can be set up in advance on tables or in centers for children in module 3.5. All the teacher must do is to tell certain children to go to the puzzle table (simple activity) and other children to go to the block center and build according to the patterns found there. Meanwhile, the teacher asks the children doing the more advanced activity in 3.2 to check three activities on a dittoed contract and to do those three activities by a certain time (when this hand points to 3 on the clock, for example). The contract may look like this:

Name _____ Contract

Wash your hands. ✓

Sweep the rug.

Water a plant. ✓

The contract should include ten to twelve easy tasks, some more time-consuming than others, and each child could check three to do in fifteen minutes. While each child is checking the contract and getting busy, the teacher is left to teach only one group—those doing the simple activity in 3.2.

The solo teacher can have four groups working in two modules at the same time period. When this is first tried with the children, it is vitally important to reassemble the children at the end of fifteen minutes and evalute with them what happened, including a report from each group as to how things went. It is very important for the teacher to note how things went for the two groups involved with simple activities. If all the children seemed to be learning, then all four groups will move to postassessment or the next step on the following day. If several children are still having problems, the teacher must plan another activity more suited to their learning styles.

Look at the activity sections in Module 3.2. The first three activities are oral (auditory). So is the simple activity. The child who is having problems is probably more visual or tactile than auditory in his/her learning style. He/she needs the teacher to create an activity with visual directions (pictures) to be held up as the oral directions are given. Then the directions should be repeated taking one or more of the pictures away. This is what is meant in the module by "design your own activity to meet the needs of individual children." After this extra help (switching or combining methods of teaching), these children can be postassessed.

If any children are having problems learning in the more advanced activities, put them through the simple activity the next day.

It is important, when you reassemble the whole class into one group, to talk about how they are expected to behave socially at the puzzle table, or in working together at some point in their contracts. Children need training in how to work independently, but in close contact with their peers. In about a week and a half or two weeks, it will not be necessary to discuss social behavior in the evaluation following the fifteen-minute activity period. Also, the solo teacher will eventually become skilled in evaluating the progress of groups working independent of the teacher without always having to reassemble the whole class. The teacher will learn to watch carefully as he/she walks around the work areas and will learn to build self-checking devices into materials.

Postassessment

The postassessment in a module is the same test as the preassessment. It must be administered individually, because it is

difficult for the teacher to assess the knowledge of a group. A recording sheet is used like the one shown earlier in Module 3.2, preassessment. The only difference is that the word *preassessment* is changed to *postassessment* on the sheet.

Those children who pass the postassessment go on to a new module the next day. Those who do not pass go on to the section in the module called "Additional Activities." After the additional activities, the children who did not pass the first postassessment are given a second postassessment. Add a column to the recording sheet for the results of the second postassessment. The number of children going through additional activities and a second postassessment will be very few. However, they are another group to plan for. For the teacher just beginning to use this book, it would be advisable to stay at a maximum of four groups operating at any one time: one in an additional activity of an old module, one in a new module, and two other groups (those who test out or are more advanced in another module). In the latter two groups, all could do the same activity, especially in the modules that do not have sequential activities.

Other Suggestions

If an activity calls for a field trip, a visitor to come in, or something to be cooked, it may be necessary to involve all the children at that time. However, those who were not in that particular module at the time of the activity will have to reexperience this when they do go through the module. It is very important that the teacher record the experience so as to be able to recreate it for each group going through the module. The experience can be video-taped, photographed, or tape-recorded. Different visitors with similar backgrounds can be invited to afford each group the same experience. Some teachers have movie cameras with sound that can be used.

If it is impossible to take the children on field trips, the teacher must go and video-tape or photograph the experience to share with the children.

The solo teacher should not feel that he/she must be the sole provider of materials. Children and parents can help. Allow a couple of weeks for children or parents to bring in materials before an activity will actually take place. Materials from the school or regional centers may have to be ordered weeks or months in advance.

The solo teacher should be very flexible in terms of materials needed for these modules. If the module calls for checkers when bottle caps would do just as well, gather bottle caps. Adapt to the situation with materials readily at hand.

Teaching solo does not mean that instruction cannot be individualized. It does mean that the teacher has to plan for more groupings and an abundance of learning materials. This book has a curriculum with individualization built in, but the teacher is the creative element that brings the curriculum to life. The solo teacher can meet the needs of individual children and help each child discover personal meaning in learning.

Learning is fun!

Acknowledgments

One of the strengths of this book is that teachers from six states contributed ideas, objectives, and activities to the author for curricular consideration. The author is indebted to Nancy Bowden, a language arts specialist, for her suggestions regarding the Language Development Component of this book.

The following teachers are acknowledged as contributors to this book: Elizabeth Barton, Kay Bauer, Kathey Blanchard, Jane Bowers, Arlander Boyd, Phillis Broadway, Janice Brown, Sandra Brown, Nancy Bruce, Nina June Burroughs, Debora Carpenter, Diane Chester, Melba Coke, Frankie DeFries, Joan C. Delong, Rose Demuth, Marcia DeSotel, Jean Evelyn Dobbins, Kathleen Drilling, Cathy R. Edwards, Coralie Elmore, Elizabeth E. Goodwin, Devra Graham, Pamela Greedy, Marilyn Hrubes, Gerald L. Jones, Vonda Kilpatrick, Barbara Kueter, Romania E. Leimer, Mildred K. Lewellen, Marjorie Malloy, Jackie Pogue, James Raby, Daisy Roehr, Alice Severe, Carol Sexton, Lindy Sexton, Julie L. Simpson, Kay Ross Sloan, Leona Smith, Christina Steele, Patricia Steele, Sharron K. Turman, Susan Vines, and JoAnn Wullenwaber.

The author is indebted to the educators and children of the Victoria Independent School District (Victoria, Texas) for appearing in the pictures of this book, and to Richard Korczynski, who photographed their spontaneity. The author would like to thank Esther Smith for manuscript preparation, Dr. Robert Stewart for ideas relating to graphics, and Dr. William Nesbitt for thoughts on curricular structure.